AFRICAN FORAGERS

The African Archaeology Series

The African Archaeology Series offers comprehensive, up-to-date syntheses of current research on the African cultural past. Though the essence of each volume comes from archaeology, they are equally dependent upon examination of the anthropological and historical records, in order to explore the African experience and the place of the African past and lifeways in the broader world. This series permits Africanists an opportunity to transform field investigations into more general syntheses, giving context and meaning to bare bones archaeological reports, utilizing innovative methods for comprehending, as well as explaining, the past.

Series Editor:
Joseph O. Vogel (University of Alabama)

Books in the Series:
- Chapurukha Kusimba, *The Rise and Fall of Swahili States* (1999)
- Michael Bisson, S. Terry Childs, Philip de Barros, Augustin F. C. Holl, *Ancient African Metallurgy: The Socio-Cultural Context* (2000)
- Innocent Pikirayi, *The Zimbabwe Culture: Origins and Decline of Southern Zambezian States* (2001)
- Sibel Barut Kusimba, *African Foragers: Environment, Technology, Interactions* (2002)

Submission Guidelines:
Prospective authors of single or coauthored books and editors of anthologies should submit a letter of introduction, the manuscript, or a four- to ten-page proposal, a book outline, and a curriculum vitae. Please send your book manuscript or proposal packet to:

The African Archaeology Series
AltaMira Press
1630 North Main Street, #367
Walnut Creek, CA 94596

AFRICAN FORAGERS

Environment, Technology, Interactions

Sibel Barut Kusimba

A Division of Rowman & Littlefield Publishers, Inc.
Walnut Creek • Lanham • New York • Oxford

AltaMira Press
A Division of Rowman & Littlefield Publishers, Inc.
1630 North Main Street, #367
Walnut Creek, CA 94596
www.altamirapress.com

Rowman & Littlefield Publishers, Inc.
A Member of the Rowman & Littlefield Publishing Group
4720 Boston Way
Lanham, MD 20706

PO Box 317
Oxford
OX2 9RU, UK

British Library Cataloguing in Publication Information Available

Library of Congress Cataloging-in-Publication Data
Kusimba, Sibel Barut, 1966–
  African foragers : environment, technology, interactions / Sibel Barut
Kusimba.
      p. cm.—(The African archaeology series)
   Includes bibliographical references and index.
   ISBN 0-7591-0153-1 (cloth : alk. paper)—ISBN 0-7591-0154-X (pbk : alk. paper)
   1. Hunting and gathering societies—Africa. I. Title. II. Series.

  GN645 .K87 2002
  306.3'64'096—dc21

                                                      2002005149

Printed in the United States of America

Cultural man has been on earth for some 2,000,000 years; for over 99 per cent of this period he has lived as a hunter-gatherer. . . . Of the estimated 80 billion men who have ever lived out a life span on earth, over 90 per cent have lived as hunter-gatherers. (Lee and DeVore 1968:3)

With a grain cache and meat on the hoof, Egyptians had resources to counterbalance the effects of lean times, thereby allowing them to go on hunting and gathering. (Wetterstrom 1993:197)

The Yao describe another legendary race of "little people" who used to live in the country and who may still be met with . . . (they are of) very small stature . . . touchy, quarrelsome, and fierce, and carr(y) spears as weapons. When anyone met one he was immediately asked: "Mumbonelekwapi?" (From how far did you see me?) and it was always as well to pretend to have seen the little man coming a long way off, and make him believe he was considered quite a big person; if you said, "Hullo, I have only just spotted you!" he would immediately spear you. They are commonly supposed to dwell on the tops of high mountains and were iron workers. They are called the Mumbonelekwapi. (Stannus 1915:131)

Contents

Figures

Tables

Foreword

The world of the few remaining hunter-gathering communities in Africa, sometimes envisioned as an idyllic state of nature, a retreat from modern work-a-day problems, remains a foreign country to most of us. To some, it suggests a kind of Edenic time, of humans in tune with nature, and the beginnings of mankind's career on Earth. To others it is a hardscrabble hand-to-mouth existence. Hunter-gatherers, worldwide, seem at ease with nature. The livelihood of the so-called gentle people takes on a different perspective when we reflect on an unrelenting chase of game across a parched Kalahari Desert, or the blood-soaked perils of an Inuit seal hunt in frigid Arctic waters, or the intense competitiveness of potlatching Kwakiutl, and the like. The universe of hunters is a tangled skein of contrasts.

This is the terrain Dr. Kusimba introduces, explaining that hunter-gatherers come in many different varieties, opportunistically blending into rich terrains, using well-honed social and technological skills to adapt the business of survival to a wide-ranging mosaic of economic prospects. By exploring the hunter-gatherers of Africa, she is able to offer a narrative of mankind's first way of life from its beginnings and subsequent evolution, up to its interaction with farmers and herdsmen and its transformations into the present-day world. It is appropriate that she examine the history of the hunter-gather in tropical Africa. Of all places on Earth, it has the longest experience of mankind's oldest and most enduring lifeway. Scattered across the continent are the remains of centuries old hunter-gatherer encampments, a silent testimony to a once flourishing way of life.

Once, sometime ago, my wife and I, seeking a change from our investigations in the Zambezi Valley, spent two seasons in central Zambia, in that part of the country, north of Mumbwa, known as the Big

Concession. In the 1920s, a district commissioner at the Mumbwa Boma had recorded a number of caves in the vicinity, attracting attention in the prewar years. Dart and Del Grande had dug into deep deposits at Mumbwa Cave, which were explored more successfully by J. Desmond Clark. The area contained not only the stratified cave at Mumbwa, but farther to the south, on the Kafue Plain, were the equally well-known localities at Gwisho Springs, reported by Gabel, van Noten, and Fagan. The survey of the Big Concession seemed an intriguing project to determine if other traces of a Wilton-kind remained to be discovered.

The Big Concession seemed a rewarding venue for discovering evidence of Later Stone Age encampments. Investigating the area was only made difficult by tall elephant grass that had not fully burnt off. Otherwise, one needed to look at the surroundings with the same eyes as a band of hunter-gatherers. The few rocks large enough to form shelters or caves stood proud above the Kafue Plain, and here and there one spied, in the distance, vapor rising above hot springs. Watercourses were all well marked, as were the tracks of game down to them. Here and there, one found places where lions slept the night before, flattening the grass, leaving claw marks where they stretched after their naps. Elsewhere were the signs of game passing in the night. The survey for ancient camps was a fruitful one. The talus slopes below the few caves were strewn with fragments of worked stone, and upon terraces ringed about the springs was ample evidence of prior use and pieces of microliths. The area is still rich in game. In ancient times, this open plain was a hunter-gatherer's paradise.

Climbing the slopes up to the caves, one could glance back, as Later Stone Age hunters would have, searching across the plain for signs of the movement of game. As in the Kalambo Falls basin, or at the painted cave at Nsalu, in northeast Zambia, one got an understanding of the ecological needs of early hunter-gatherer communities, using these places in their seasonal round of economic and social activities. One came to understand the intricacies of site selection, rationalizing water sources to the availability of food and material resources. Seated in front of one cave, Chambabulele, you easily visualized the life of a busy camp filling the two small caves in the rock. We dug there, and it was later redug, analyzed, and reported by Karla Savage. The material culture differed from that in nearby Mumbwa Cave. The Big Concession fit a pattern described by Dr. Kusimba; that distinctive toolkits were produced in one place or another to suit particular activities.

It is this understanding of the ways of the hunter-gatherer through space and time that Dr. Kusimba, drawing upon her own research in East Africa and familiarity with the Howeison's Poort Industry, as well as the interesting material culture from Lukenya Hill, brings to this discussion of hunter-gatherers in subtropical Africa. She explores not only the evolution of hunter-gatherer routines, but also shifting fashions of archaeological and anthropological scrutiny of them. It is important to understand that hunter-gatherers have been perceived differently from time to time. Once, they were viewed as a model of the "noble savage"; while at other times they were regarded as the epitome of primitive preagricultural humanity, trapped in impoverished hand-to-mouth existences. Dr. Kusimba offers us an opportunity to evaluate hunter-gatherer lifeways quite differently: not as the hopeless precursors of food producers, but as a rich, accomplished way of life of its own. She explains that it was a successful strategy, and that humanity lived as hunter-gatherers for a far longer time than any other cultural style developed over the past two and a half million years. As she makes clear, it worked, was opportunistic and adaptive. She draws inference from the ethnography of recent hunter-gatherers to describe their survival into the twentieth century.

Dr. Kusimba explains why the various social organizations that we bundle together as hunter-gatherers worked. Not only how they sought out appropriate encampments, but also how they garnered a wherewithal of stone, wood, and bone, as well as the rest of their material needs. She discusses how food was obtained, and, how after it was brought back to camp, it served a political, as well as a dietary, purpose. She explains how tools were fashioned and how they functioned in hunter-gatherer food getting, and demonstrates the intellectual capabilities of early hominids and their successors. Equally, she lays out how archaeologists examine different facets of stone acquisition or choice, as well as features of stone working to single out ethnically bound traditions, demonstrating the transfer of material and ideas within socially obligated, but, otherwise, disparate groups. It is these three factors, the ecological situation of particular groups, their technological response to their surroundings, and their social interaction with others, ensuring intergroup, as well as intragroup, permission-giving, that she underscores, rightly, believing that these traits constitute a solid basis for comprehending the evolution of humanity, and its cultures, in the distant past, and the continued presence of hunter-gatherers into the present.

This is a history of science discovering anew the hunter-gatherer lifeway, as well the story of humanity's earliest experiments, building upon certain hominid habits to use an emergent transmittable culture to evolutionary advantage. She details the later growth and adaptations of that culture over many hundreds of thousands of years, as well as the spread of humans, and the adaptive capacity of the hunter-gatherer lifeway, out of Africa into far distant places. She not only sets out the results of archaeology's explorations of this interesting and long-lived cultural pattern, but she details the ways archaeologists go about it, setting out the history of perception of hunter-gatherers, as well as the methods available for comprehending the residues of the past. It is a worthwhile story, well told, and one we are pleased to bring you.

Joseph O. Vogel

Preface

In a recent review of a hunter-gatherer conference, R. Foley (1999) lamented the rift in the anthropology of hunter-gatherers between those with evolutionary interests on one hand, and those practicing a historical approach on the other. The Harvard Kalahari Project had revolutionized the study of hunter-gatherers in the 1960s, though many took it as a revelation when revisionists countered in the 1980s that most, if not all, present-day hunter-gatherers had had long relationships with farmers or pastoralists lasting for centuries. If salient characteristics of modern hunter-gatherers are in fact a product of that interaction, then some of the essential characteristics of hunter-gatherers (see Lee and DeVore 1968:12, or Lee and Daly 1999) are not appropriate analogies to the past. Even more damaging, many have argued that the term *hunter-gatherer* assembles far too much variation to be really meaningful (Feit 1994).

After twenty years of critique, the field of hunter-gatherer studies remains sharply divided (E. A. Smith 2001). Yet such divisions seem unnecessary. Yellen (cited in Stiles 1992:16) commented that "The confrontation between the 'historical' and the 'traditional' or 'evolutionary' approaches . . . dissolves, for the most part, into the unanswerable question of which . . . alternate . . . goal is most worthy of anthropological pursuit." In this book, I have taken an archaeological approach to hunter-gatherers both as an evolutionary problem and as one of historical survival. I link these two approaches in one story to attempt to bridge the gap in methods and perspective between historical and evolutionary interests. My perspective stretches back to the earliest archaeological indications of hunter-gatherer behavior, searching for signs of characteristic behaviors resembling those we already know ethnographically. I end with a discussion of the transformation of hunting and gathering into an economic strategy that coexisted with food producers in the early Neolithic and with the complex societies of our times.

I use the concepts of environment, technology, and interaction in examining hunter-gatherers both over evolutionary time and, in the final chapters, in their relationships with food-producing societies. The importance of these three concepts is obvious. The environment includes the natural and cultural setting of a hunter-gatherer society, including not only the economic opportunities present, but also the ways that humans choose to use them. Technology is the body of knowledge through which people interact with their environment. In the case of archaeological peoples, the implements they left behind and the signs of their manufacturing procedures form the basis of our knowledge of their technology. We shall need to consider the function of these technologies and the effects, and causes, of technological change. If technology is the means by which humans relate to their surroundings, interaction, in the broadest sense, is the way that we humans act with one another. Hunter-gatherers form social groupings of various sizes and complexity that are part of networks of relationships that define mutual responsibilities and the inherent obligations of social membership. These social relationships reach out to a wide range of interaction spheres, in which people, near and far, are bound in a social matrix that allows for the flow of information, culture, and genes. As far we can determine, these three factors have been a constant feature of humanity's adaptation since the very beginning of cultural time. The earliest humans in East Africa have left us ample proof of their ability to solve environmental dilemmas through the institutions of tool making and community. Therefore, we can use the conditions of environment, differences in technology, and the structure of their societies to describe and compare hunter-gatherers through time. At the same time, in the latter part of this book, I describe hunter-gatherers' interaction with the other lifeways developing in their vicinity that came to dominate their social and physical environment.

Beyond describing the development of the hunter-gatherer lifeway, my interest abides in determining the time when we can detect definitively "modern" cultural behaviors. To this end, I have categorized different food-getting strategies. The first of these is Early Foragers, early hominids of highlands of eastern and southern Africa (and other regions of the Old World) who were forager/scavengers. A wealth of archaeological research has tried to characterize the behavior of hominids of the Oldowan and Acheulian cultural periods, and the extent to which these hominids constructed campsites, hunted animals, or used the landscape with the kind of planning and patterning that characterizes modern hunter-gatherers. Although I briefly review this question, it is not my goal to examine the difficult and equivocal archaeological record of this period in any detail.

Rather, the first problem I tackle is that of Advanced Foragers. It is clear from the archaeological record that hunter-gatherers of the Later Stone Age belong to this category and were fully "modern" in their behavior in an evolutionary sense. They used complex multicomponent tools, and in some areas, they intensified their economic effort to an extent not seen earlier, and practiced reciprocity and exchange. Their economic and environmental specializations had long-term implications, as well. In some areas people became more sedentary, relieving themselves of the stresses of mobility. At the same time, the more limited purview of sedentary residence required an intensification of social contact, enabling them to access a broad range of material and informational sources.

When does this fully "modern" hunter-gatherer lifeway appear? To answer this question, the first archaeological period that I examine is the Middle Stone Age, the first culture associated with hominids more or less fully human, *Homo sapiens sapiens*, in their morphology. Middle Stone Age people resemble present-day hunter-gathers in terms of the environments they inhabited, their technologies, and possibly the means through which they formed societies and interacted. Were these the first "modern" hunter-gatherers? The Howeison's Poort Industry of South Africa is often thought of as a harbinger of advanced technological procedures. By implication, it is regarded a forerunner of other "modern" hunter-gatherer behaviors. I thought to test the first proposition with an analysis of the archaeological residues from Nelson Bay Cave, a Howeison's Poort site, near Cape Town, South Africa. The basis of my investigation is a collection of artifacts kept at the Field Museum in Chicago.

I compare the Middle Stone Age from Nelson Bay Cave in South Africa, which has some of the features of this modern way of life, with a slightly later archaeological sequence from Lukenya Hill in Kenya, which a team and I excavated in 1994. Although some of the pieces of modernity are in place at Nelson Bay Cave, a fuller picture is realized during the Lukenya Hill period.

The second category I examine is Foragers and Food Producers. From time to time, foraging peoples experimented with harnessing their food sources, by cultivation or the tending of game animals. Following the demise of the last glacial period, humans, continuing their settlement of the world, developed ways of life in which the expense of preparing fields or the full-time keeping of animals became cost-effective. With the advent of food production, hunting and gathering became one of many flexible economic strategies practiced. Hunter-gatherers were not relegated to the margins, but participated vicariously and sometimes directly in food production, engaging in exchanges with neighboring food producers and performing crucially important services in this new world. They even took part in transcontinental mercantile economies of the last few hundred years. Given the low returns of hunting and gathering, it should have been overwhelmed by innovative food-getting strategies and novel societies. Can we use our observations of environment, technology, and interaction to explain its persistence into the present day? I use archaeological data to show how "Neolithic hunter-gatherers" modified their hunting practices, their mobility, and the type of social interactions they forged to suit a new economic world—the most constant were, paradoxically, the most flexible.

One positive outcome of the hunter-gatherer revisionist debate has been that people are realizing the value of studying the interdependent, intermediate, or "encapsulated" (Woodburn 1988) forager society as important in and of itself, but also as a source of analogy for studying the transition to food production. By realizing the important role that hunter-gatherer groups have played, we no longer see them as isolated remnants. Were hunter-gatherers important players in cultural processes in later prehistory, or are they a source of analogies for understanding the evolution of humanity writ large? I believe they can be both.

Acknowledgments

This book would not have been written without the encouragement and support of Chapurukha Kusimba, who encouraged me to write it, inspired me with his grandfather's stories of the *mumbonelekwapi*, critiqued and edited the entire manuscript, held our family up during my absences, and reassured me it would one day be done. Dorcas Makokha and Pierrette Barut have proven that the Hadza are not the only hardworking grandmothers. Our excavations of Kisio Rock Shelter were supported by an NSF grant to Chapurukha M. Kusimba, and

I thank him for suggesting that the data be used in this book. Briana Pobiner and David Braun analyzed the faunal remains and lithic artifacts from Kisio Rockshelter. James Phillips added his great knowledge of lithic technology to the analysis of the Nelson Bay Cave tools, and I'm grateful to him for his expert tutelage. William Pestle of the Field Museum facilitated my analyses. The excavation of GvJm62 was supported by an NSF predoctoral grant and by the Fulbright program and guided by Charles Nelson. In the excavation I am also grateful to Dr. Chapurukha Kusimba and the support and staff of the National Museums of Kenya. I would like to give thanks to my dissertation advisor, R. Barry Lewis, for all his support and encouragement, and to the colleagues and teachers I have had who have influenced this manuscript, including Stanley Ambrose, Bennett Bronson, James Brown, Rick Davis, Jack Harris, Chuimei Ho, Augustin Holl, Philip Kilbride, David Kuehn, Sally MacBrearty, Curtis Marean, Harry Merrick, Charles Nelson, Peter Peregrine, James Phillips, Ronald Mason, Carol Mason, Anna Roosevelt, Fred Smith, Olga Soffer, Gil Stein, Thomas J. Riley, John Terrell, and Edward Yastrow. The bibliography was masterfully and patiently assembled by Brittany Russell, and Jill Seagard, John Weinstein, and Ted Grevstad-Nordbrock assisted immeasurably with the photographs and illustrations. The index was prepared by Amanda Halpin. She and Edward Yastrow read and commented on the entire manuscript. I am indebted as well to Peter Mitchell whose extensive comments have greatly improved this manuscript. Jennifer Ringberg drew the illustrations of the Nelson Bay Cave tools. I also thank the following for permission to use images and photographs: J. Adams and H. Faure (1997) for the QEN Atlas of Paleovegetation; R. Klein for photographs of the Nelson Bay Cave sites; *American Anthropologist* for Figure 4.1; David Philip Publishers for Figures 7.1, 7.2, and 7.3; Chapurukha Kusimba for photographs of Kisio Rockshelter; and John Weinstein and The Field Museum for photographs of the Nelson Bay Cave tools. I am grateful to Mitch Allen for taking on and supporting this project and to Grace Ebron and John Calderone for making it a real book. Finally, Joe Vogel went above and beyond the call of duty in faithfully editing the manuscript at several stages, providing his expertise in guiding the manuscript along, encouraging me, and holding a vision of the finished product up for me every step of the way.

1

Monuments of the Past

Foraging—the hunting and gathering of naturally occurring seasonal harvests—is the longest-lived of humanity's economic activities. It is a way of life forged in the cultural experiments of the earliest hominids, sustaining human endeavors for thousands of years. It supported the first human societies developing on the highlands of eastern Africa. It was the economic instrument for the spread of humans throughout most of the world's land surface. Its roots extend far back into the Pleistocene, yet hunter-gatherers occupied as much as one-third of the world's land at the beginning of the twentieth century (Lee and Daly 1999:3). They could be found everywhere, on the Australian continent, in large parts of South America, Africa and Asia, as well as much of western and arctic North America.

In the twentieth century, many of the world's hunting and gathering people turned away from foraging and the societies it engendered. Yet, we continue to be fascinated by them. Anthropologists study the intricacies of a seemly simple lifeway. Archaeologists research them, seeking means to explain the leavings of past hunter-gathering societies. A popular image is formed from characterizations of the "gentle people" of the Kalahari or the "flower children" of Shanidar Cave. The popular idea of a hunter-gatherer may be an Andamanese with his blowgun or a Kalahari "Bushman" stalking a giraffe. However, the foraging lifeway was capable of fueling the prosperity of Upper Paleolithic cave dwellers in Europe, and the potlatching peoples of North America's Northwest Coast. It was a versatile and fertile lifeway, which eventually engendered the lifeways of pastoralists and agriculturists who would come to take the foragers' place.

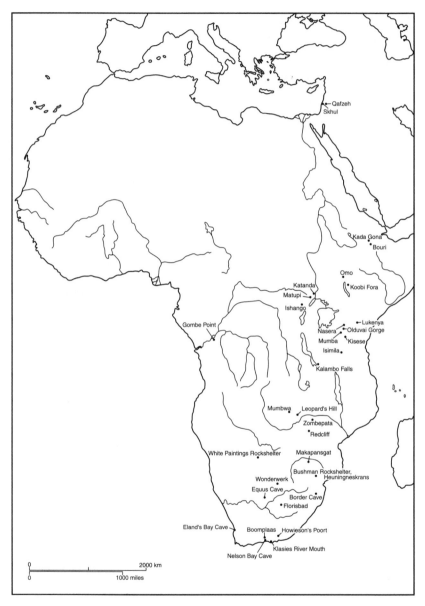

Figure 1.1. Map of Africa showing sites mentioned in chapters 1, 2, and 3.

At their most basic, we tend to think of foragers by their economy. Hunting and gathering groups subsist on the killing, capture, or scavenging of wild animals, as well as the gathering of wild food plants, fowling, and fishing. They tend not to be cultivators, yet they usually possess an intimate knowledge of their floral surroundings. Though they keep no animals, except for dogs, they retain a profound grasp of the comings and goings of game in their vicinity. Hunter-gatherers are mobile, and their movements, regulated by well-rehearsed sequences of economic opportunities, form an intrinsic part of their worldview. Folklore, myth, and story telling preserve a vital comprehension of the world and their relationship to it.

Many features distinguishing the hunter-gatherer way of life, such as particular cosmologies, kinship systems, marriage rules, and social arrangements, tend to be more variable (Kent 1997). Because of the obvious diversity of cultures traditionally bundled within the hunter-gatherer rubric, many doubt the utility of the portmanteau term *hunter-gatherers* at all (Burch 1998:211; Keeley 1995; Smith 2001). However, most lay people and many anthropologists continue to think of foraging folk as a natural or "basic substratum" of human cultural life. To many they are living museum specimens, living fossils frozen in cultural time from mankind's beginnings. As such, they are valued more as a window into the wellsprings of humanity than as examples of a highly successful lifeway in its own right (Lee and Daly 1999).

Modern hunter-gatherers enjoy a highly evolved lifeway that has stood a test of time. As we have seen, the popular idea is of a "failed" or "primitive" condition. Hunter-gatherers have long been thought of as "natural" human beings, portrayed, according to fad, as either "nasty" or "noble" savages. However, neither traditional depiction fills the bill. A third, more scientific view of "natural man" accepts extant hunter-gathering groups as historical models of evolutionarily or essentially significant human biological and cultural traits. Although this view may not always be accurate, it has renewed scholarly interest in foragers. In this vein, Lee and DeVore (1968b:ix) wrote that "the human condition is likely to be more clearly drawn here than among other kinds of societies."

At the same time, others view matters differently. In opposition to the use of today's hunter-gatherers as models of Paleolithic behavior, some "revisionist" or historical anthropologists argue that hunter-gatherers are no more "natural" than any other society (Schrire 1980; Wilmsen 1989). Their diverse lifeways and ideologies are not the expression of a basic human nature, but the product of adaptive history (Schrire 1984). The revisionist perspective has even questioned the use of the generic lexeme *hunter-gatherer* to denote a particular kind of society. It is their position that the hunter-gatherer of the ethnographic record is a result of a marginal status in a world dominated by herding and farming neighbors (Wilmsen 1989). As such, present-day foragers are the end result of historical processes rather than their starting point.

A series of academic exchanges highlight the strong points of these differing attitudes (Lee and Guenther 1991; Solway and Lee 1990; Wilmsen and Denbow 1990). As in most such academic squabbles, we can find virtue and fault in both sides of the argument. Modern foragers have had a long and varied history, but their modes of cultural adaptation do permit the careful observer to posit hypothetical models of archaeological phenomena not otherwise observable today. Some of the behavior of modern counterparts may reflect on the past, but the present-day hunter-gatherer is not a leftover from prehistory.

The theoretical rift between an evolutionary and the historical perspective remains deep (Foley 1999). I attempt to merge both approaches in order to tell the story of the hunting and gathering lifeway in Africa. Africa not only has the world's longest, most continuous history of hunting and gathering, but it also has a record of hunting and gathering peoples that persist into the present (Bollig 1987; Kent 1997). In Africa, the forager lifeway is not a hypothetical construct or a "throwback" but a recently living and long-lived mechanism through which human communities were melded into ecologically sound arrangements. It is a way of life that creates a delicate, fluctuating stasis between humans and the landscapes they inhabit.

Hunter-Gatherers as "Original Man"

In the seventeenth and eighteenth centuries, Europeans also thought of hunting and gathering peoples as living representatives of ancient, even precultural, humanity. They were savages living in a "state of nature" (Barnard 1999). One's opinion of the virtues of these *savages* depended on one's view of the state of nature. To some, it was viewed favorably, but to others it was a "continuall feare, and danger of violent death; And the life of man, solitary, poore, nasty, brutish and short" as Hobbes (1973 [1651]:64–65) put it. However, for others the hunter-gatherer "satisfy(ies) his hunger at the first oak, and slak(es) his thirst at the first brook . . . and, with that, all his wants supplied" (Rousseau 1973[1755]:52, as cited in Barnard 1999). Rousseau said that their "savage" social systems somehow reflected favorably the aspirations of the revolutionary ideals of liberty, equality, and fraternity (Rousseau 1973[1750–62]) as cited in Barnard 1999). In any event, these philosophers viewed their foraging contemporaries as representatives of primitive and ancient ways of life. To these armchair savants, foraging humans were a rhetorical convenience, rather than objects of informed observation and comprehension.

By the nineteenth century, although reliable knowledge of the world's foragers was still limited, an evolutionary perspective on hunting and gathering was developing. It implicitly assumed, in the writings of Adam Smith and Friedrich Engels, that hunting was a universal first stage of society. To Marx, it was associated with a primitive form of communism and governance by consensus (Barnard 1999; Wilmsen 1989:20). Something akin to this point of view informed most precolonial and colonial encounters with hunter-gatherers. It was taken for granted that Europeans had progressed to a higher level of biological and cultural evolution. By their own estimation, they were superior to the prehistoric stage still exhibited by hunter-gatherers. At the time, many held that their non-Western contemporaries were living holdovers from earlier states of being. Indeed, this position is not superficially different from the view that contemporary societies are ready models for past behavior. In 1915, Sollas published his *Ancient Hunters and Their Modern Representatives*. The title alone expresses a trenchant point of view. Nevertheless, as in many such expositions of cultural evolution, living and archaeological examples were used indiscriminately to illustrate cultural types and stages. Earlier, in *Ancient Society*, Morgan had claimed that savagery was a formative period of the human race. He explicitly linked archaeological findings with his contemporary hunter-gatherers:

> the inferiority of savage man . . . is, nevertheless, substantially demonstrated by the remains of ancient art in flint stone and bone implements, by his cave life in certain areas. . . . It is still further illustrated by the present condition of tribes of savages in a low state of development, left in isolated sections of the earth as monuments of the past. (Morgan 1877, in Wilmsen 1989:14)

Evolutionary Perspectives

In the early part of the twentieth century, the study of hunting societies took a back seat to questions of modernization and urbanization in the wake of the colonial effort and its aftermath. Nevertheless, a negative view of the "state of nature" prevailed. Braidwood, in 1957, expressed an opinion common among those investigating early agriculture, that a man who spends a lifetime tracking wild animals to eat is little more than a wild animal himself (Braidwood, in Sahlins 1998[1972]:8). Likewise, hunter-gatherer social organization was fit into the cozy ideal of the patrilineal band (as in Service 1962) on the basic assumption that patrilocality retained needed ecological information concerning band territories, although few empirical studies corroborated it. In the face of this absence of substantive data, others, working with the hunter-gatherers of Africa, Australia, Canada, and the rain forests of South America, began a new appraisal of this lifeway. At the time this scientific effort began, hunters and gatherers, especially those of Africa, were still very poorly known.

The work of professional anthropologists—above all, Marshall, Lee, Silberbauer, and others—overturned previous opinions about the lives of hunter-gatherers leading to a vital consensus. An important step on the road toward this new understanding was the synthesis presented at a 1966 University of Chicago conference and published as *Man the Hunter* by Lee and DeVore (1968a). This important interchange offered a more balanced, positive evaluation of the cultural and ecological situation of modern hunter-gatherers. Nevertheless, it sought an evolutionary perspective of hunter-gatherers as clues to humanity's original state of affairs.

Based on available data, *Man the Hunter* set forth some of the diversity found in the world's hunter-gatherer societies. At the same time, Lee and DeVore (1968b:11–12) produced a composite view of hunter-gatherer society. It was designed to encapsulate the many variations in hunter-gatherer lifeways. It also attempted to provide an empirical model of what human society was like before "advanced technology and formal institutions have come to play a more and more dominant role in the human adaptation" (Lee and DeVore 1968b:12). Hunter-gatherers were once more relegated to the role of monuments to the past. Nevertheless, conflating ethnographic evidence, but emphasizing their observations in the Kalahari, Lee and DeVore (1968b:11–12; see also Lee 1979:2) developed a model of the ideal hunting and gathering society.

According to their paradigm, hunter-gatherers were likely to live in small bands, with a variable and changing membership. They are residentially mobile, moving their settlements throughout the year for social reasons and the search of food. This mobility is characterized by periods of band aggregation and dispersal, responding to the seasonal fluctuations in food or water. They have reciprocal visiting, and marriage, alliances that interweave each band into a larger breeding unit and linguistic community. They possess economic arrangements that include home bases or camps and a sexual division of labor where, for the most part, men hunt and women gather. Their most telling characteristic is the act of sharing collected food, which they seldom have the means to store, reenforcing a sort of egalitarianism that characterizes them politically. Their wider political world is tied to reciprocated rights to forage on other peoples' lands.

It is a nonspecific model, but very much in the spirit of the times. During the 1960s, science reached the moon and archaeology was reinvigorated by the application of radiometric dating, which spurred a new class of investigators to comprehend the organization of piles of trash or anything else that illuminated the task of exploring foreign cultures of the past. In this interesting time of novel approaches, anthropological archaeologists hoped to update the idea of ethnographic analogy, reviving a discipline that, for the most part, avoided the reality that anthropology dealt with people and culture process. The "new archaeologists," with an anthropological bent, conflated disparate bodies of information searching for underlying patterns. They sought regularities that would somehow rival the "theoretical laws" of other sciences.

Both the *Man the Hunter* conference and the Lee–DeVore generalization relied on information from the Kalahari Ju/'hoansi, called !Kung San, among whom Lee did his pioneering studies. Following their lead, many others went into the field in the 1970s and 1980s to capture this vanishing way of life. Their enthusiasm to preserve a record of these "monuments to the past" recalls that of the nineteenth-century founders of anthropology, hoping to document "native" peoples before they became extinct. To some researchers reconstructing ancient human behaviors was an implicit, and occasionally, explicit goal. The study of hunter-gatherers was a way to comprehend how ideas of property, social organization, and politics were invented (Lee and DeVore 1968b:12), to complete a "picture of the hunting and gathering way of life" (Lee 1976:3).

The observations of the anthropologists were becoming a valuable asset. As we have seen, at the same time as the *Man the Hunter* conference, a "New Archaeology" was emerging. It was steeped in anthropological theory and field observation and founded on a solid footing of rigorous scientific inquiry (Binford 1962). *Man the Hunter* gave practitioners of anthropological archaeology, including many working in

Africa, a model for hunter-gatherer society. It approximated the kinds of regularities practitioners of the "new archaeology" sought. It was used to evaluate situations from eastern African fossil hominids to late prehistoric groups in the northeastern United States (Shott 1992:846). By the end of the 1960s, an announced goal of African archaeology was reconstruction of prehistoric behavioral patterns (Clark, J. D. 1970). Clark, who had studied hunter-gatherers in the flesh, as well as in archaeological deposits, had an ethnographic ideal of them similar to that of Lee and DeVore's in mind when he ascribed patterns of behavior to prehistoric settlements. These behaviors included such things as the duration and periodicity of site occupations; the numbers of inhabitants; settlement patterns; territorial range; economic activity; and communication and intergroup relationships (Clark, J. D. 1970:80).

These are very different considerations from an archaeology predicated on description and classification. From this time onward, archaeological investigation was to transcend classification and enumeration of finds, to explain associations and contexts it met while delving into the archaeological record. Africanists came to reflect this new perspective. Novel field methods were introduced. The old-fashioned idea of searching transported river gravels for worked stone was eschewed. The exploration of erstwhile living floors was a desired goal. Techniques for uncovering floors were devised. Once, deep, narrow cuttings sought to expose cultural-stratigraphic units. Now, field workers, like Clark, the Leakeys, and Howell, opened broad horizontal excavations, baring human settlements, communal settings, and the foci for particular activities (Binford 1987:17, 22). The spatial organization of ancient cultural formations was laid bare.

As archaeology came to understand the long-standing complexities of the hunter-gatherer lifeway, others were coming to a comprehension of their intricate economic patterns. Hunting and gathering was no longer thought of as "a precarious and arduous struggle for existence" (Lee 1968:30). On the contrary, in the 1960s and 1970s cultural ecologists argued that foragers were perfectly adapted to shifting equilibria in the environment, varying their procurement to suit availability and yet never overexploiting. Cultural practices kept foragers in a homeostatic balance with nature (Vayda and McCay 1975). Man the Hunter was also Man the Conservationist. Although the concept may be somewhat overwrought, common sense tells us that foraging is a product of experience, of generations of foragers stockpiling crucial ecological knowledge as their birthright, and that sustainable use and management is widespread (Smith and Wishnie 2000).

As more work was done among hunter-gathering groups, it became obvious that their life was not necessarily a precarious one. It was equally apparent that many groups were well adapted to their local circumstances. Lee (1968) calculated the caloric needs and time spent working by the !Kung San and determined that they were able to collect relatively abundant high-quality foods at short distances from their camps. A modest work effort seemed to provide them with sufficient means to support not only the active adults, but a number of middle-aged and elderly people, as well (Lee 1968:39). He was able to suggest that the !Kung's average daily caloric intake was adequate by USDA standards, and that the average adult spent only twelve to nineteen hours a week in the food quest. The ostensibly hand-to-mouth existence of the forager was seen to be not only more than adequate, but also replete with a fair amount of leisure. This kind of anecdote was contrasted with contemporary subsistence farmers, usually to the disadvantage of the farming folk. A totally new attitude and admiration for the hunter-gatherer people of the world was emerging.

Sahlins (1972) later reiterated the economic satisfaction of hunter-gatherers. His essay "The Original Affluent Society" claimed that foragers "enjoyed lives in many ways richer and more rewarding than ours . . . hunter-gatherers had structured their lives so that they needed little, wanted little, and for the most part, had all the means of fulfilling their needs at their immediate disposal." His take, so very different from Braidwood's, made two distinct arguments: that first hunter-gatherers were affluent, in the sense that they met all their wants, and second that they lacked the acquisitive nature and assumption of future scarcity that underlies most other economic behavior (1972:29). After all, they had structured their lives around the periodic pulses of nature and had learned from long experience what would be available and when. He attributed the lack of food storage to the material context of their lives. As transhumant foragers reliant on nature's rhythms, they were in no position, or need, to keep reserves. Moreover, they trusted in the bounty of the environment; it would provide, as it always had. He concluded that hunters were affluent because they met their wants with little effort. Using ethnographic studies from Africa and Australia, he pointed out that hunter-gatherers kept "bankers' hours," satisfying their needs in as little as three to five hours a day. This was far less work than that of the average horticulturist. These observations promoted a more positive view of hunter-gatherer life (Sampson 1988:14). The prevailing view of foragers was of the "noble savage" type. The "harmless people," with their sharing, flexible social units, periodic movement, and lack of aggression, became the very model of hunter-gatherers.

Human Behavioral Ecology

It was known at the time, of course, that a large number of hunter-gatherer groups did not fit into Lee and DeVore's (1968:11–12) model (Murdock 1968). Their trait list is a poor fit to temperate and high-latitude hunter-gatherers, such as the Inuit, who require substantial dwellings, tools, and clothing; store food; and are characterized by long stays in seasonal villages. Among complex groups like those of the Northwest Coast of North America, corporate ownership of resources, large group sizes, settled villages, and prestige competition clearly set them apart from the societies described by Lee and DeVore. This significant variability in the record of hunter-gatherers, worldwide, is explainable in some part as environmental adaptation (Kelly 1995).

The ahistorical perspective epitomized by Lee and DeVore was eventually refined on a number of fronts. Their kind of model had a use in describing the parameters of the hunter-gatherer lifeway. However, like other such models it was limited in its application to specific cases or specific behaviors. Anthropological archaeologists came to recognize that each instance was to be evaluated on its own terms. Novel kinds of data were needed to meet the demands of exploring past human activities in all their diversity. Their way of life was foraging. Anthropologists needed to know as much about foraging as did their subjects.

Human behavioral ecology (Winterhalder and Smith 2000) developed from attempts to model optimal foraging behavior. This was, in part, an attempt to examine questions of hunter-gatherer work and productivity. The subject matter may sound like the purview of an efficiency expert, but it was inspired by and intended to complement and expand Lee's study. Anthropologists have since examined the foraging habits and caloric yields of men, women, grandmothers, and children; the energy expenditure involved in food processing and transport; and habits of food sharing and their consequences in many foraging societies—creating a balance sheet of the day-to-day affairs of the even the smallest band (for example, Hawkes, Hill, and O'Connell 1982, 1991, 1995; Hawkes, O'Connell, and Blurton-Jones 2001a; Winterhalder and Smith 1981; Smith 1983, 1988; Smith and Winterhalder 1992). A close look at the domestic life of the camp led to a different view of its purported affluence. Hawkes and O'Connell (1981) demonstrated that after considering all forms of work, the hunter-gatherer workday was considerably longer and the caloric return for work expended was considerably smaller. Forager caloric yields were considerably smaller than Lee first suggested. Studies of their diet and health suggested that supposedly "affluent" !Kung and Mbuti were underfed and undernourished (Bailey 1991; Jenike 2001; Truswell and Hansen 1976; Wilmsen 1989:303–315). Interestingly, some still use Lee's and Sahlins' concepts to assert the affluence of hunter-gatherers, a people "who . . . hav(e) everything they need and want little more" (Gowdy 1999:392).

Human behavioral ecologists, building on these work-time studies, developed a set of sophisticated models describing hunter-gatherer economics. The diet breadth model, for example, describes how hunter-gatherers choose their diet within a range of foods and whether they used a broad-spectrum strategy or one stressing a more limited range of foodstuffs (Hawkes, Hill, and O'Connell 1982). The choice of food-getting strategy influences decisions about moving camp, transporting and processing foods, or, if feasible, whether they will intensify production (Smith and Winterhalder 1992; Smith 1983). Most of the answers developed by behavioral ecology stress energetic efficiency and the different reproductive goals of males and females (Hawkes, O'Connell, and Rogers 1997). These questions delve into the most crucial features of the hunter-gatherer lifestyle. Why, for example, the common division of labor between female gatherers and male hunters (Hawkes 1993a,b)? In spite of the potential power of behavioral ecology, questions like this one remain unsolved (Hill and Kaplan 1993; Hawkes 1993a, b and comments; Hawkes, O'Connell, and Blurton-Jones 2001b and comments). Further, the behavioral ecology approach is a poor fit to concerns about the ideological, cultural, and psychological motivations of human behavior (Stiles 1994; Yee 1994).

The Revisionist Perspective

Though critical in detail, many practitioners of human behavioral ecology were in general agreement with the idea of Man the Hunter. However, another more clear-cut critique was inherent to the investigation of long-term interaction between hunter-gatherers with their food-producing neighbors, in particular those of the Kalahari Desert. Schrire (1980) questioned the use of !Kung San as exemplars employed to explain Paleolithic life. This undercut the premises of the "ethnographic analogy" school of explanation, giving rise to what came to be called the "revisionist perspective" (Stiles 1992; Lee and Daly 1999). The revisionists' criticisms arose from the Paleolithic modeling based on modern examples. Therefore, some sought to understand the individual history of hunting and gathering within regional economies (Schrire 1980, 1984; Wilmsen, 1989; Wilmsen and Denbow 1990). In most modern instances, foraging, farming, and herding societies were interconnected through trade, clientship, marriage, land usage, or cattle ownership.

In *Land Filled with Flies*, Wilmsen (1989) used archaeological and linguistic data to claim a long history of interaction between San and other groups and erstwhile cattle herding by San-speakers. They had lost their cattle and the practice of stock management due to exploitative or inequitable client-patron relations. The Ju/'hoansi were the poorest groups in the region; not because they were culturally inadequate, but as a result of long-term exploitation by neighboring agriculturists and European settlers.

The Ju/'hoansi circumstances were the product of several millenia of historical process (Wilmsen 1989:3). Furthermore, inherent similarities between many present-day hunter-gatherer communities reflected a common history of domination by nonforaging neighbors. Theirs is a search for compromises that would allow them to persist with a semblance of their traditional way of life. At a time when anthropology was becoming more sensitive to the importance of history and transglobal interactions (Wolf 1982), Wilmsen and Schrire emphasized that the ethnographic present was a product of long-term interaction. The present had a history that must be heeded.

However, others affirmed the legitimacy of the Ju/'hoansi as hunter-gatherers, emphasizing a sense of ethnic identity as foragers, even after centuries of interaction with others (Silberbauer 1991; Solway and Lee 1990; Kent 1992, 1997). Others pointed out the inadequacies in Wilmsen and Denbow's archaeological findings (Yellen and Brooks 1989; Sadr 1997). Nevertheless, revisionist critiques focused attention on the diversity in hunting and gathering societies, rather than emphasizing the common elements apparent in Lee and DeVore's model (Kelly 1995; Kent 1997).

In the same critical vein, other anthropologists questioned the presumption of forager harmony with their surroundings and ideologies of "conservation" that ensured this rapport (Headland 1997). The inescapable fact was that they shared environments with nonforaging neighbors. Theirs was not a simple backyard that they could manage as they pleased. It was a field of interaction where differing cultural priorities were played out. Sometimes these interests coincided, while at others they were in marked conflict. It was obvious that the ethnographic present was far different from the times met with in archaeological excavations. Huntingford (1963) suggested that "pure" hunter-gatherers could be set apart from "symbiotic hunters." Similarly, Lee and Daly (1999) made a distinction between foragers, who were direct descendants of hunter-gatherers, and those who lived in degrees of contact and integration with nonhunting societies. These include some whose histories include periods as farmers or herders. The revisionist debate, on the other hand, posited that only "pristine" cases had value to prehistory and questioned our ability to reliably discern "pure" hunter-gatherers (Stiles 1992).

Present Legitimacy of the Term *Hunter-Gatherer*

A primary result of the revisionist debate was a rejection of the generic hunter-gatherer. At a time when different people possess a large repertoire of food-producing routines, the term seemed to make little sense (Feit 1994). Furthermore, all hunter-gatherers are known to modify their environment and help out natural productivity in ways very close to the control over species exercised by farmers (Keeley 1995; Roscoe 2002; Yen 1989). Humans, it seems, have always successfully manipulated their environmental interaction, effectively raising its productivity (Bailey and Headland 1991:266). To address diversity and the preagricultural environmental management exhibited by most, if not all "hunter-gatherers," some have even advocated rejecting the dichotomy between "foraging" and "farming" and focusing on the complexity of people's relationships with food species (B. Smith 2001). Some people collect from natural stands of grain, while others tend or sow them. This last may not be agriculture, in the pure sense, but it certainly is not gathering in the accepted sense of that concept, either.

Recognizing the different ways that people interact with their surroundings, Woodburn (1982) and Testart (1982) prefer to differentiate between *immediate return* economies and *delayed return* ones. In the first case, people obtain a direct and immediate return from their labor. In the second, there is an interval between the labor and the enjoyment of its fruits. The time lag may include investments in food storage, valuable tools, or other artifacts meant to be used over a period of years, or used as wealth to be exchanged, or the tending of stands of wild produce nurtured until they bear fruit. Delayed return societies, whether ethnographically or archaeologically known, are often characterized by competitiveness, wealth differences, status, and acquisitive behavior (Hayden 1990). This behavior is quite different from the variable social groupings, individual social freedoms, and emphasis on sharing and mutual accountability we ascribe to hunter-gatherer communities. Explored in their diversity, the idea of *typical* hunter-gatherers makes little sense.

Now, we can see that even the substitution of a multivariant model for simplistic philosophic depictions does not satisfy our desire to define, conveniently, the many kinds of activity subsumed by this way of life. The *Man the Hunter* model was criticized for a lack of breadth. Even the concept of modern hunter-gatherers as a paradigm of ancient societies has drawn fire. Perhaps the field of hunter-gatherer studies is so contentious because it lies at an intersection of prehistory, ethnography, ecology, and physical evolution (Bird-David 1992:19). Its subject matter calls us back to humanity's origins. In many instances, instead of viewing existing cultures as things of interest in themselves, researchers have searched the world's foraging communities for insights into the origins of human capacities and inclinations, reducing them to mere testing grounds for anthropological theory (Winterhalder 2001a). Consequently, theoretical debates tend to be more prominent than the empirical details. Given all this, we still search the record of mankind's career for a Holy Grail, some unique feature contributory to the foundation of social life. To many, the practice of sharing, so key to the hunter-gatherer way of life, seems to supply us with a sensible explanation of early hominid interaction.

Some Perspectives on Hunter-Gatherer Sharing

Hunter-gatherers provide us with some of the best examples of sharing and reciprocity. In its most basic form it occurs around the consumption of large animal kills. Meat is an important nutritional source and it is customary to distribute it through the immediate group. Consequently, people gather in the camps of skilled and successful hunters (Woodburn 1968:106; Clastres 1972; Bahuchet 1990a; Griffin 1984). Meat-eating, of course, encourages congregation around ready supplies and skilled hunters, weaving a strong net of reciprocal obligation. Many suggest that sharing is linked to other socially reinforcing behaviors; these include the ideal of an equal entitlement to the hunter's spoils and an equal say in decision making (Wiessner 1994). The product is the egalitarianism we so often attribute to hunter-gatherer bands and that seems the most salient feature of so many hunter-gatherer ethnographies. It is an important concomitant of the survival strategy of small formations, assuaging conflicts and melding individual egos into a group endeavor (Bahuchet 1990b; Balikci 1968; Clastres 1972; Damas 1972; Gubser 1965; Lee 1984; Testart 1987).

Lee suggested that sharing serves to downplay the hunter's arrogance (see also Wiessner 1996). He hunts to fulfill a social role, not necessarily to elicit esteem. Among the !Kung San, the owner of the first arrow to hit the prey, not the shooter, is responsible for apportioning the meat. The weapon, as among the Inuit for instance, belongs to the *role* of the hunter, rather than to the individual hunter. Men using "borrowed" arrows cede the opportunity to share out the meat. The meat is needed, and the skill to get it is valuable, but the hunter submerges his ego. The individual retains moral standing among his fellows by affirming communal ownership of the meat. The hunter relinquishes possession, assuaging any likely envy or conflict (Marshall 1976:297). Turnbull (1965:158) also asserted that the Mbuti, when dividing the meat from a kill, shared one "recognized goal—equitable division of the spoils."

Sharing, therefore, not only apportions provisions, but also acts as a means of conflict avoidance. Hunters are required by custom to be modest, to avoid calling undue attention to their skills. This, at least, is the ideal case. The reality is sometimes different, but the principle of "community" generated is constant. People in small hunter-gatherer communities are dependent upon one another for their daily sustenance. Sharing is the means of assuring access to it, today through your effort and tomorrow by a colleague's.

Many believe that sharing is intrinsic to the hunter-gatherer way of life (Lee and Daly 1999). It may be the most significant form of interaction in these communities, and one of our oldest socially sanctioned behaviors (Bahuchet 1990b; Balikci 1968). Sharing systems seem to be an outgrowth of the small mobile band and functionally related to mediating risk (Cashdan 1985). The proceeds of the kill bring a benefit to the whole group. In this way, the hunter's effort contributes to the perpetuation of the community as a whole (Winterhalder 1986). From this perspective, sharing is a form of insurance policy, reinforced by custom and the necessity to return the gesture someday. Sometimes, an explicit moral imperative contributes to adherence. To the Mbuti of Central Africa, the Nayaka of southern India, and the Batek of Malaysia, the environment as a giving parent acts as a "metaphor" structuring or informing the foragers' sharing behavior as part of a "cosmic economy of sharing" (Bird-David 1998:125). The moral imperative suggests that the act is not only a necessary one, but also manifest in the workings of the universe.

Some revisionists, especially on the behavioral ecology side, have questioned the underlying effects and purpose of sharing. In their view, sharing of kills is less amicable and more competitive than previous characterizations would lead us to believe. Ethnographers report disparities and conflict in the division of the meat (Flanagan 1989; Speth 1990). Hunters use others' arrows not to limit possibilities for arrogance but to avoid the responsibility of cutting and parceling out meat. This implies that they are avoiding the consequences to be incurred from an apportionment considered unfair. Furthermore, females, who are often excluded by practice or taboo from the choicest portions, have significantly lower body fats and other indices of health than men in the same societies (Jenike 2001). On the one hand, then, inequities occur in these societies and they upset people. On the other, the rules of propriety are affirmed in that transgressions are easily come by and vigorously prosecuted.

In some instances, disagreements over sharing rights are a pretext for argument, a time to vent personal grievances (Turnbull 1965:158). The choice parts of the animals might be inequitably distributed, the etiquette giving preference to elders or mothers' parents avoided (Turnbull 1965; Lee 1979). Sometimes, as with the Hadza and !Kung, inequity is marked along sex or age lines, women or children being prohibited from approaching the men as they eat (Woodburn 1979:254). To the Hadza, the meat is sacred. A similar ideologically founded prohibition among the Ju/'hoansi limits the parts given to women. Continued hunting success prohibits women eating the men's part of the game (Lee 1979:247). Many other accounts demonstrate meat apportionment rules denying women and children the richest parts (Speth 1990). Whatever we make of these inequities, it is obvious that the sharing custom reinforces a variety of complex social behaviors, from modesty to knowing one's place.

Recognizing the evidence for conflict and inequalities in meat-sharing rules due to age, sex, and kin relationship, many still insist that they are symbolic, for the most part, and not meant to create a social order of priority (Gibson 1988:176). One ought not to seek preeminence at the expense of one's fellows. While competition is considered a virtue in most societies founded on a concept of rank, it is best avoided in those formations requiring a submergence of self into the group effort. This may be a naïve way to look at the interaction in hunter-gatherer communities, but it seems a fair evaluation of the kinds of social risk they entail. Nevertheless, competitiveness is evident in some sharing systems. Gift exchanges involve competing for choice partners and prestigious exchange items (Wiessner 1982a).

Based on the foregoing, it is apparent that sharing acts to assuage ill feelings in some instances and exacerbate them in others. This is hardly the basis for describing a polished touchstone. The assumption of a cosmic economy of sharing describes hunter-gatherer interaction, but does not explain it (Winterhalder 1996). If human society began with the act of food sharing, then its many paradoxes need to be accounted for.

The human behavioral ecology point of view views sharing as a diverse, complex, yet extremely important behavior (Winterhalder 2001b), but is more pragmatic about its workings. Sharing and other food transfers exist because those who perform them foresee a benefit accrued in the act. Some aspect of cost-benefit analysis pervades participants' thinking. This may sound sterile, but it acknowledges that most people have some inkling of the value of their efforts. They respond to this perception in their social and economic relationships.

We can describe a broader universe of styles of transfer. These include *tolerated theft*, found frequently in other animals, *reciprocal altruism*, rarely found in nonhuman animals, and *delayed transfer*. In reciprocal altruism, one performs an action that benefits another. If the favor is returned consistently, then reciprocity is said to evolve. It cannot evolve without some mutual assurance that the participants will reciprocate. Reciprocal altruism, which is practiced by some animals (Winterhalder 2001b), is the basis of most human institutions. Tolerated theft, on the other hand, is common among animals and is a much simpler case where one gives up something when the cost of defense exceeds the benefits of keeping it. Delayed transfer includes the many social benefits that may incur from gift giving (Hawkes 1993a, b). This nexus of systems of transfer regulates the movement of necessities within social formations. More often than not, a particular transfer involves aspects of all of these reasons.

If sharing was the touchstone informing the interaction of early hominids, then each of these styles of transfer played some role in the development of society. There are those who feel that the social systems of early humans involved an ability to recognize and shun those who would not reciprocate (Winterhalder 1996). This, after all, is the basis for evaluating one's social relationships, determining whether there truly is a benefit to be derived. In evolutionary terms, reciprocity may be the outcome of earlier systems among early hominids, where tolerated theft, carrying no obligation to reciprocate, was a means of food transfer (Hawkes 1993a). Sharing, in whatever form, satisfied a need in the procurement programs of early hominids and equalized access to resources, while granting a strategic advantage to those who practiced it.

Sharing is particularly beneficial when the diet is dependent upon an unpredictable resource. Foragers, who pool and parcel out their catch, equalize the differences in individual foraging yields (Cashdan 1985; Lee 1979; Winterhalder 1986). In other words, by sharing, variances in yield due to differences in individual skills or scant harvests are leveled out, and everyone in the group receives something. Group survival is enhanced. Sharing is an important component of the set of behaviors we term the hunter-gatherer lifeway. Even when we do not agree on the details, there is a consensus that food sharing is a critical part of the founding and adaptation of these societies.

Humanity's Earliest Communities

Tropical Africa seems an ideal place to study the evolutionary and historical processes resulting in the foundation of human society. For one thing, Africa's foraging societies have the world's longest history. They began in the middle Pleistocene, experimenting with social and technological modes of adaptation that separated them from their nearest hominid relatives. They still inhabit the modern world. They even successfully reside in much the same landscapes they did so many thousands of years ago. Intimately engaged in the intricacies of ecosystems, over that period they adapted to significant climatic oscillations, changes in natural surroundings, and movement onto their land by herdsmen and farmers. New forms of economy flourish in the vicinity in which they participate. This indicates a remarkable adaptability. There are palpable signs of accomplished adjustment to modern conditions. Nevertheless, their lifeway has been studied by a generation of ethno-archaeologists that wanted the "actual . . . environment occupied by early man" (Lee 1976:10). The best-known application of "Bushman anthropology" to the archaeological record was Isaac's (1978a, b) food-sharing model explaining the rise of early societies.

Isaac's insight was spurred by the remarkable set of archaeological discoveries of early hominid activity in East Africa since the 1950s (Leakey 1965; Leakey and Leakey 1964). Archaeological localities at Olduvai, dating from between 1.8 and 1.3 million years ago, appeared to be ancient living sites, places visited by small troupes of early hominids. It would seem that these camps were visited on a periodic basis, as small groups of early foragers moved from one economic opportunity to another, reclaiming old campsites. The refuse of these "camps" were dense clusters of worked stone and animal bone of many species (Leakey, M. D. 1971). Several decades of research have revealed that the sites are complex and often ambiguous palimpsests of hominid and other animal behaviors (Potts 1996). Although these hominids, especially *Homo habilis,* may not yet have been predators, they were partly carnivorous and possessed stone technology.

The discovery of the early settlements of the Oldowan, and successor Acheulian, Industrial Complex at Olduvai Gorge was later corroborated elsewhere. At one time or another similar Acheulian concentrations were found at Koobi Fora, Isimila, Kalambo Falls, and sites in the Omo Formation, to name a few (Kusimba, S. and Smith 2001). Acheulian hunter-gatherers roamed widely over Africa and Eurasia. Almost from the very beginning of humanity's career, settlements show signs of specialized usage. A chert quarry from Bed II at Olduvai, for example, shows the manufacture and selection of flakes of particular shape and size (Stiles 1979). These camps were not the random leavings of meandering animals, but the trash of early hominids conducting culturally conditioned tasks, and at least some of the components of typically human behavior, at that.

Given the apparent diversity of settlement attributable to these early communities, Isaac (1984) developed a classification of Oldowan Industrial Complex sites. Type A was sites in which only stone tools were found. Type B ones included stone tools, along with the bones of single species of animal; and Type C sites included stone tools as well as bones of several different animal species. Some of the game bone exhibited cut marks as the result of hominid butchering (Bunn and Kroll 1986). So early humans were out and about gathering natural subsidies, responding to pulses in their environment, enjoying the fruits of natural harvests. They used tools considerably more "manufactured" than those of chimps—in what other way was their foraging different from that of other animals?

The Food-Sharing Model

To Isaac (1978a, b), type C sites were the loci of the first societies. Isaac thought that food sharing was one of the distinct features separating humans from their closest relatives. Certain kinds of tool use, communication, and society could be attributed on a rudimentary level to other primates. The wonder was not the "cultural skills" of other primates, but that humans evolved so much complexity out of the basic stock of hominoid behaviors. To Isaac, food sharing was the impetus for long-term communal living, the engine driving societal practices. Man the Hunter was becoming, of necessity, a highly involved social animal.

According to this view, early hominid societies were not unlike those of the San. Here in small encampments, occupied as family groups, perhaps even ringed with grass "bomas," they lived out a life not unlike that of today's foraging folk. They manufactured stone tools, cut up and apportioned gathered meat, and fed themselves with plant foods collected nearby. Men and women pursued different kinds of labor, and children frolicked, gathering fruits or digging out rats. Bound by the communal bonds of kinship and labor, the community survived.

The archaeological concentrations, then, were the durable residue of the shifting camps of wandering troupes of hominids. In these home bases, as opposed to those near a kill site, the refuse of sundry kinds of game are found. The meat from many initially dispersed carcasses was brought home, shared, and consumed (Isaac 1978a:319).

In Isaac's model, food sharing among Oldowan hominids was part of a complex adaptation that included sexual division of labor, technologically assisted food getting, and the return of hunted and gathered foods to a repeatedly occupied central place. He describes the essence of the "hunter-gatherer lifeway." The precedents to this lifeway, as tolerated theft, hunting, and tool use, already existed as part of the hominid behavioral repertoire and were still demonstrated by chimpanzees. The early hominid pattern eventually evolved into the complicated array of behaviors found among modern humans. Isaac visualized a food quest requiring frequent separations and reunions with exchanges of food. He surmised the significance of information transfers in this social context as an incentive to the eventual development of language (Isaac 1986:323).

Over more than two decades, the home base model and the role of sharing in the origins of human society inspired a great deal of research. It is worth noting that the home base theory was earlier posited by Leakey (1971), Howell, Cole, and Kleindienst (1962), and Clark (1974). However, there were naysayers. Binford (1984, 1987), for instance, argued that the home base theory of Isaac was founded upon inadequately tested ethnographic analogies. He pointed out that field workers were too eager to declare any stratigraphic concentration of tools and its associated fauna a camp. His call for scrupulous testing initiated new research examining the role of alternative processes, especially natural ones and the activities of carnivores, capable of producing the faunal accumulations detected. These taphonomic studies involved analysis of archaeological sites, sediments, artifacts, and observations of carnivore behavior and carcass taphonomy. It was demonstrated that quite palpable accumulations could have been laid down without any human involvement.

Other taphonomic studies of bones focused on the animal species represented, especially their size, the body and limb parts represented, or evidences of carnivore involvement, such as gnaw marks. These could be compared to the very different marks made by tools. Blumenschine (1988) observed present-day carcass taphonomy to develop a sequential pattern of depletion of body parts. This model was used to appraise the role and timing of hominid and carnivore involvement in reaching, processing, and moving carcasses. It sought to determine the timing of early hominid access to carcasses. One asked whether hominids appeared before or after carnivores had their fill; whether they had access to meaty parts or less desirable ones; and whether this access varied according to the size of the animal. If early hominids scavenged kills of other predators, their access would have been more limited and later than if they were the hunters.

The new information was very useful to understanding the activities of early human ancestors. As so often happens, integrating this new data and testing the food-sharing model had less than conclusive results. Hominids may have had access to carcasses before other scavengers at the FLK Zinjanthropus site at Olduvai Gorge (Bunn and Kroll 1986). On the other hand, others thought hominids were some of the last in line (Blumenschine 1995; Blumenschine, Cavallo, and Capaldo 1994). Getting to the meat was one thing—bringing it home was another matter. Some investigators seriously questioned the ability of early hominids to defend their home bases from predators. Tunnell (1996:328) summed up his opinion:

> The last thing I would want to do in the Serengeti is to sleep among scavenged or hunted bones and meat remnants and be expected to organize a defense against lions and hyenas. . . . I believe that the early hominids slept in trees or possibly shelters . . . and avoided close association between meat and those trees or shelters.

The suggestion that early hominids lacked the technological and cognitive skills needed to maintain home bases cast a long shadow on the likelihood of hominid food sharing as a prime mover. However, some overlooked the obstacle of predatory animals and held to the opinion that meat was returned home by early hominids and actively shared at type C loci. Reciprocal altruism, with people sharing in the expectation of a suitable return, could have favored early hominids with an evolutionary advantage. Echoing Isaac (1978a), Winterhalder (2001b) proposed that reciprocal altruism might have evolved out of the system of tolerated theft. This does not answer the criticisms per se, but it does imply that the meat having been obtained was worth any cost to keep it. As early humans gained control of fire, any sensory advantage from predators' ability to see in dim light was diminished and the advantage swung to the humans.

However, more was involved in the sharing habits of early hominids. The food-sharing hypothesis suggested that a system of gender-separate food quests and a regular pattern of sharing provided strong selective pressure on effective communication systems (Isaac 1978a). Lovejoy (1993) added that it would have encouraged lasting male-female bonds. In his view, the sexual division of labor coexisted with assurance of paternity and a reduction of male competition for mates. More recently, Deacon's (1997) idea of language origins suggests that a shift to meat eating and provisioning of females led to recognized sexual partnerships. Sexual partnerships were formed that divided subsistence and parenting activities between the couple. According to Deacon, this first symbolic social relationship led to other uses of symbolic communication as an organizing tool in hominid social groups. Although some consider the pair bond an anthropological myth (Hawkes, O'Connell, and Blurton-Jones 2001b), reciprocal altruism, at least in general, could have formed the basis of the first symbolic relationships. For its symbolic and economic roles, then, sharing is fundamental to hunter-gatherer societies.

A Summing Up

Hunter-gatherers first intrigued Europeans in the years following their expansion into the tropics and other areas formerly isolated from them. Natural philosophy first saw in them models of "natural man," who were lionized as "noble savages" uncorrupted by the vices of the modern world, or as "a brutish state" from which condition modern man had lifted himself. An element of Rousseauian romanticism remains in many of our current ideas (Dowson, 1996). Their purportedly egalitarian politics and emphasis on sharing caused them to become of the stereotypical "primitive communist." Only in the latter decades of the nineteenth, and during the twentieth, century did trained anthropologists observe them with any consistency. In Darwinian terms, they were viewed as "throwbacks" to the most primitive stage of human society. They were characterized by a peripatetic, hand-to-mouth existence of limited material means, little by way of formal political structure and a nature-based ideology, barely more complex than that of nonhuman hominoids. What interest that archaeologists had in foragers was as analogs for prehistoric cultures.

Throughout much of the twentieth century, archaeology was for the most part a descriptive process. It spent its time collecting, classifying, and enumerating the residues located in the sites of former occupations. Field methodology was constantly improved. However, the archaeologists limited their inquiry to matters of when in time something originated. The growth of a self-styled "new archaeology" in the 1960s changed this. New attitudes toward archaeological residues were formulated. The discipline came to see in the leavings of human activity valuable clues to not only that activity but also to other aspects of organization and cultural process inherent in human societies. Archaeology demanded answers to questions, which lie deeper in an extinct culture, than observations on material culture. The once disregarded practice of *ethnographic analogy* was resurrected, within a context of strict regard for "scientific protocols" and the definition of "cultural laws." That such laws were difficult to find was not a deterrent. Models of a generalized hunter-gatherer pattern, as well as other behaviors, were devised and very specific ethnographic studies undertaken in order to provide a means for explaining phenomena encountered in the archaeological record. These models, though not in themselves "laws," were a suitable platform for reviewing field data.

To understand better the idea of a generalized hunter-gatherer pattern, various scientific approaches to the evaluation of their communities developed. That the subject communities no longer lived in times past posed a problem. What were we to think of the behavior of modern foragers as an aid to explaining the past? Should we disregard their adaptation to present-day conditions and use them as stereotypic Ice Age hunters, if it suited our purposes? Alternatively, should we factor in all the cultural influences on transhumant peoples? Sometimes these approaches seem to compete with one another, while at other times they may be said to be complementary. In any event, the different schools of thought attempted to get a clearer vision of the foggiest and most distant passages of humanity's journey.

Different approaches still exist in an uncomfortable balance. A "classic" or ethnographic one describes the sociopolitical, economic, and ideological whole of hunter-gatherer societies. To some extent, it views "hunter-gatherer" communities as a discrete category of society. The essence of this societal type is more than an economic mode, but a constellation of other cultural practices and ideologies as well.

In contrast to this somewhat classificatory attitude, historical revisionists and practitioners of human behavioral ecology explain particular features inherent in any particular hunting and gathering culture as a consequence of context. For historical revisionists, the context is the history of socioeconomic interaction in specific regions where foraging is practiced. For behavioral ecologists, the important context is the process of adaptation to the environment and human attempts to maximize payoffs of food and prestige within it. To both, specific occurrences of hunter-gatherer communities are the result of historical processes that shaped each case uniquely, no matter how superficially they resemble some generalized ideal.

Arising in this debate is the question of whether we should even discuss hunters and gatherers as a societal type. The disparate answers to this query fuel contemporary study of hunter-gatherers (Lee and Daly 1999:11). Whether a simplistic characterization of hunter-gatherers is still useful is a quandary for anthropology. Archaeology, on the other hand, is left with the problem of explaining past behavior. However, the obvious greater diversity of the archaeological record as opposed to the ethnographic one (Kuhn and Stiner 2001; Panter-Brick, Layton, and Rowley-Conwy 2001) again belies the utility of essential models.

In any event, these arguments become moot if our comprehension of the hunter-gatherer lifeway does not somehow illuminate our understanding of past human behaviors or explain how distinctly human behavior developed in the first place. The debate over the significance of food sharing as an engine driving the formation of the first human societies is an important one, testing both our assumptions of the past and our means of uncovering the reality of that past. That is, did some intrinsically simple hominid habit, like food sharing, give rise to cultural constructs? Did these newly learned patterns effect permanent human congregations, living within sets of mutually understood constraints? Had humankind become a cultural, symbolic animal as the result of gift giving? This debate implies the possibilities available to thoughtful practitioners and points up the difficulties of construing the past from highly evolved modern examples. All we can really know is the end result of processes begun many thousands of years ago.

Over the past twenty years, anthropology has concluded that hunting and gathering, humanity, and the early hominid way of life are three different but overlapping sets. Although Isaac's food-sharing paradigm was criticized for overhumanizing early hominids and oversimplifying their social life, it seems to retain its allure while being difficult to evaluate empirically. Most instances of resource transfer are motivated by many social, cultural, and psychological factors that might have varying implications for evolution (Winterhalder 2001a). Furthermore, there is much controversy over how these essential factors are interrelated (Hill and Kaplan 1993). Sharing, care of offspring, and food transfers between adults and children are radically different from group to group. Among the Hadza, women and children especially procure much of their own food. On the other hand, Ju/'hoansi children get most of their food from adults (Hawkes, Hill, and O'Connell 1995). The use of a single format to depict hunter-gatherer behavior is fraught with difficulties, causing explanation in archaeology to be equally difficult.

Archaeology can develop strong theory about hunter-gatherers if it moves away from a single model of essential characteristics to a comparative perspective reflecting the historical diversity of hunter-gatherer communities (Panter-Brick et al. 2001; Kelly 1995). Isaac's model has garnered greater appreciation for its identification of important variables, including food transfers, symbolic communication, and gender-distinct tasks. Deacon (1997) used the same variable-cluster, elaborating on how their interaction was related to the evolution of language. As we can see, our avenues to the past are many. Like Dante, we may be lost in a dark wood from time to time, but we seem to find our way by posing different kinds of questions and expecting different kinds of answers. Within this now centuries-old debate over the meaning of our cultural cousins, the hunter-gatherers, lies the seeds of our inquiry. To this end, we may now explore the archaeological record left by those that came before.

2

Human Landscapes

Heretofore, we have examined empirical models of early hunter-gatherers. Isaac's model depicts an immediate return of the hunter-gatherer society. It drew inspiration from the behavior of some present-day hunter-gatherers, but it represents an idea of how troupes of early hominids not only exploited economic opportunities, but also arranged the tactical transfer of foodstuffs to the benefit of their collective. The variables posited by Isaac—hunting, communication, sharing, and sexual differences in economic function—are still useful to our consideration of evolutionary models (Deacon 1997). They help explain the rationale for early hominid social organization.

Hunter-gatherers in Africa, as elsewhere, depended upon natural bounties in their surroundings, harvesting often seasonally available resources. Their only means of achieving critical survival activities were their technology and social arrangements. The first permitted them to derive natural subsidies from their surroundings, and the second organized not only the collecting but also the distribution of gathered resources. It was also the mechanism for binding people into a sometimes mobile but stable subsistence unit. Human society is often about much more than subsistence. However, we can make the naïve argument that culture ultimately is about the survival of the group. Implicit in this is the idea that technology and social interaction are the means humans developed to ensure an effective adaptation to their surroundings. Environments are wavering in their bounty. Some are richly endowed, some less so, and many resources are scattered and unpredictable. Hunter-gatherers are required to breach these lacunae with a repertoire of culturally determined behaviors. Before we examine the development of hunter-gatherer technology and social interaction, we should look at the opportunities African landscapes offered them.

Environment is more than the sum of the plants and animals and other natural resources in one place or another. It includes other people living in one's vicinity and their sometimes competing land use. For most of their history, the numbers of hunter-gatherers on Earth was small. Their only competitors were other hominids, scavengers, and predatory beasts. Throughout most of the Pleistocene, hunter-gatherers were the only people on Earth. They created the means to interact with other groups much like themselves. In time, other social and economic lifeways developed around food production, and the remaining hunter-gatherers learned to avoid or interact with them as well. This latter interaction forms a significant part of the history of hunter-gatherers. The crucial interplay between environments and mankind, though, is an important part of our story. It is a tale of complex multivariable rapport. Human landscapes are in a constant state of flux. They differ not only in their resources but also with regard to different cultures' perceptions of them and organized arrangements adopted to exploit them.

Adaptation is multidimensional. Over time, the biological, geological, and social universes affecting how each group of hunter-gatherers makes its living shape the broader process of natural selection. Humans act upon their surroundings in destructive as well as nurturing ways. They manage environments to make them more habitable. Human communities over time modify the contexts in which evolution takes place. Technology, in the broadest sense—implements, as well as a body of industrial knowledge, material choices, and strategies, developed, modified, and passed on—permits humans to shape their present circumstances and influence future outcomes. Technology may be a key to using natural resources, but social interaction is its complement, a way of articulating groups of people into favorable ecological arrangements.

Interaction is, at its most basic, a system of permission-granting behaviors (Kelly 1995). People agree to interaction, to be bound by certain rules and conventions, to form social arrangements. These include such things as sharing, exchanges, and arbitrated land useage, as well as rules defining mating, kinship, and whatever else organizes society. It is the mechanism framing humanity's social environment, facilitating the application of technologies.

The World We Live In

Now we concern ourselves with the whole of the nonhuman setting, including climate, topography, terrain, as well as resources of benefit to hunter-gatherers within it. Temporarily we can defer discussion of that other crucial part of the environment, other human or proto-human communities. Sometimes, these other humans interdict access to necessities, while at other times they ease access through organized exchange.

The significance of the physical environs has long been understood. Sometimes, it was characterized as an agent shaping human character, while at others it was thought of as a passive stage for human actions, a constraint on human potentials, or as a storehouse of resources existing for human benefit (Redman 1999:17–25). In some basic ways, the environment does constrain many kinds of activity. This is obvious. It is the unique ability of human populations to meet such challenges as extremes of temperature, altitude, drought, or famine by resorting to cultural solutions. These solutions permit a given population to be successful. They persist from generation to generation and adjust to inconstant circumstances. Over time, favorable solutions become normalized and shared with contemporaries through interaction. As successful solutions are integrated into the cultural pattern, not only is the cognitive environment altered, but also participating cultural populations attain a selective advantage. Their survival chances are enhanced. The constantly changing perceived environment, as well as mutable effects of other evolutionary agents, such as population drift and gene flow, make adaptation an ongoing biological process.

Because of long-held beliefs about the austerity of hunter-gatherer lifeways, many have erroneously assumed their economies and social organizations to be a direct product of the environments in which they live. However, there is no reason to attribute a more determining role to environment among hunter-gatherer cultures than with any other cultural group (Wiessner 1982). As cultures adapt to their surroundings, their inherent technological, social, and ideological systems influence how they arrange adjustment. More basically, the relationship between hunter-gatherers and the environment is bidirectional. Humans evolved, culturally, as well as biologically, by this continuing process of environmental interaction, meeting daily urgencies with enduring answers. This process of flux, change, transformation, and evolution, apparently, even affected the sort of early hominid that would be successful. In other words, intelligent early hominids affected their own evolution by their invention of technology and social interaction. They adjusted to situational changes as they modified their social and environmental circumstances. No other idea of human development is more compelling.

Hunter-gathering peoples are sometimes portrayed negatively, as people living within environments but having little effect on their surroundings. Hunter-gatherers in reality significantly modify their environmental circumstances (Yen 1989). As I have suggested, they are quite adept at this and have been so from the very beginning. When not being characterized as the hapless victims of nature, hunter-gatherers are often portrayed as resource managers, living in equilibrium with their environments (Williams and Hunn 1982).

Natural Conservationists

Though our discussion seems to imply a beneficial "symbiotic" relationship, this is not always the case. Sorting through the patent admiration for the "conservationist" habits of forager ideologies, anthropologists have become increasingly aware that some hunter-gatherers practiced a profligate use of resources, leading to destructive overexploitation (Klein 1992; Headland 1997; Redman 1999). One has only to consider the massive kill sites left by European Upper Paleolithic hunters, or suggestions that Pleistocene megafauna were hunted to extinction by bands of Paleoindians (Haynes 2002).

The past offers other examples of environmental degradation, deforestation, soil erosion, soil depletion, and mass overkilling of herds (Errington and Gewertz 1993; as cited in Headland 1997). In more recent times, the record is no better, indicating that hunter-gatherers, and other small-scale formations, will overexploit and damage their surroundings (Rambo 1985; Headland 1997; Edgerton 1992). The hunting practices of the Piro of Amazonian Peru seem to be governed more by near-term benefit than some long-term conservation (Alvard 1993).

A "Symbiotic" Relationship

Whether any hunter-gatherers ever had "conservation" on their minds, here and there they had a profound environmental impact through quasi-agricultural and other practices (Keeley 1999). Deleterious consequences aside, foragers for the most part invest in activities that yield future benefit (Smith 2001; Woodburn 1982; Yen 1989). They selectively hunt male animals and replant food plants, irrigate wild stands, and stimulate plant growth through burning to revitalize the soil. They will take only a portion of the honey from a hive, and so forth. Many others take explicit steps to control and safe-guard resources, developing a somewhat more symbiotic than a truly "dependent" relationship. The effect was to produce circumstances more congenial to human habitation. In Africa, botanists credit the widespread dispersal of semidomesticates like the baobab to human influence. This tree has many human uses and is often a marker of past human habitation (Wickens 1982). Indeed, the long-term impact of hunter-gatherer modification of the environment may be strongest in Africa, where they have lived the longest. In some areas, human clearing of vegetation has maintained tracts of savanna grassland (Waller 1990). Hunter-gatherers may in fact have spent much of their evolutionary history as "low-level food producers," selectively culling and replanting species only partially under their control. Low-level hunter-gatherer plant cultivation was an important pre-cursor to later agriculturist strategies (Smith 2001). Animal hus-bandry, as well, was obviously an outgrowth of the accumulated knowledge of hunters and of experiments at control (di Lernia 1997). These examples of hunter-gatherer resource control show the depth of human-environment involvement.

Diet, Mobility, and Resources

The *Man the Hunter* conference set forth a framework for under-standing the environment and its effect on hunter-gatherer diet and mobility. Most of this effect is obvious; foraging is an opportunistic food-getting strategy, as many recent examples indicate (Kelly 1995). Low- to moderate-latitude foragers, such as Kalahari hunter-gatherers, the Aché of Paraguay, the Hadza, and the Mbuti, focus on plant foods, consuming up to 65 percent of their caloric intake from them. Often, these consist of a couple of staples, such as the *mongongo* nut, piñon nuts, or tubers. High-latitude hunter-gatherers, such as the Inuit and Northwest Coast groups, have a diet rich in animal foods, including large animals and fish. For some of these, between 50 and 70 percent of their diet comes from large terrestrial mammals. While for some others, such as the Nunivak, the Yaghan and Tareumiut, and the Copper Es-kimo, fish make up 60 to 70 percent of the diet. People will make di-etary choices from what is relatively plentiful, or what is economically harvested.

It is perhaps simplistic to point out the correlations between the proportion of meat or plant foods in the diet and latitude. Hunter-gathering is not only opportunistic; it is a low-cost strategy. Hunter-gatherers reap what nature makes available. To this extent, environment determines their emphases. For some high-latitude groups, fish stands in the place of plant foods as an important source of oils and fats (Binford 1980; Keeley 1999; Kelly 1995). To others, in the tropics and subtropics, plant foods are more important. For tropical hunter-gatherers in Africa, Southeast Asia, or Australia, these plant foods are usually tubers and fruit. In midlatitudes, however, for such groups as the Washo, Shasta, Tolowa, and the coastal Yuki of North America, nuts and seeds make up nearly half of the diet. These resources are seasonal, plentiful, and easily stored (Figure 2.1). Therefore, the food quest is less demanding and a certain level of sedentism is possible. For some others, foodstuffs are seasonal and widely dispersed, demanding high mobility. The latitude-diet correlation is a direct

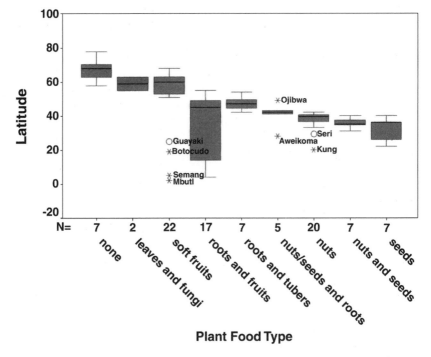

Figure 2.1.   Types of plant foods in the diet based on latitude (data from Keeley 1999).

result of the different opportunities available in one place or another. For-agers adapt their diet, and the means of achieving it, to the opportunities made available to them.

Just as environments influence dietary regimens, dietary choice affects how hunter-gatherers view the landscape. A broad correlation between latitude and residential mobility is evident (Binford 1980). Residential mobility occurs for the same reasons that effect dietary choice: what is available, where, and when. In other words, when food resources are geographically and seasonally dispersed, people are apt to be mobile. They need to be where their provisions are handy. In stable woodlands, foragers have a comparatively easier job than do hunting parties stalking lone animals across a parched desert. Just as hunters need a variety of specialized implements, so too do woodland foragers require means to boil water to process ground seeds or leach tannic acid from acorns (Basgall 1987). The environment offers sustenance, but human ingenuity grants access to nature's bounty.

Just as environment affects diet, so diets impacts how hunter-gatherers use the landscape. Again, some broad correlations between latitude and mobility are evident in comparing hunter-gatherer data. Binford (1980) and Kelly (1983, 1995) examined the relationship between effective temperature (essentially a function of latitude and a kind of proxy measure for the overall abundance of food in the environment) and the frequency and kind of movements groups made. Nomadic groups who move often tend to be found in tropical areas and the arctic, while more sedentary groups are often found in mid-latitudes near water, where they construct large winter villages and live on stored food, especially fish. Binford also noted the frequent presence of logistical mobility among high-latitude hunter-gatherers. Logistical mobility is the formation of special task groups who collect certain resources and return them to residences for processing and storage by the social group as a whole. Logistical mobility and storage allow successful adaptation to areas of scarce resources where resources are only seasonally abundant. Where food storage is not possible, social storage is practiced—a kind of "lein" on others created by the debt incurred in exchanges and gifts (Testart 1982). In sum then, several dimensions of the hunter-gatherer adaptation correlate with latitude—in general, the frequency of residential moves, the distance moved, the size of territories, and the quantity of meat in the diet all increase with latitude (Lee 1968).

Where resources are scarce and unpredictable, mobility is high, both in terms of how often people move and the amount of territory they move over. Similarly, the degree of sedentism increases with abundance, predictability, and diversity of resources, and the need to move is, theoretically, lowest where resources are the most predictable and dense. In other words, people tend to go where the food goes. The size of groupings is also a function of the predictability and density, or "structure," of resources. Horn's model (Kelly 1995:214) defines three basic kinds of forager-spatial organization. First, where food is evenly distributed, stable, and predictable, people form small, dispersed settlements. The camps of Mbuti hunter-gatherers of Central Africa are an example. Second, when resources are clumped, mobile, and unpredictable, a large settlement in a central location is an optimal choice. A camp of Paleoindian hunters might be an example. Third, resources can be clumped and unpredictable, which results in large temporary aggregations. The Shoshone of the American Great Basin formed these aggregations for pinion nut harvesting or rabbit drives (Steward 1938). One can also recognize a fourth category of resource structure, aggregated and predictable resources (Dyson-Hudson and Smith 1978). An example might be the seasonal salmon runs of the Northwest Coast, which were associated with seasonal group aggregations (deLaguna 1990). Indeed, all hunter-gatherer settlements are temporary, if revisited seasonally, and are responses to seasonal or periodic resource pulses. Another pan-forager pattern is that, across all environments, regardless of their resource structure, seasonal variation in the quantity of foodstuffs enforced a pattern of aggregation and dispersal. That is, the seasonal mobility pattern has a period when the group is dispersed and mobile and another sedentary one where groups come back together. Aggregation and dispersal patterns are a response to resource seasonality that is a feature of all environments, whether tropical, temperate, or subarctic and arctic (Lee and Daly 1999).

As we can see, hunter-gatherers respond to their conception of the environment in different ways in different settings. However, all these responses are rational. The changing environment affects choice of diet, settlement patterns, and much else shaping the life of foragers. In the past, as now, different places presented varied mixes of opportunities. Game moved across their horizons and plants came to fruition in their season. In response, people travel in anticipation of these natural pulses; and game or other produce flourished or not in accord with alterations in the biosphere. Climatic episodes came and went. The cognitive universe reflected people's worldview of a natural reality. This worldview was subject to change. People hesitantly modified it at times, and adapted to it, and through it, at all times.

African Landscapes

"Landscape is the external world mediated through subjective human experience" (Cosgrove 1985). A landscape contains, of course, such natural features as rain, stone, soils, distances, and whatever else we can imagine as part of the world around us, as well as the artificial features of technology, social ordering, belief systems, and whatever else eases a people's way in the world. It is an interplay of elements, as we have seen, maturing under the influence of physical and cultural entities. It facilitates the transfer of energy from nature to culture, the circulation of materials from one place to another, and the movement of information from one group to another. Landscapes pass from one generation to another as reservoirs of vital environmental knowledge. This is the cognitive universe. However, the cognitive ecosystem has a very real physical presence that we can describe, as a geographer depicts the natural features of the Earth.

In order to understand the challenges of early hominids, we must first discern the trials they faced, the physical environments that shaped human evolution. Only then can we begin to recognize the human genius of getting by in the strange new world of cultural adaptation. Paleoenvironments are reconstructed from animal and plant remains, links to modern analogs, geological, soil morphological, lake level, and tree ring studies, and many other methods. Once we have a clear picture of the physical world ancient humans traversed, we can reconstruct, from the evidence of their cultural residues, a better idea of their cognitive world, places where they gained provisions or raw materials, people with whom they interacted and exchanged information, and all the rest that makes up the how and why of culture process.

Lately, there has been a greater appreciation of the interplay of environment in long-term culture change. Much of this renewed interest comes from more refined chronologies of environmental change (deMenocal 2001). Of immediate interest to us are studies of the isotopic chemistry of marine sediments, which reflect changing oxygen isotopes in the oceans as temperatures changed. These studies imply that major climatic events, such as the transition from Pleistocene to Holocene conditions, often occurred abruptly, in a few decades, rather than the usual protracted processes that we associate with geological eras (deMenocal et al. 2000). The world of the late Pleistocene hunter was one of great flux, of extinctions of familiar prey, shifts in weather patterns, "wild Nile" floods, and the passing away of well-known habitats, requiring replacement of old habits with a whole new suite of behaviors. Furthermore, over the last twenty millennia, Africa has undergone a series of sudden, nearly eighty-year-long, arid periods when the seasonal rains failed every 1500 years or so (DeMenocal et al. 2000). The world was no stable stage on which to play out preconceived survival strategies, but an arena testing humanity's mettle.

In Africa's present position straddling the Equator, much of the climate and plant life of its Northern Hemisphere mirrors that of its southern half (Figure 2.2). It is a rich mosaic of biomes. Tropical rain forests near its center, at the Equator, are a result of high amounts of solar radiation and heavy precipitation. There are two prominent periods of rain, due to movement of the Intertropical Convergence Zone, an area of low pressure drawing the trade wind moisture from the north and south, producing rainfall. This zone moves north and south of the Equator during the year effecting the characteristic rainy seasons in the woodlands and grasslands on either side of the tropical rain forest. These rains, and their accompanying monsoon winds, derive from

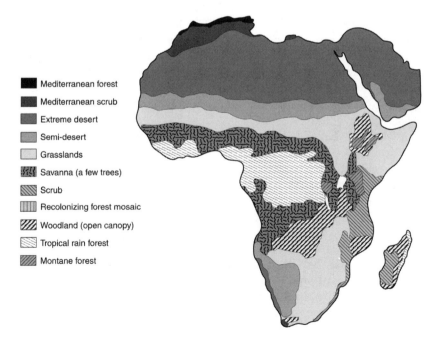

Figure 2.2. Present vegetation in Africa, assuming no human modification.

evaporation of surrounding oceans. Between the monsoon seasons, skies are cloudless and months pass without a hint of rain. The rainy season is more than a colorful or annoying feature of life in grasslands and woodlands. It gives life to vegetation and the game dependent upon it. To people dependent upon plant foods or fodder for animals, wild or domestic, the patterned reliability of the rains is critical. To herdsmen and agriculturists, as well as hunter-gatherers, the rhythm of the alternating rainy and dry seasons shapes their way of life. Yet, these rhythms are unpredictable.

Further to the north and south, the Sahara and Kalahari Deserts formed because the same wind currents that bring moisture toward the Equator deplete these areas of moisture. These deserts seem forbidding. Yet, humans entered these domains as soon as ameliorating conditions brought even the slightest rains to these areas (Close 1992; Wendorf and Schild 1992). In general, we might assume that most of the human population in Africa was largely centered on the middle of the continent, reaching out into the northern and southern extremes only intermittently (Avery 1995). Equatorial Africa today has the most environmental diversity. The region around Lake Victoria, for example, is a varied mosaic of rain forest, woodland, scrub forest, and semievergreen bushland and thicket (White 1983:46, 180). The lake is the main contributor to rainfall in the area. This Lake Victoria Regional Mosaic has a long, well-known history as a home not only to hunter-gatherers but also to generations of pastoralists and subsistence farmers. It has abundant resources, a high rainfall, and much small game. It also seems to have acted as a refuge during the cold, dry periods of the Pleistocene (Hamilton 2000).

Montane East Africa is a steep escarpment through the center of tropical Africa. Distinct Afromontane vegetation is characterized by altitudinally zoned belts of bushland and montane forest, sometimes including bamboo, ericaceous bushland and thicket, and Afroalpine vegetation (White 1983:162–169). In East Africa, the mountains have a profound rain shadow effect. As a result, equatorial rainfall falls almost year-round, and is heavier to the west, averaging about 1,500 to 2,000 mm per annum, than to the east of the escarpment, where rainfall is a third or less of that farther west. These moderate highlands have long been home to humans and their ancestors; the rainfall is seasonal, shifting south of the Equator for a few months before moving north. The monsoons set the traditional rhythms of life there. Farming people time their planting by them and herdsmen follow the grasslands' greening in its passage. In times past, herds of game heeded the same cycle, seeking forage. For at least some of human history they were followed by bands of hunters. The broad sweep of the savannas of eastern and south-central Africa is broken by the Rift Valley and the Great Lakes, except at the chokepoints, like Kalambo Falls or south of Lake Malawi, where hunters periodically camped to await migrating game. It was here on these moderate highlands, amid the lakes and vistas of East Africa, that some of the first hunter-gatherers learned their trade.

The physical environments of Africa are varied, offering many a varied range of possibilities for hunter-gatherers. Technological change over time demonstrates that any environment represents a changing set of problems to be surmounted rather than a constraint on human activity. For example, in Zimbabwe's Matopo Hills, Middle Stone Age people hunted large game with stone-tipped spears. Later hunters focused on smaller animals using traps. By the same token, an optimization perspective, though it permits us to understand the rationale of food choices, does not fully predict the range of technological solutions that cultural evolution is capable of generating, since food energy values are an expression of human technology. For example, processing technologies affect caloric returns (Hawkes and O'Connell 1981).

Botanists recognize some nineteen vegetation zones on the continent (White 1983; Figure 2.3). Each zone is the result of varied altitude, temperature, and rainfall. Besides the Lake Victoria Regional Mosaic, the other zones relevant to our review of hunter-gatherer adaptations include the Sahara-Sahelian, Somalia-Masai, Guinea-Congolian, Zambezian, Kalahari/Highveld, and Karoo-Namib and Cape vegetation zones. The Afromontane zone is found on high altitudes throughout the continent.

Each zone offers challenges and special opportunities to hunter-gatherers. Few areas have a complete ethnographic record, but taken with the archaeological one, we can assess relationships of these vegetational zones to human habitation. In general, areas where resources are abundant support higher densities of more sedentary people. Areas of low-resource density and predictability tend to encourage higher mobility, residential flexibility, visiting, and other means of creating social networks. The diverse nature of African ecosystems shows many points between these extremes, with many kinds of dietary diversity as well. Although Lee, Kelly, and Binford demonstrated relationships between latitude and hunter-gatherer settlement patterns and diet, the predominantly tropical environments of Africa also exhibit patterns of diversity, even within the same latitude.

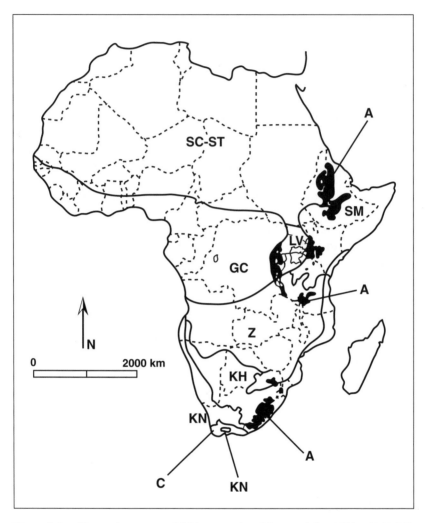

Figure 2.3.   Vegetation zones of Africa mentioned in text (after White 1983:38).
SC-ST, *Saharan Center and Sahelian Transition Zone;* SM, *Somalia-Masai Center;* Z, *Zambezian Center;* KH, *Kalahari/Highveld Transition Zone:* KN, *Karoo-Namib Center;* C, *Cape Center;* A, *Afromontane Centers;* M, *Masai Center;* LV, *Lake Victoria Regional Mosaic;* GC, *Guineo-Congolian Center and Transition Zone.*

Afromontane Zone

The classic example of a high-altitude adaptation are the Okiek, whose territories, shaped like narrow strips called *konito*, extend up and down the mountain from 1,800- to 2,600-m (Blackburn 1982). These land strips are owned by lineages and include four types of vegetation from low-lying dry woodland, dense forest, large treed forest, and finally open highland glades above 2,600-m. This allows them access to the different resources of each zone. Low-latitude resources are found on the plains and include a breadth of game from tiny dik-dik to elephants hunted by individuals or small parties tracking, stalking, and killing with poison-tipped arrows or spears. In the forests small browsing antelope are hunted with dogs, traps, and spears. In the region of the Rift Valley plants are a less-used provision than is meat, though honey is collected as the main source of carbohydrates and traded to Masai. The Okiek offer an example of human technological adaptability to local circumstances, adopting different hunting strategies according to the game, terrain, and altitude, as well as engaging in trade with food-producing neighbors.

The Saharan Center and Sahel Transition Zones

The Sahara is the world's largest and most extreme desert. Woody vegetation is limited to those places where the minimal rainfall may reach as much 200 mm per year. Otherwise, it is a region of grasses adapted to aridity and excessively salty soils. Now, about a third of the Sahara has no vegetation at all. Its southern fringe includes bushland and grassland. Only a zone north of Ahoggar and from Mauritania to the Gulf of Suez has always been a desert. Under different rainfall regimens, hunters stalking game at long vanished watercourses occupied parts of the present desert. Its southern fringe has long been the home of transhumant herdsmen.

The Sahara was probably never consistently occupied when it was desiccated. The Acheulian tenancy was during pluvial episodes, when the desert was at its slightest. Even during the Middle Stone Age, Aterian people rarely entered the desert, living along the Mediterranean littoral, at oases, or around a much larger Lake Chad. The key to living here, as well as in the Kalahari, was to search out watery areas. During the early Holocene, the desert retreated and many hunter-gatherers lived on long vanished wetlands, exploiting riverine and lacustrine resources.

The Somalia-Masai Center

The generally flat peneplain of the Somalia-Masai Center, dominated by *Acacia* and *Commiphora* bushland and thicket, has low (less than 500 mm per annum), erratic rainfall, spread over two rainy seasons. The area's aridity, despite its equatorial location, is a result of a rain shadow formed by the eastern escarpment of the Great Rift Valley. Its main characteristics are arid bushlands and mobile game. The prominent rocky hills, or inselbergs and *burrs*, seem to have been magnets for early humans on the lookout for shelter, game, and plant foods (Figure 2.4). However, pastoralists rapidly colonized many of these areas. The Hadza consume a fair amount of plant food, particularly tubers, berries, and the baobab (*Adansonia digtata*). Baobab is a particularly useful tree since it produces fruit used to quench thirst, stores water, and produces bark that can be stripped to make baskets and the like, without killing the tree. The Hadza pattern was one we should expect for other hunter-gatherers living in the region. The annual round consisted of residential mobility and a seasonal aggregation and dispersal dependent upon water sources.

Figure 2.4. Acacia/Commiphora *bushland of the Athi Plains, Kenya, with inselbergs.*

lived as hunter-gatherers, but after contact with Bantu-speaking cattle owners they adapted to pastoralism, moving their herds from one water-hole to another. It would appear that the Kalahari was not as inhospitable as it would appear at first sight.

The Karoo-Namib and Cape Centers

The Karoo-Namib area is a desert, including some of the Kalahari, low in rainfall (from 100 to 250 mm per year) with shrubland vegetation and sand. The Namib Desert, itself, is very like the Sahara, a vast wasteland of sand. Though bordering on the Atlantic Ocean, the region receives very little wind-derived moisture, which drifts overhead to fall far inland. Nevertheless, hunter-gatherers have intermittently lived in this area since the Acheulian Period (Klein 1999:334).

The Cape lowlands, fringing the southern limits of the continent, have like the northern extreme of Africa a moderate, Mediterranean climate marked by a widely variable rainfall pattern (between 250 and 2,500 mm per year). In vegetation the region is an ericaceous shrubland called *fynbos* and includes coastal and riparian bushland and thicket (White 1983:132, 137). This zone borders two biomes, an inland one replete with small game and a coastal one that also affords ready access to marine resources. The Cape Center is rich in archaeological sites of the Stone Age and the recent era.

African Interglacial and Glacial Cycles

As rainfall patterns structure modern biomes, other longer-term phenomena shaped the ecosystems of the past. The climate of Africa has changed many times over the past millennia. Once, African environments had distinctly different flora and fauna. These changes affected human endeavors on the continent. We have already referred to rapid alterations in rainfall patterns. In higher latitudes, the most dramatic complementary changes were the imposition and removal of glacial ice. The effect of altered patterns of solar-radiated land surface, atmospheric and oceanic flow was new climatic regimens, which in turn affected land-based phenomena. In the north of Eurasia, frigid conditions reduced boreal zones to tundra or covered them with ice. Hunters living in the north adapted to the changing climates with new tool assemblages, material culture, and living arrangements. In contemporary Africa, warm and generally wet periods were alternated with dry and generally cold ones. Vegetation zones, and the game they harbored, expanded and contracted with the ebb and flow of continent-wide changing ambient temperatures, altered monsoon winds, and so forth.

To make an obvious point, the climatic tendencies we examine—now, as well as then—are part of complex ecological systems caused by a myriad of factors. The ancient ecosystems, their stability as well as their intensity, all shaped history to the extent that humans reacted to them, modifying old behaviors and inventing new ones.

Glacial Climates

Since the end of the Miocene, the Earth's climate has oscillated between cold glacial and warmer interglacial regimens. In general, African climates, during the period associated with early hominids, were generally wetter than today's. However, at the same time, the Earth underwent long periods of desiccation. In other words, a cyclical pattern of glacial and interglacial episodes and including a general drying trend has, coincident with the evolution of humanity, prevailed over the Earth's surface (deMenocal 1995). At the same time, as the major rhythms were playing out, lesser cycles affected local conditions. Beginning at least by 2.8 million years ago, climates oscillated in cycles of cooler, drier glacial regimens lasting around 100,000 years each and wetter interglacial intervals of around 15,000 years. Over time, the magnitude of these oscillations increased. During the past two to three million years, there have been around twenty-one major periods of glaciation. For the most part, then, mankind's early tenure on Earth was sustained during times of climatic flux, composed of many interludes of relative colder and arid weather, interfused with warm and wet conditions (Potts 1996).

Paleoenvironments of the Last 50,000 Years

Our ability to reconstruct ancient environments and vegetation zones is most secure for the last 50,000 years. This time period included great extremes of climate, including the Last Glacial Maximum (LGM) at around 18,000 years ago, the coldest period of at least the last 100,000 years. The paleoenvironmental reconstruction of the Last Glacial Maximum in Africa gives us an idea of what conditions the continent experienced during cold pulses, when dry vegetation zones expanded and those dependent on water contracted (Adams and Faure 1997; Figure 2.5).

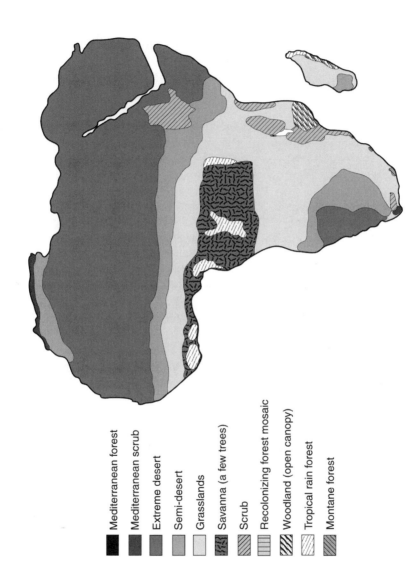

Figure 2.5. Reconstructed vegetation in Africa from 16,000 to 20,000 years ago, during the Last Glacial Maximum.

Mediterranean forest

Mediterranean scrub

Extreme desert

Semi-desert

Grasslands

Savanna (a few trees)

Scrub

Recolonizing forest mosaic

Woodland (open canopy)

Tropical rain forest

Montane forest

The Somalia-Masai Center

For the last 50,000 years, data from lake-level studies, sedimentology, palynology, glacial features on East African mountains, and faunal data support a picture of cold and greater aridity than today. However, most studies are from high-altitude areas, where distinct Afromontane vegetation is characterized by altitudinally zoned belts of bushland, montane forest, sometimes including bamboo, ericaceous bushland and thicket, and Afroalpine vegetation (White 1983:162–169). During the Last Glacial Maximum, glaciers on Mount Kenya, Mt. Elgon, Kilimanjaro, the Aberdares, and the Ruwenzoris reached their greatest extent. Underlying vegetation belts of Afroalpine grassland, ericaceous bushland and thicket, and dry montane forest shifted 700- to 1,000-m downward in altitude (Hamilton 1982, 1987). At Sacred Lake on Mount Kenya, cold and dryness reac: ed their maximum at 21,800–17,000 years ago (Coetzee 1967). Moist montane forest on Mount Elgon was replaced with grassland and patches of dry forest (Hamilton 1982). Rift Valley lakes dried up, including Nakuru, Elmentietia, and Lake Abhé, while lakes in the Ziway-Shala basin reached low stands (Gasse and Street 1978; Haberyan and Hecky 1987; Hastenrath and Kutzbach 1983; Richardson and Dussinger 1986; Richardson and Richardson 1972; Street and Grove 1976).

Pollen data from Sacred Lake on Mount Kenya suggest an average drop in temperature of from 5.1° to 8.8° C at the Last Glacial Maximum, and depressions of 1,000-m of altitude in vegetation zones (Coetzee 1967). Similar temperature estimates come from studies of former snowlines on Mount Kenya and Mount Kilimanjaro (Coetzee and van Zinderen Bakker 1989:192) and from interpolated age results from amino acid racemization of ostrich eggshells from the Naisiusiu Beds (Manega 1993). Using lake-level data, Hastenrath and Kutzbach (1983:151) estimate precipitation decreases of 10–15 percent below present levels before 12,000 B.P. in the Central Rift Valley.

Archaeological faunal assemblages show that although some areas were colder and more arid in the later Pleistocene, others remained well-watered. At Lukenya Hill (Marean and Gifford-Gonzalez 1991), faunal assemblages are dominated by an extinct small alcelaphine similar to the extinct *Damaliscus agelaius*. This alcelaphine is smaller than any living member of the family except the bontebok and blesbok, both of which it approaches in size; its teeth, however, are significantly more hypsodont (high-crowned and providing much extra material for wear). This animal is also found in faunal assemblages at Kisese II in northern Tanzania (Marean, Ehrhart, and Mudida 1990), but it is absent from Holocene levels at Lukenya, suggesting it became extinct at the end of the Pleistocene. Another extinct animal found in Holocene-dated faunal assemblages from Lukenya is the giant buffalo. Species common in the area historically, such as wildebeest, Thomson's gazelle, and impala, are rare or absent (Marean 1992a). The presence of oryx and Grevy's zebra in the assemblages, both of which are dry-adapted species presently found generally in areas with less than 750 and 500 mm of rainfall, respectively, also suggests expansion of dry grasslands during the last half of the Upper Pleistocene (Marean and Gifford-Gonzalez 1991:420). The rarer wildebeest, a species that may require more regular water and greener grass, suggests seasonal availability of water in the Lukenya area. Although the behavior of the most common herbivore, the extinct small alcelaphine, is unknown, its extreme hyp-sodonty may indicate an adaptation to poor-quality grass, which was possibly more common locally during the Pleistocene (Marean 1992a).

The fauna from Kisese II imply a contrasting pattern of environmental change. Marean et al. (1990) list the proportion of the Kisese II bovid fauna (as percent of the Minimum Number of Individuals [MNI]) from pre-Last Glacial Maximum, Last Glacial Maximum, and Holocene levels that are found today in closed, open, or mixed vegetation covers, and the proportion that can be classified as browsers, grazers, or mixed feeders. The Kisese sequence shows little change in the proportions of bovid types through time. In all three assemblages, closed habitat species make up around 20 percent of Minimum Number of Individuals and open feeders make up between 50 percent of Minimum Number of Individuals during the Holocene and 70 percent of Minimum Number of Individuals during the Last Glacial Maximum. The proportion of browsing species increases by only 10 percent in the Holocene compared to Last Glacial Maximum. The Kisese data dispute the Lukenya Hill evidence of marked aridity in East African grasslands. Kisese is located on a hilltop ecotone between an open grassland plain and the closed woodlands of the hill itself, where more browsing species could have thrived than in the open surroundings of Lukenya. Similarly, Upper Pleistocene fauna from Nasera Rockshelter, presently in semiarid grassland and woodland (White 1983:123), include species typical of such habitats, as well as water-loving reduncine antelope and duikers, suggesting more vegetated areas were nearby (Mehlman 1989). Contemporaneous faunal community differences at Lukenya Hill, Kisese, and Nasera underscore just how locally variable environmental change can be.

The Lake Victoria Regional Mosaic

The Lake Victoria regional mosaic was considerably drier and its vegetation less diverse during the Pleistocene. Today, Lake Victoria contributes 50 percent of the region's moisture, but extensive coring shows that it dried up during several thousand years of the Late Pleistocene, especially around 17,300 years ago (Johnson et al. 1996). Before 30,000 years ago, a montane conifer forest covered Kashiru Swamp, Burundi (2,104 m), today a humid forest, indicating conditions cooler and drier than today, but less dry than at the Last Glacial Maximum, when grass dominated and rainfall was an estimated 30 percent less than at present (Aucour, Hillaire-Marcel, and Bonnefille 1994; Bonnefille, Roeland, and Gruot 1990; Bonnefille and Riollet 1988).

Sowunmi's (1991) palynology of Lake Mobutu shows evidence of climates cooler and drier than today at this time. From 23,000 to 15,000 years ago pollen and organic matter were scarce to absent, indicating very dry regional conditions, as well as cold temperatures, and the lake dried up into a swamp (Sowunmi 1991:233).

The Guineo-Congolian Center

Rain forests located in lower altitudes contracted and fragmented during the late Upper Pleistocene, while high-altitude woodlands and montane forest expanded into lower elevations in Ghana, northeastern Angola, Cameroon, and the Bilanko Plateau in the Congo. As in East Africa, Afromontane vegetation descended 1,000-m from present altitudes, suggesting temperature drops of 6° C during the late Pleistocene (Elenga, Vincens, and Schwartz 1991; Elenga, Schwartz, and Vincens 1994; Maley 1987; van Zinderen Bakker 1976).

Pollen records from Matupi in western Uganda include both grassland and forest species, suggesting that the cave's immediate environment included more grassland during the Later Stone Age than at present. The pollen is mostly grass and forest ferns. Percentages of these plant and animal types, however, are unavailable (van Noten 1977). Pollen from this area show that "tropical forests with more open canopies than those of the Holocene may have persisted in this part of the Congo Basin" (Mercader and Brooks 2001:202). Preliminary analysis of pollen cores from Lac Tumba, indicate that the region, presently a tropical rain forest, was "an open landscape of savanna type close to marshy areas and gallery forests" (Fiedler and Preuss 1985:181). The distribution of birds, plants, mammals, amphibians, butterflies, and mollusks in Africa suggests that equatorial rain forest was reduced to three main refugia in eastern Congo, especially the Ituri, Cameroon and Gabon, and coastal Tanzania, with a minor refugium in western Rwanda and southwestern Uganda (Hamilton 1982:212–213; Hamilton 2000). Present-day plant and animal diversities are highest in these areas and decrease with increasing distance.

Fauna from the Later Stone Age site of Matupi, on the eastern edge of the Guineo-Congolean Center, are dominated by forest species, including squirrel, giant forest hog, okapi, bongo, forest duikers, Bates' dwarf antelope, and sitatunga, but also include open-habitat species like roan antelope and oribi (Van Neer 1989). The fauna from Ishango (Peters 1989) also include both forest species, such as red forest buffalo and duiker, as well as grassland and woodland-dwelling topi and Cape buffalo, suggesting a mosaic environment, as at Matupi. Pollen support this reconstruction (Brook, Burney, and Cowart 1990).

The Zambezian Center

Last Glacial Maximum pollen data are consistent with greater cold and aridity here, although vegetational changes were not as great as in the Lake Victoria or Somalia-Masai regions. At Kalambo Falls, late Pleistocene pollen data show that montane vegetation zones shifted downward in elevation 600- to 900-m, indicating drops in temperature of 3° to 5° C from modern averages (Van Zinderen Bakker 1969), compared with 1,000-m and 6° C drops from Kenyan studies (Coetzee and van Zinderen Bakker 1989). At Shiwa Ngandu, 282-km south of Kalambo Falls, Livingstone (1971) found very little change in the pollen record from 22,000 B.P. until the present, during which time a miombo woodland prevailed, as it does today. Livingstone notes that *Brachystegia* pollen become more common relative to grasses during the Holocene, but that the change is not dramatic. A nearby pollen core in the Mpulungu Basin at the southern end of Lake Tanganyika (780 m) also shows that *miombo* woodland prevailed, although tree density was less than at present and overlying montane vegetation belts were depressed in altitude from present locations (Vincens 1991). The relative continuity in the Zambezian woodland vegetation through time, as evinced by the Mpulungu core, contrasts with the pattern from a similar altitude at Lake Mobutu in the Lake Victoria regional mosaic (Sowunmi 1991), which was almost devoid of vegetation at the Last Glacial Maximum.

Faunal analysis indicates that vegetation in southern Zimbabwe was more open than today (Cruz-Uribe 1983; Klein 1978). Fauna at Redcliff Cave show a more open habitat and include small hartebeest, tsessebe/hartebeest, and springbok, all of which are found today only on South Africa's highveld grasslands. Klein's (1984) comparison of faunal change in the Zambezian region at Leopard's Hill Cave and in southern Africa at Heuningneskrans demonstrates that the shift from open-grassland large grazers to browsing species at the close of the Pleistocene was not as drastic in the Zambezian region as it was in areas farther south.

The Kalahari/Highveld Regional Transitional Zone

This zone of low (250- to 500-mm/year), single-season rainfall has diverse vegetation, but two main types are the Highveld grassland and the Acacia bushland and wooded grassland of the Kalahari (White 1983). Pre-Last Glacial Maximum fauna from the Highveld grasslands at Heuningneskrans, Bushman Rockshelter, and Border Cave are similar to modern-day inhabitants (Wadley 1993). Last Glacial Maximum vegetation was cold- and dry-adapted and low in diversity, for example the ericaceous vegetation that dominated around Rose Cottage Cave (Wadley 1993). Last Glacial Maximum fauna from Heuningneskrans suggest more arid, open conditions than today (Klein 1984). Increased grass cover in Last Glacial Maximum pollen spectra at Equus Cave indicates temperatures 4° colder than at present, and bovids from this site are more open-living than present fauna.

In contrast to the Highveld, the Kalahari and Namibia were wetter than at present throughout much of the Upper Pleistocene (Brook, Haberyan, De Filippis 1991; Cooke 1984; Deacon, J. and Lancaster 1988; Shaw and Thomas 1996; Wadley 1993). At White Paintings Rockshelter in the Tsodilo Hills, a large lake supporting fishing communities existed in what is now desert during much of the later Pleistocene (Robbins, Murphy, Stewart, Campbell, and Brook 1994).

The Karoo-Namib and Cape Centers

The Karoo Desert has long been a no-man's-land (Wadley 1993:261). By contrast, the Cape's *fynbos* and coastal and riparian bushland and thicket areas were well inhabited. Study of caves, lakes, coasts, and pollen and charcoal shows that climate was cooler and dryer than at present (Deacon and Lancaster 1988). Latest Pleistocene fauna found in Cape archaeological sites, including Elands Bay Cave, Boomplaas, and Nelson Bay Cave, were dominated by migratory grazers, including quagga, wildebeest, bontebok, and springbok, consistent with an open grassland environment (Klein 1972, 1980). Today, small browsers inhabit the *fynbos*. A detailed pollen record from Boomplaas shows low plant species diversity. Seventy-eight percent of the pollen are attributable to *Elytroppappus*, just one of many genuses of ericaceous shrubs in the *fynbos* today (White 1983:132). Oxygen isotopes from speleothems at the Cango Caves, and from fossil water at Uitenhage aquifer, show 5.5° C drops in average temperature from 28,000 to 15,000 B.P. (Deacon and Lancaster 1988).

Summary: Africa at the Last Glacial Maximum

Most of the African continent experienced dramatic drying and cooling during the Last Glacial Maximum. However, continuity between present and Pleistocene vegetation in the Central African rain forest and Zambezian zones is greater than in the drier areas of eastern and southern Africa. Pocket refugia existed in parts of Central Africa. The *miombo* woodlands may have been rather similar to today (Vincens 1991). The Matupi and Ishango fauna (van Neer 1989; Peters 1989) contain primarily forest species with some savanna species, showing that forest still dominated late Pleistocene vegetation in Central Africa. By contrast, southern and eastern Africa were sometimes drier than at present. Although our data permit us to reconstruct only the most recent cold event, the cyclical and repetitive nature of climate change suggests strongly that previous glacial periods had similar effects on African climate and vegetation.

Holocene (Interglacial) Climates

The Holocene period was a dramatic change to a warm and wet period around the world. It began around 15,000 years ago (Deacon and Deacon 1999:119; deMenocal et al. 2000). In Africa, for the most part, the transition to it is marked by distinctly warm and wet period that lasted until about 6,000 years ago (Lamb et al. 1995; Jolly, Prentice, and Bonnefille 1998). However, this is not evident in South Africa, which was drier than at present. During this African Humid Period, eastern African lakes, like Eyasi, Olduvai, and Natron, as well as the

Kalambo basin swelled, attracting game and hunter-fishers camping on their margins. There was a brief return to more arid glacial conditions around 12,000 years ago (Roberts et al. 1993).

The African Humid Period had many dramatic effects. Eastern Africa became a hunter's paradise. During its florescence, a broad swath of the Sahel and the southern reaches of the Sahara saw substantial occupation by hunting and fishing people (Figure 2.6). They were dispersed in semisedentary fishing villages, reaping a rich harvest from a lacustrine domain in what is now desiccated (MacDonald and van Neer 1994; Holl 1998a; Smith, A. 1992). The "green Sahara" was virtually covered by vegetation, its landscape marked by scores of lakes, and lakeside camps throughout the region. Some of the fisher-fowler-grain collectors were experimenting with the husbanding of herds. The onset of the African Humid Period was as sudden as its end. Both occurred in periods of less than four centuries. With its demise, the active life of the bone-using hippo hunters and gatherers of lakeside resources, occupying an interaction sphere from the Niger to the Nile, came to its end, as well.

During the Humid Period, Africa experienced the warmest temperatures of the last 100,000 years (Deacon and Deacon 1999). Afterward, a period of aridity began that produced the Sahara Desert as we now know it. Elsewhere, the continent became cooler and drier. Cold periods reoccurred about every 1,500 years. The most recent was the Little Ice Age from 1300 to 1850 A.D. In southern Africa, however, rainfall increased due to El Niño effects. Discounting such variation, African climates became generally warmer and drier (deMenocal et al. 2000). The long dry spells of recent years have had an adverse effect on the human environment that we can confidently project into the distant past.

Because of the cyclical nature of climate change, there are similarities in the climatic history of our present interglacial period, and the last interglacial, from 130,000 to 117,000 years ago (deMenocal 2001). Both began with about 6,000 years of warm and humid conditions, culminating in about 4,000 years of peak humid conditions. The previous interglacial terminated with nearly 6,000 years of warm, but dry conditions, similar to those we experience today. This was succeeded by an abrupt reversion to glacial cold and aridity. Whether this will be our fate is yet to be determined.

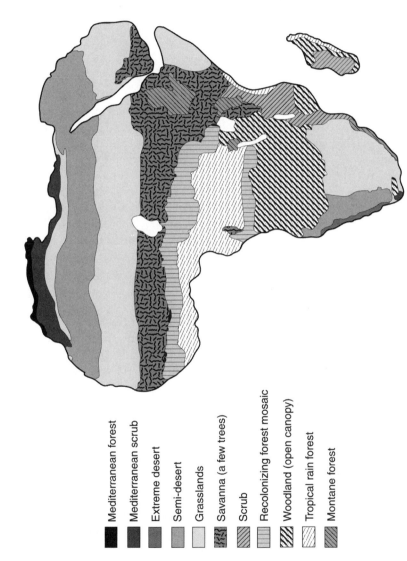

Figure 2.6.   *Reconstructed vegetation in Africa 9,000 years ago, during the African Humid Period.*

Mediterranean forest
Mediterranean scrub
Extreme desert
Semi-desert
Grasslands
Savanna (a few trees)
Scrub
Recolonizing forest mosaic
Woodland (open canopy)
Tropical rain forest
Montane forest

Summing Up

A fine-grained climate record gives archaeologists a chance to understand the impact of climatic change on African cultures. Significant events in human evolution—such as the appearance of robust australopithecines and the invention of stone tools 2.7 million years ago, or the evolution of early *Homo erectus* 1.8 million years ago and the demise of the robust australopithecines around a million years ago—have been allied to abrupt and dramatic climatic cooling episodes. It is thought that these events overwhelmed the adaptive ability of hominids (deMenocal 1995; Potts 1996; Vrba 1988). Altered conditions tested their inventiveness. In much the same way, abrupt and small-scale climatic events such as the Younger Dryas period near the end of the Pleistocene would give successful impetus to the ongoing trials of agriculture (Bar-Yosef and Kislev 1989). Climate changes in northeast Africa have been implicated in the beginnings of pastoralism there (Wendorf and Schild 1998). It only stands to reason that anything that has a significant effect on long-standing, well-rehearsed behavior stimulates appropriate adaptive responses. Failure to respond would, of course, spell disaster. Early hominids seem too resourceful to permit this. It is not that climate was the prime mover in human evolution, but that the history of humanity's development is a tangled skein of environmental influences, technological novelties, and social responses. It is an interplay of many forces, some accidental and some designed (Terrell 1986).

Clark (1994) suggested that alternating glacial and interglacial interludes caused cyclical changes in the vegetation belts of Africa. He hypothesized that during glacial periods, lowland forests such as those in Central Africa and the woodlands of southeastern Africa shrank, while desert, savanna, and steppe conditions expanded into tropical regions. In this scenario, a few places in equatorial Africa would have been warm, wet refuges, during repeated cold episodes, offering hunter-gatherers moderately moist conditions even during colder, arid periods. Indeed, some areas of tropical Africa in Gabon, Cameroon, the Shaba region, and Gombe Point in the Congo, or the Serengeti in eastern Africa demonstrate long histories of human use, with many deep stratified sites, continuously inhabited over long periods of time (Mehlman 1989; Brooks and Robertshaw 1990; Klein 1992; Cornellison 1997).

On the other hand, lacunae in human settlement occur in the more temperate northern and southern extremes of the continent (Avery 1995;

Clark 1994; Wendorf and Schild 1992; Klein 1989). The Sahara effectively emptied during glacial periods, when it was a dry desert, but became populated again during interglacial times, when it became "the green Sahara." Similarly, South Africa was often poorly populated or empty. On the other hand, African populations were arguably the world's largest, throughout much of prehistory, when ice sheets hindered human settlements elsewhere (Relethford 1998; McBrearty and Brooks 2000). Overall, the very diversity of African environments is reflected in significant cultural diversity from the Middle Stone Age onward.

Much of the African continent is seasonally arid, an effect of the shifting pattern of the monsoons. Historians and archaeologists alike have discussed the influence of aridity, drought, and other environmental constraints; unpredictable seasonal rainfall; poor soils; and disease on the adaptive responses of African cultures (Avery 1995; Gifford-Gonzalez 1998; Klein 1992). It is apparent that these constraints encouraged African populations to be mobile and expansive "colonizers" of vast internal frontiers (Iliffe 1996). Pastoralism, in particular, a shifting food-producing strategy, and shifting cultivation are highly adaptive to African conditions. It is no surprise that herding developed in Africa long before agriculture, as it initially furthered the transhumant habits of hunter-gatherers (Holl 1998a; Marshall and Hildebrand 2002).

Africans, in adapting to their sometimes marginal surroundings, developed an expertise in managing their situation through extensive techniques—segmentary kinship, shifting cultivation, mobility, and seasonal transhumance readily come to mind. In other words, effective food-getting strategies were ones based on shifting cycles, rather than long-term modifications of single areas. However, it should be noted that shifting cultivators invest time and effort on real estate intended to be of long-term benefit. Mobile people—whether foragers or herdsmen—invest in technologies and social arrangements that permit an extension of their activities across large territories. It is fair to say that their habits are consistent with those of African shifting cultivators, who generally exploit their home territories in an extensive, rather than an intensive fashion (Sutton 1994–1995). The territories of African cultivators often seem poorly populated to eyes accustomed to the densities of the more temperate latitudes.

However, not only cultivators used social systems creatively. Africans of all ilk seek to protect themselves against environmental stress, using a number of technological as well as social strategies. Hunter-gatherer bands, traveling through and utilizing multiple environments, wove intricate social bonds between their communities, using far-reaching interaction spheres to forge access to resources otherwise far over the horizon. This sort of social construct was not unique to Africa, but Africans used it in proficient fashion. At the same time, they cultivated skills that not only allowed them to explore the rich environmental mosaic of their homeland but also to venture out into the wider world.

3

Humans, Tool Makers

Imagine a time when, scattered across the highlands and peneplained spine of a continent, troupes of early australopithecines plied the trade of scavenger-foragers. If we discount Dart's (1957) extravagant claims for the tool-making abilities of these creatures at sites like Makapansgat, the circumstantial evidence suggests they were not stone-tool makers or users, although the use of minimally modified objects was probably part of their repertoire (Brain and Shipman 1993). Sometime later, at least 2.5 million years ago at Kada Gona in Ethiopia, a group of clever hominids transformed themselves from tool users to tool makers (Semaw et al. 1997). At nearby Bouri, these *Australopithecus garhi* butchered the carcasses of antelopes and horses and left cut and batter marks on the animals' leg bones (Asfaw et al. 1999; de Heinzelin et al. 1999).

Tool use is a behavior found among higher primates and other animals such as birds. It permits a variety of tasks beyond the capacity of flesh alone. Things can be cut, sawn, rubbed, scraped, and abraded or battered with the right instrument. Among chimpanzees at least (Whiten et al. 1999), and certainly the human lineage, tool making was and is a learned, repetitive behavior. It is a skill to be stored in memory and used again. Once grasped, it can be taught to one's fellows and progeny. Some hominids had discovered technology, a learned extrasomatic behavior. The many animals who keep a repertoire of learned behaviors and pass them onto their offspring can share information and adapt much more quickly than those for whom behavior is innate (Avital and Jablonka 2000:325). To early hominids, it gave an evolutionary advantage, especially in rapidly changing and unpredictable environments (Potts 1996).

Simply stated, the history of stone-tool making is one of experiment, ingenuity, and efficiency. The first tool makers not only perceived the value of sharp edged stone, but they understood its fracturing qualities and intelligently tested different sorts of stone and ways to chip useful edges (Roche et al. 1999). They ingeniously found inventive ways to flake it, progressing from the simple shaping of cores to the intricacies of blade manufacture and core preparation. Each new method was a clever way to impart force and efficiently cleave useful product from a rock. Over the course of millennia, stoneworkers learned to produce larger quantities of edge, the working part of a tool, from a minimum of stone. Over time, generally speaking, the finished product itself and the stages involved in its production became more predetermined, and the number of different tools made increased (Isaac 1986). The earliest tools made involved a simple sequence of flake removals—both the flakes and the flaked object or core were useable, handheld tools. Over time the form and subsequent modification of the flakes themselves became the focus of tool making, especially with the evolution of hafting—the placement of the flakes in handles of various shapes and sizes. When humans began to place increasing emphasis on hafting, the shape and size of the hafted flakes needed to be controlled. This began a "leptolithic" age of smaller, narrower blade tools that were mere components of complex, multicomponent tools. Stone slivers, or microliths, were combined with bone, bone or leather, and adhesives in the production of composite tools. Smaller quantities of raw material were needed, saving on the cost of acquisition and transport. The microlithic advantage permitted hunters in the field to conveniently repair broken implements, sharpen a dull edge, or assemble a new weapon as needed. The discard or loss of a stone microlith entailed little cost (Mitchell 1988; Bleed 1986). Humans had become not only capable tool makers but also highly effective ones.

The "survival" strategies of human populations needed more than sticks and stones, or knives and spears, no matter how cleverly they were contrived. Nevertheless, the product of technology, the objects themselves, and the modes of manufacture or utilization, as well as their symbolic value or social significance, are often the only hints we have of bygone behaviors. For good reason, archaeologists view technology as a significant component of the human condition and reconstruction of past technologies as a primary goal of their research. Appreciating the diverse ways and wherefore of human ingenuity, we gain a special insight into other aspects of culture as well. We discern the finished product and reconstruct its manufacturing techniques, realizing that every tool was used in a functional capacity. The stone tools so readily preserved in archaeological excavations once had a job to perform in subsistence and commerce, and as part of daily life, as well as in social arrangements and belief systems. Understanding technology is a keystone to comprehending the people who conveniently left the remains we find in our excavations.

Approaches to Technology in African Archaeology

Like most archaeologists of the early twentieth century, those studying Africa prehistory once used a simple classificatory scheme, placing similar shapes of worked stone into niches, space-time pigeon holes that are presumed to reflect a generalized, evolving tool-making tradition, possibly associated with an ethnic group or "culture" (Deacon, J. 1990; Robertshaw 1990). Such categorizations aided the initial comprehension of the growing collections of stone tools from a very large continent, understood to have housed the earliest human cultures. By the 1950s, many Africanists were uncomfortable with the prevailing descriptive, intuitive archaeology (Parkington 1986; Trigger 1990:313).

The next few decades saw an increase in the numbers of investigators in Africa, and in the numbers and diversity of the sites uncovered by them. New sorts of questions were asked, or at least new ways toward solving old problems. Archaeology sought to understand the appearance of new metallurgical technologies and food production on the continent, but the discovery of previously unknown hominids perpetuated the chronicle of early forms of humanity. Along with the fossils of early hominids were the remains of their culture. Material studies were key to understanding the origins and evolution of mankind.

Over the past twenty years, the "technological organization" approach to stone-tool analysis, which we will say more about in this chapter, has tried to move stone-tool studies away from the descriptive and technical and more toward an anthropological view of context and use (Nelson 1992). Whether these approaches have advanced our understanding of ancient stone tools has been disputed (Torrence 1994). Whatever else was accomplished, there has been greater appreciation of human behavioral patterns as an instigator of archaeological deposits. Though, one should say that Africanists had long been pursuing an understanding of behavior and adaptation, especially through the functional analysis of stone tools. Clark, as early as the 1960s (1970:80), was attempting to reconstruct the behavioral patterns of Early Stone Age times at Kalambo Falls. There and elsewhere, his research sought answers to questions beyond descriptive typology and stratigraphy. His excavations at the many camps buried in the silts of the Kalambo Basin (Clark, J. D. 1974) uncovered not only a rich sequence of Stone Age culture but also the very context of its use. Land once trod by Pleistocene families disclosed an even richer lode of behavioral details.

To understand these behavioral patterns, Clark (1958) examined the many kinds of tool types found throughout eastern and southern Africa and used ethnographic analogies with Native Australian and African tool use to propose tools' function as woodworking, rasping, or scraping. He noted (1958:148–149) use wear on woodworking tools. Using this understanding of function he was able to interpret lithic assemblage variation as caused by raw material or manufacturing or use strategies, as opposed to using the *portmanteau* "culture" to sidestep the problem of why stone-tool assemblages are different from one another. Howell, Cole, and Kleindienst (1962) began the process of differentiating the special functional toolkits of Acheulian hunter-gatherers. They were able to show that different localities along the streams of Isimila had different sets of implements. This suggested that hominids had different sets of tools they applied to different purposes.

The importance of activity differences led Clark (1970:38) to define an industry not according to percentages of shaped tools and blades—the most striking axis of variation in European Paleolithic sites—but as a group of occurrences that share technological and typological similarities that nevertheless encompass variation, particularly that related to raw materials, flaking techniques, and site functions. For example, Clark reasoned that Hope Fountain "culture," distinguished by a block-on-block stoneworking technique, was, in fact, a specialized sort of Acheulian adapted to the conditions of southern Africa. Similarly, the appearance of handaxes in Acheulian assemblages indicated the addition of a new and important activity to a previously established lifeway, rather than an influx of immigrant culture-bearers (Clark 1970:84). Similarly, he posited the Sangoan and Lupemban, forest-based industries of the Middle Stone Age derived from the Acheulian and marked by large woodworking tools, were a specialized adaptation to the spread of forest, rather than to a "degeneration in ability" as was previously thought (Clark 1970:112; but see McBrearty 1991; Clark and Brown 2001). As one can see, the uses of the tools became an important factor in the analysis of Paleolithic residues.

Africanist archaeologists sought confirmation of their functional arguments in early attempts to study use wear. Keller (1966:501) conducted controlled experiments to investigate factors that influenced edge damage in such a way that the results could be applied to any archaeological assemblage. He discussed factors that affect variations in observable microscarring. These included scarring attributable to the hardness of the raw material, edge angle, the motion of the tool in use, the duration of the motion, and the material upon which the tool is used. Phillipson and Phillipson (1970) examined edge wear on quartz artifacts from Chiwemupula in Zambia, carrying out experiments meant to replicate observed wear. They also determined that the materials, edge angle, and the type and duration of force all influenced the kind of damage found on artifacts. The real significance of these investigations was their attempt to draw from the field data more than just the morphology, or even the knapping process, of the worked stone. These were pioneering attempts at ascertaining, with a certainty, what sort of work the implements performed, although the study of polishes (Binneman 1997; Wadley and Binneman 1995), rather than microscarring, is sometimes considered a more reliable use signature.

Since archaeology was concerned with categorizing the implements it found and generalizing about their cultural identity, it was necessary to reflect on the reasons for variability. Differences in the quality of available stone have an obvious effect on the finished product. It may allow stoneknappers to excel, or it may thwart efforts to produce a precise cultural ideal. There may be other reasons for differences, but it is best to first consider the simplest cause.

Africa is a continent of vast expanses, where cultural territories may spread over thousands of miles. The workable stone may vary in availability and quality within this range, and different materials may yield serious variation even when worked using the same manufacturing procedures. Beyond considerations of the transport of quality stone from one place to another, we are forced to consider the characteristics of different raw material on finished artifacts (Clark 1980a). Isaac (1986) contended that the core-tool forms of the Karari Industry were a result of an efficient least-effort flaking, adapted to the original shape of the split cobbles used. The interplay of nature and culture made for a characteristic tool type. Variation in the archaeological record can be seen to have many causes—different assemblages at different locations, different tools for different jobs, poor craftsmanship, or variable quality of the stone used. Acknowledging this fact challenged many traditional modes of expressing the content of archaeological localities. It also opens new pathways to understanding the past and the people who inhabited it.

Archaeologists in Africa sometimes work with remote time periods, as well, and investigate the behavior of hominids of unknown capacities. Nevertheless, we hope to identify the products of these differing faculties from the distant past. Being assured that variation might be due to the unreliable skills of the earliest stoneworkers (Kibunjia 1994) gave little comfort to those who sought to perceive the genesis and development of the tool makers' earliest efforts. To this end, Isaac (1986) proposed an analysis of residuals, sorting out the effects of differences in material quality, function, and cultural format. This analysis first identified aspects of assemblage variability due to efficient working of a particular sort of stone before evaluating the influences of raw material availability and economical transport, and then it considered any consequences of use. Having produced a picture of a culturally discrete assemblage, differences that could not be accounted for were ascribed to differences in "culture." That is, it represented a cultural "style," a deviation intended by the makers. If, over space or time, differences in cultural intent involved variation in the number of steps involved in a technological process, the imposition of an arbitrary form, or an elaboration of the number of forms in an assemblage, than some perceptible change in cultural style was indicated (Isaac 1986:226–227). That is, we had encountered culture process, a designed alteration of customary formats.

Acknowledging the formation and alteration of cultural formats led to an interest in describing the evolution of cultural and intellectual capacity (Wynn 1989). To this end, Wynn (1993a) examined worked stone as a clue to early hominid abilities to conceptualize space. He posited that the makers of Oldowan Industry tools had spatial competency levels of modern chimpanzees, whereas the makers of Acheulian Industrial Complex tools understood and reproduced symmetry, a more complex judgment of outline. Furthermore, Acheulians could put together a greater number and variety of spatial concepts, showing the greater complexity of Acheulian tool making.

At the other end of the time scale, Africanists have long used ethnoarchaeology as a source of theory. Clark (1984) studied the manufacture gunflints in the Congo, where a punch technique was used. He noted a debitage of waste flakes similar to those littering sites of the Middle and Later Stone Age, suggestive of analogous modes of manufacture. Having an experience of African hunters, he was able to use his personal observations in other interpretations of sites and artifacts (Clark, J. D. 1958, 1969, 1970, 1974, 1989). For example, he drew attention to the use of poison on the lightweight projectiles of the Later Stone Age (Clark 1970:157; Clark, Phillips, and Staley 1976) and showed an interest in the worked stone tools of Native Australians as a clue to the function of archaeological implements (Clark 1958). He posited that ash lenses in Middle Stone Age sites in southern Africa were indicative of meat-drying racks (Clark 1989), and so forth. The close observation of modern behavior often shows that variation in the archaeological record can come from individual as well as cultural variation. Weedman (2000) has studied obsidian hide scrapers used in the Ethiopian highlands, observing that the social contexts of use vary dramatically among three different ethnic groups and noting the influence of individual skill and experience on the shapes of manufactured scrapers.

Other approaches involving lithic data and the deciphering of behavior include the use of a technological organization approach, which seeks to understand how settlement and mobility patterns influence how people procure, design, and use tools. Mitchell (1992) noted similarities between late Pleistocene Robberg lifeways and technology in South Africa and those of roughly contemporaneous Paleoindians of North America. These similarities included a varied settlement pattern and the hunting of large, mobile game. Comparing the technology of these two groups, he sought to find out whether identical canons of technological design and organization characterized both industries.

The Paleoindians used bifacial cores to produce large, flat flakes. It is assumed that transporting raw material such as large bifaces in this way is an optimal way of carrying raw material (Kelly and Todd 1988). By contrast, Robberg hunter-gatherers employed a great many microlithics, hafted into a wide variety of specialized tools and weapons. This could be considered a way of optimizing raw material as well (Barham 1987), allowing one to create a great many cutting edges from a single piece of stone. Mitchell considers both technologies an efficient use of raw material. The types of tools made in these two cultures differed dramatically, however. Paleoindian tools were made on high-quality raw materials and their projectile points in particular were painstakingly designed, while the Robberg bladelets were produced as needed with a minimum of retouch, using the many different kinds of stone found close at hand (Mitchell 1992). Although both populations of big game hunters shared many common features—a mobile land-use pattern and the hunting of large, mobile mammals—their technologies are quite different.

If, as we suppose, people will attempt to find the most efficient way to carry out survival strategies, why should these two groups with similar subsistence goals develop such radically different technologies? Kuhn (1994) suggested that carrying several, small specialized implements was more efficient use than carrying a few large multifunctional ones. By this measure, the more numerous, highly standardized bladelets of the Robberg were a more efficient way of transporting raw material than larger bifacial cores. We can only suggest that the contrasting technologies came about because each group used very different initial kinds of raw material. Robberg people used local supplies, for the most part, while the Paleoindians acquired stone, whose blanks were large and suited for the manufacture of large bifacial cores. Paleoindian stone procurement seems to have been a more "costly" business, relying on a few, distant material sources, requiring trade and maintenance. Robberg hunters, on the other hand, used "inexpensive" stone destined to a short life, transported, used, and discarded not far from its source. In contrast to locally discarded Robberg worked stone, the Paleoindians kept theirs longer and carried it as far away as 500-miles from its source. In other words, Paleoindian and Robberg technology differ because Paleoindians required long-distance exchange to acquire raw material and factored this into their "cost benefit analysis" (Goodyear 1989; Seeman 1994). Furthermore and efficiency counting aside, the knappers in each group were part of a very different evolved tradition of tool making—purely cultural differences must be reckoned with. It is this kind of technological variation that often clouds our reading of the palimpsest left us by past events. To understand technological choices, we cannot limit ourselves to reading any one factor in the archaeological record. Instead, we need to consider the whole context of a technology, the physical and social environments binding any assembly of people to a particular web of earth.

Thinking about Technology

Stone tools, traditionally, have been catalogued according to their shape, along with ideas about their mode of manufacture or function. In order to get more information from our collections, it may be necessary to look more closely at other aspects of tools, especially at the motives and styles of the makers. It is, therefore, useful to think of the manufacturing process and subsequent use of the tool as a set of actions, or choices. These stages of the technological process are the raw materials, the transforming forces, the finished objects, the manufacturing sequence, and the technological knowledge needed to successfully carry out the operation (Lemonnier 1992). The artifacts themselves are an outcome of all of these actions and choices. If there is a choice between two different sorts of stone nearby, we can speculate on why one was chosen and not the other. The stone may be from some distant locale. We can then speculate on the mode of acquisition and whether the makers traveled to the source themselves or engaged in some kind of exchange network that brought it to them. We can ask whether the stone was transported as raw material or as a completed object. Examination of reduction sequences will suggest one or the other, by identifying styles of manufacture that differ from one place to the other. If the transported stone was received through intermediary agency, we can question the organization of the exchange network. If the makers went to the stone source themselves, we can surmise the manner of their social interaction with the "owners" of the stone. We can ask whether the contact had a social or religious sanction, and so forth. The interplay of all aspects of human culture and society is open to inspection, because that complex organization that we signify as culture is at work.

The certain value of tool use in human lifeways has led many to espouse a kind of technological determinism. V. Gordon Childe, for example, once emphasized the role of technology in driving cultural evolution, an idea common to many working in Africa, where the idea that technology has driven successive waves of cultural change is well established. It's hard to deny the crucial role of the first stone tools in broadening the dietary possibilities of early hominids; the earliest stone tools are associated with equally early evidence of carcass butchery at the Bouri site. In more recent archaeology, iron was thought to have created a domino effect of population increases, large-scale migration, and cultural complexity, in effect moving African culture from a hunting and gathering stage to a Neolithic stage. This technological determinism is misplaced. More accurate is the view that technological systems—which include not just implements but the cultural knowledge of how to make and use them—are deeply embedded in the cultures they are a part of (Lemonnier 1992).

At the same time, fulfilling such a cultural agenda requires, in the first instance, skilled artisans schooled, somehow, in the necessary craft, its rituals, and whatever else is needed to successfully author consistent, tried-and-true products. Sometimes the ritual prescriptions contain technological knowledge, other times they are obscurant. Content may be less significant than performance. Adherence to a cultural format is paramount to continuity. Survival strategies imply strict adherence to cultural ideals. This insinuates much about the cultural role of technology and consistency of practice by the application of social constraints. These restraints may lie outside the physics of the manufacturing process and only be hinted at in an archaeological situation. Nevertheless, they are always on our mind. As a result, if we identify the aspects of any technological process, we can use this as an entrée to the culture it was a part of. In particular for students of foragers, the application of technology is important to the creation of ecological solutions to environmentally posed problems.

Exploring *Chaînes Opératoires*

Flaked stone tools are, by far, the most plentiful sort of artifact found in African pre–Iron Age archaeological sites. As a result, we have tended to give them a certain importance in our analyses. At one time, collections were made on the surface or from river gravels. These offered an essentially unprovenienced context, but a liberal introduction to ancient stoneworking. As a result, these lithic collections were tirelessly assessed. Once, we were satisfied simply to describe prehistoric assemblages, illustrating and counting the various bits of shaped worked stone. Elaborate typological schemes evolved. In Africa, as elsewhere, whole industries or "cultures" were identified by the presence of particular tool types, flaking procedures, or the relative numbers of one kind or another of worked stone (Robertshaw 1990). Recently though, we have begun to rethink this somewhat one-dimensional view of technology. Archaeology now prefers a more holistic portrayal, viewing technology and culture process, generally, as a series of choices that have social and ideological as well as economic implications (Holl 2000).

African archaeologists, perhaps because of the great diversity in material culture and the expanses of space they have had to deal with, have long been concerned with the influence of environment and economy on technology. For example, the Burg-Wartenstein Conference suggested a hierarchical organization of stone artifact occurrences, proposing the "techno-complex" as a general way to use technology to mark cultural-stratigraphic units, recognizing that variation in local industries was conditioned by raw materials, function, and economy, as well as social context (Clark, J. D. 1970:38).

As a result, our attitude toward artifacts we find has changed as well. Until the mid-twentieth century, tool types and their frequencies at one site or another were often taken as markers of an "ethnically defined" preference of the makers. They were used to delineate groups separate from all other similar groups, contemporary or otherwise. This was the approach usually associated with Francois Bordes. It had the museological advantage of conveniently pigeonholing everything found. It was unclear whether these categories corresponded to any sort of reality. No one knew how cultures, so defined, related to one another. Binford (1972), working with European material, initiated criticism of the ethnic-comparison concept. He posited that tool classes, and especially, their relative occurrence in one place or another, were a reflection of functional difference rather than totally separate tool manufacturing traditions. He contended that differences in observed assemblages did not necessarily indicate different people, but a suggestion that the same people did different things from time to time and place to place.

There are many ethnographic observations of hunter-gatherer tool manufacture, transport, and use suggesting the influence of activity differences on interassemblage variation across space (Binford 1979; Binford and O'Connell 1984; Kelly 1988; Carr 1994). By determining the different toolkits used in one place or another to perform one set of activities or another, we can also understand how toolkits might vary from one archaeological locality to another.

This began the function versus style debate (Sampson 1988). One side argued that stone tools change within a sequence because tool functions and activities changed. The other side claimed that sequential change resulted from different traditions of stoneworkers occupying the site. This reminded some of the arguments attributing sequential change to movement of new people into a region. The great "migration hypothesis" may be unsatisfactory, but as in many academic arguments, one can cherry-pick useful tidbits from either point of view.

The "style" side held that stylistic information marking an ethnic identity was encoded into artifacts through time-honored manufacturing processes, replicated loyally from one generation to the next (Sackett 1982). In other words, it emphasizes that the educational process conserves certain ethnically ordained ideals. This is undoubtedly true, and archaeologists are justified in pinpointing the importance of technological traditions. On the other hand, function gives reason to making things in the first place. Some functional aspects can be tested by analysis of use wear, especially polishes formed on the worked edges of siliceous stone (Keeley 1981). Edge war studies seemed a scientific way to solve questions archaeology had always answered intuitively. However, these analyses did not always indicate a convenient correlation between shape and function (Odell 1981). They suggested that shape variation stemmed from different technological choices, sometimes a product of the knapper's creativity and sometimes learned and practiced subliminally; there is, indeed, an "ethnic" component to be reckoned with.

This recognition of several "ways to skin a cat" accompanied a shift in focus from the style or function argument to the sorts of analyses of technological process Lemonnier proposed. He posited examining the complete manufacturing process, from the acquisition of raw material to the fabrication procedures, use, reuse, and discard. This casts a light on "technological style" or "ways of doing things." It has the advantage of revealing variation in prehistoric manufacturing strategies. Using such a technological approach, French archaeologists examined the steps in stoneworking, or *chaîne opératoire*, and surmised a rationale for technological choices leading to the finished product (Pelegrin 1990). Pelegrin states the now obvious truth that encoded in stone tools is evidence of a far-reaching spectrum of human behavior—technical, economic, and social. The technological approach permits an insight into this spectrum, while avoiding the dilemma of deciding between culture or function, or "real" versus "invented types" (Pelegrin 1990:116). This method elicits an idea of the cultural format of the makers, as well as their training and skill. To take a non-stone tool example, Knecht (1992) has shown that the manufacture of Upper Paleolithic Aurignacian split-based points followed certain underlying principles that were a choice from among several other, equally workable possibilities.

This approach derives, in part, from a French tradition of experimental replication of stone tools, practiced by Bordes, Tixier, Pelegrin, and others. It requires close scrutiny of the stone tools and involves perception of behavior through an in-depth reading of the process of successively reducing a core piece to a finished tool. This reduction process is conceived of as a stylized, learned process constraining craftsmen to a series of culturally defined formats. Throughout the knapping process, knappers monitor and adapt their expectations to a particular core and raw stone material. Whether it is that so many French analysts experiment with stoneworking, or because of a long-standing academic interest in psychology, the technological approach seeks to detail not only the "mental formats" envisioned by stoneworkers but also the use of these in the production of implements (Pelegrin 1993).

The end result of this careful scrutiny is the description of many sorts of stone-reduction procedures (Boëda 1991, 1993; Boëda, Geneste, and Meignen 1990; Pelegrin, Karlin, and Bodu 1988). For example, the production of Acheulian bifacial handaxes and cleavers is a process of *façonnage,* or the patterned removal of flakes to produce a core tool (Figure 3.1). Prepared core reduction, typical of the African Middle Stone Age, is a more complex process. The core is conceived of as two opposing, convex surfaces. On one surface, platforms are prepared, facilitating removal of flakes from the other (Figure 3.2). In blade production, typical of the Later Stone Age, the core is conceived of as a discrete piece from which a large number of blades are produced (Figure 3.3).

What is important to our analyses as archaeologists is ascertaining where in the sequence some excavated piece finds itself, whether early in the process of core selection and testing, or as a flake of waste from core reduction or shaping, or from tool retouch. Certain types of debitage, such as cortical flakes, crested blades, flakes removed in repair or readjustment of platforms, or flake release surfaces, or tool retouch or resharpening flakes, all provide clues to the sequence (Movius et al. 1968). The core type and especially the morphology of the flake can also reveal flaking techniques such as bipolar or freehand core reduction (Cotterell and Kamminga 1987). Each sequence, and steps within it, may be conceivable as a signature, cultural or individual; hence, the importance of determining the *chaîne opératoire.* The more detailed our understanding of the reductive sequence, the more attributes—such as flake size, shape, presence of cortex, the direction, pattern, and number of dorsal scars, or platform type and faceting—can be used to assign pieces to stages along it. Once the knapping protocols are known, artifacts can be categorized and characterized as to their place in the fabrication sequence, whether core reduction, platform preparation, flake or blade production, core readjustment, tool manufacture, or subsequent modification of tools (Pelegrin, Karlin, and Bodu 1988; Inizan, Roche, and Tixier 1992).

For all this may tell us about individual artifacts, there is a still bigger fish to fry: the assemblage as a whole. Evaluation of relative quantities of worked stone, in varying stages of manufacture, permits an insight to the technological behaviors that produced the assemblage in the first place. This, after all, is the point to this analysis. For example, a quarry site should have a preponderance of artifacts early in a *chaîne opératoire.* On the other hand, a stoneworker's *atelier* will contain many waste flakes, while a use site will have every evidence of knapping, except for the resharpening of tools and the discard of broken or expended tools.

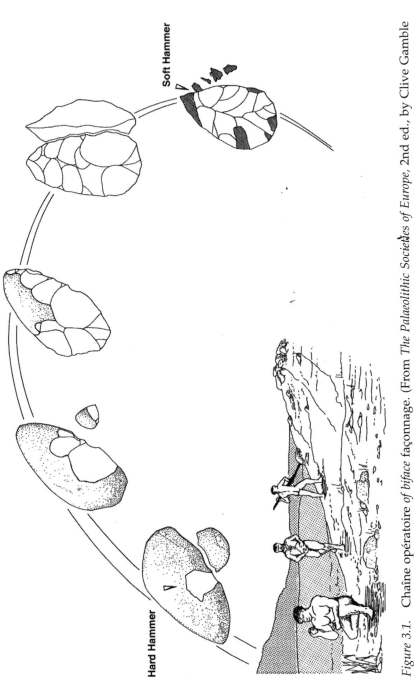

Hard Hammer

Soft Hammer

Figure 3.1. Chaîne opératoire *of biface* façonnage. (From *The Palaeolithic Societies of Europe*, 2nd ed., by Clive Gamble [Cambridge: Cambridge University Press]. Copyright © Cambridge University Press. Reprinted by permission of the publisher and Clive Gamble.)

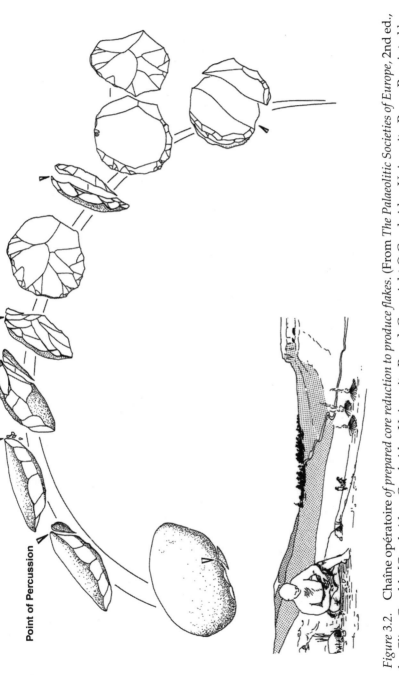

Point of Percussion

Figure 3.2. Chaîne opératoire of *prepared core reduction to produce flakes*. (From *The Palaeolitic Societies of Europe*, 2nd ed., by Clive Gamble [Cambridge: Cambridge University Press]. Copyright © Cambridge University Press. Reprinted by permission of the publisher and Clive Gamble.)

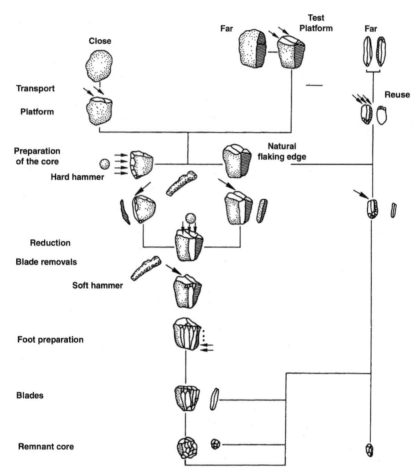

Figure 3.3. *A complex* chaîne opératoire *based on blade tool reduction.* (From *The Palaeolithic Societies of Europe,* 2nd ed., by Clive Gamble [Cambridge: Cambridge University Press]. Copyright © Cambridge University Press. Reprinted by permission of the publisher and Clive Gamble.)

These are obvious examples, but they illustrate an ability to highlight behavior beyond the counting of stone tools. At the same time, we uncover an ongoing rationale for transhumant strategies. To this end, *chaîne opératoire* analyses suggest neighboring localities will exhibit different emphases on the component stages (Ebert 1992). By observing the type and kind of stone recovered, we start to say something about what people were doing. They allow us to form images of hunters in ambush, where some keep a lookout, while their companions check their weapons, replacing a broken point, sharpening dulled edges. Uniform workmanship may suggest a single skilled craftsman producing tools for his companions, with all its social implications. Imported stone or varying quality of workmanship may imply social contact of a broader sort, or the presence of knappers of varied ages or experience levels (Weedman 2000). We are allowed to get closer to the human element in the archaeological record.

Such sequences are discoverable in other technologies such as pottery or metals. However, the idea of a perceptible sequence of technological stages lends itself particularly well to analyses of stone-tool manufacture, because detritus from all stages of lithic work—cores, debitage, decortification flakes, retouch flakes, and so on—are retrievable in archaeological sites.

Technological Strategies

Once the technological information inherent in a cultural assemblage is analyzed, we can interpret these patterns in any number of ways, deciding the relationship of the inherent technological strategy and choices to broader issues of residential mobility or subsistence. For example, acquisition and transport of raw material should be an economical routine of relatively low cost. To be otherwise stresses patterns of residential mobility or social connectivity, requiring movement to particular resource areas, or involvement with those commanding access to a critical resource.

Many archaeologists take a raw material economy approach, in which ways of transporting and reducing raw material are read from the relative proportions of different technological stages in an assemblage. There seem to be four different kinds of acquisition strategy— the transport of either unworked stone blocks, shaped cores, unretouched blanks, or finished artifacts (Inizan, Roche, and Tixier 1992). Any of these practices may be evident in a cultural deposit. Each leaves its distinctive footprint, as it were, in the form of a particular proportion of artifacts from different stages of the *chaîne opératoire*, such as cortical material or spent cores. The extent to which these procurement strategies were practiced is measured by the relative abundance of these lithic residues in the assemblage. The conservation and continued use of acquired stone is recognized by indications of tool recycling and resharpening.

A further question revolves around how the stone was acquired, whether by direct or indirect means. The identification of transport patterns opens up another stage in our analyses, in which one can ascertain the site's relationship to raw material sources, other sites, or geographical features, and how patterns of communication changed from time to time. In this way, we obtain information on a people's range or their cycle of interaction and exchange (Féblot-Augustins 1993; Geneste 1988, 1989), as well as other material concerns, such as the extent to which people anticipate future needs, particularly in the case of more evolutionary concerns such as the extent to which early hominids were able to plan ahead for their stone raw material needs (Roebroeks, Kolen, and Rensink 1988). We must assume that since stone transported over long distances is generally of high quality, it was worth the extra effort (Perlès 1993:279). Sometimes, using the raw material economy approach attempts to detect individual knappers through particular idiosyncrasies or skills (Karlin, Ploux, Bodu, and Pigeot 1993). Such identifications indicate to us the numbers of craftsmen in any group, or the reach of exchange networks, as distinctive workmanship moves out of a local sphere. At the same time, we can uncover an ongoing rationale for mobility routines, as *chaîne opératoire* studies display differing stages in the reduction process in neighboring localities, as people make implements to perform a different variety of functions (Ebert 1992).

Most studies of hunter-gatherer land use take as a starting point the idea that subsistence needs are the primary cause of mobile strategies. Regional and seasonal distribution of food plants, game, and water as well as the quality and availability of raw materials play significant roles in deciding where and when technological activities take place (Andrevsky 1994; Kelly 1988; Shott 1986; Torrence 1983). Fragments of stone flaked in the sharpening of a tool represent a different activity from blocks of stone at a quarry site or the detritus of stoneworking at a base camp. Knowing how and where stone was worked is important to us. To this end, the archaeology shows that people will make, use, and store a variety of activity-specific artifacts at an appropriate place, in expectation of using them at a future point in their subsistence cycle. That is, people anticipating some future need will obtain the materials and fabricate tools, which they will transport, if necessary, to the work site. Tools having little use elsewhere will be left behind.

The geographical variations in the types and numbers of artifacts from different stages of the *chaîne opératoire* are explainable as part of established routines. Having already alluded to some causes for variation in the archaeological record, we should note *curation* and *expediency* as recognized strategies, carefully preserving some artifacts and randomly producing others. Curation refers to any kind of technological behavior that anticipates future need (Nelson 1992). Manufacture in advance of use, transport, reshaping, caching, storing, and large expenditures of manufacturing energy are all examples of curation (Bamforth 1986). Curation is an investment in anticipated need, while expediency denotes the use of tools at the time and place of their manufacture. Expedient strategies generally involve minimal expenditure of energy in fabrication, less conformity to standardized canons, and rapid replacement (Binford 1979).

Regardless of how many organizational strategies are recognized, an important tenet of technological organization is that different strategies may exist simultaneously. For example, among Western Desert Native Australians, blanks for curated tools are formed at the quarry and then carried about, while cores for expedient flake tools are transported back to camp whole for finishing (Binford and O'Connell 1984). The same tool or work piece may be a part of curated, expedient, or opportunistic strategies at different times within its use life (Nelson 1992). Having recognized these different strategies does not make the archaeologist's task any easier, but it does offer a starting point for comment. Knowing that stone artifacts have complex life histories, including their "past lives" as part of other artifacts, is an important insight. One's goal becomes the recognition of different technological strategies within the same assemblage, and interpreting them with regard to the natural and social environment.

Actually recognizing technological strategies in an assemblage of stone tools is not always easy. Expediency is easily recognized, since it is usually associated with local raw materials, little expenditure of energy, little investment in retouch or the shaping and reduction of formal cores, and the presence of all technological stages in a discrete local assemblage (Binford 1979; Nelson 1992; Parry and Kelly 1987). Bipolar core and informal core reduction are the common manifestations of expedient production. There are thirteen ethnographic cases of bipolar core reduction, from five continents; in all cases the flakes were intended for immediate, brief use (Masao 1982; Shott 1989). These were transient sites of unanticipated, opportunistic activity.

The identification of curation for future use is difficult, but recognizable through context. For example, although bipolar core reduction is often associated with expedient tool manufacture, it is also used when raw materials are scarce or very small. Therefore, a recycling strategy may be at work (Barham 1987; White and Thomas 1972). Since we associate expediency with the bipolar technique and amorphous, informal cores and tools, we tend to infer curation from indicators of greater effort or formality in manufacture. However, this may be a misguided approach, implying a self-reifying paradigm. As a result, Nash (1996) says that prepared cores are more likely to be curated objects than are informal or amorphous cores, and that the intensity of retouch is a measure of curation. However, it is equally sure that neither prepared cores nor retouch intensity is necessarily an indicator of anticipated future use. What this all means is that even with the best of scientific intentions, archaeology remains a somewhat intuitive art, or at least a science highly dependent on the judicious use of analogical reasoning.

Transport is a more obvious type of curation behavior (Marks 1988; Kuhn 1992, 1995). It may also be one of the most important. Whether one is discussing early hominids or complex Later Stone Age huntergatherers, a major challenge for any mobile stone-tool–using group had to have been ensuring a steady supply of lithic raw material, while at the same time maintaining their schedules of food procurement and the manufacture and transport of tools (Kuhn 1995:18–19). Juggling all of these needs must surely have required planning. Kuhn (1994) contrasts two different strategies for planning that might involve both curation and expediency: provisioning *people* with tools (the hunter's "personal gear," Binford 1979) and provisioning *places* with tools. A hunter's personal gear should be highly portable and multifunctional, and archaeologically is often characterized by flakes or perhaps bifaces functioning as "flake dispensers" (Kuhn 1994; Kelly and Todd 1988). To provision places, on the other hand, requires a different set of considerations—the timing and type of tools needed at a future site should ideally be known if this strategy is to be effective. It is usually marked by the transport of cores, unmodified blocks, or other materials found at the beginning of the *chaîne opératoire*. Needless to say, the latter strategy requires the most planning, and probably became more important in times and places where people had the ability or the luxury to plan their use of sites and to stay at them for longer periods of time. More mobile people probably depended more on personal gear.

Our understanding of technological strategies and their distribution in space aids, as we have seen, in the identification of prehistoric settlement systems. They are usually based on a combination of two different kinds of mobility: residential mobility, in which the entire band moves from one residence to another, and logistical mobility, in which small task groups go out to gather specific resources on a logistical basis before returning to the home group (Binford 1980). As a result, the task parties produce a number of different site types, each specific to distinct activities. Curated and expediently produced strategies will be associated with different site types within a settlement system. Some tools require higher-quality raw materials and a complex design. Such tools imply a greater investment than casually produced ones. We should expect such tools to be linked to mobile settlements where implements were transported from place to place or left in situ. Expediently made tools, on the other hand, are more commonly found discarded where they were made and used, sometimes at temporary camps but often at longer-term, more sedentary base camps, such as the winter villages (Andrevsky 1994; Kelly 1992; Parry and Kelly 1987).

Ethnographic studies suggest what we should expect to find in various site types. For example, all aspects of stone technology should occur at residences, particularly evidence of tool making and repair, as well as exhausted or broken tools (Binford 1977, 1979, 1980). By contrast, short-term camps should contain debris from refurbishing of tools, as well as expedient tools from locally available raw materials. Drawing upon these inferences, Ebert (1992) developed a scheme for recognizing site types, proposing some different kinds of occupation. These include short-term foraging bases, semipermanent multifamily bases, logistic locations, and traveling camps. These could, in turn, be identified by an evaluation of the debris remaining from different stages of the stone-reduction process, the degree of variability and diversity of assemblages, and the ratio of expedient to curated tool types. Because of the many factors involved in the formation of a lithic assemblage, including function, raw materials, social arrangements, mobility, skill, and style, combined with the difficulty of easily distinguishing one strategy from another in the analysis of stone artifacts, and the complexity of identifying reduction sequences, even Kelly (1992:56) admits that "many interpretations of stone tool assemblages as indicators of mobility are subjective, intuitive, and sometimes contradictory."

Site type identification can be more secure when identified with respect to independent, nonlithic data, such that interpretation becomes a multivariate affair. For example, Stiner and Kuhn's (1992) analysis of Mousterian lithic assemblages from Italy suggested a scavenging strategy, surmised from a bias for older individuals and selective transport of head parts. They further determined that this was associated with short-term camps and the transport and continued production of large flake tools from centripetal cores. Hunting, on the other hand, they deduced would be associated with longer occupations and the use of smaller, shorter use-life tools and a broader range of body parts. In this case, the faunal data provided a useful background for understanding the lithic data.

Most of our ideas of the technological organization of typical hunter-gatherers derive from ethnographic observation (particularly Binford 1977, 1979; Binford and O'Connell 1984), or the extensive hunter-gatherer literature (Kelly 1983; Torrence 1983; Shott 1986). Given the paucity of stone-tool users left to study (Weedman 2000), investigators have begun to model their ostensible behavior. Shott (1986) showed the importance of portability to mobile hunter-gatherers. Kuhn (1994) constructed mathematical models to ascertain the most efficiently transported toolkits. That is, he determined that the most easily transported kind of gear was as light as possible, yet provided the most serviceable edges in surroundings where raw material availability was uncertain (Kuhn 1994:428).

Kuhn, seeking to find a measurement of portability in archaeological contexts, saw the problem as a search for artifacts that would allow the greatest potential utility and the lightest weight, enabling mobile individuals to be unencumbered by bulky *impedimenta*. His analyses indicate an obvious situation of diminishing return. Calculating supposed utility, or usable mass, of a series of flakes and cores of different sizes, he demonstrated that while core utility and the utility of flakes increase with size, permitting a larger amount of useable working edge, usefulness and portability are soon lost, defeated by large size and high weight. Greatest utility occurred in relatively small flakes. If large flakes were needed, the most efficiently carried ones were about three times their minimum useable size. Therefore, stone-tool production was not a haphazard occupation, but a skilled craft, comprehending many needs. Though Shott (1986) and Nelson (1992) posit that mobile toolkits should include multifunctional items, Kuhn suggests that several smaller tools might be more efficient. The carrying of core pieces is a debatable subject. Since they tend to be heavy and since much of their mass will be discarded, they are often deemed inefficient as personal gear. Kuhn, on the other hand, suggests that they are very versatile, being easily reduced into a number of desired implements, or used as pounders (Kuhn 1994:427). It can be said that smaller cores, used to produce blades or microliths, could easily be carried to be used as convenient dispensers of working edges—a curated expediency.

Our brief look at technological strategies and organization suggested useful ways to survey the behavior of the past. We ventured fruitfully, if sometimes debatably, from the knapping process to social organization and the mobility and acquisition patterns of stone users. We have been left, though, with some of the same problems that have vexed us since archaeology decided to eschew description to explore prehistoric behavior. The value of our evaluations is still dependent upon the intuitive powers of investigators, as much as it is dependent on the quality of the evidence.

Technological Design

Technological design comprises the form and composition of tools. More broadly, a look at technological design helps us to see how a particular tool assemblage was put together to meet basic needs: whether those needs relate to settlement mobility (Shott 1986) or resource distribution or hunting methods (Bleed 1986; Torrence 1983). Bleed (1986) proposed that prehistoric hunting weapons be grouped into *maintainable* and *reliable* designs. The second sort is counted on to work. They are overdesigned, strengthened, and sturdily put together. They are best suited to specific situations when failure has a high cost, such as encounter hunting in highly seasonal, risky environments, where game availability and pursuit times are short. They are needed when failure spells calamity as among the Inuit, where failure to reap highly seasonal Arctic resources has a high penalty over a long desolate winter (Bleed 1986).

Maintainable tools, by contrast, are generally lighter and more portable, with a conveniently maintained modular design. That is, they are made of readily available and easily replaceable components. They are suitable for general, continuous needs, ad hoc scheduling, and low-failure penalties (Bleed 1986). They are likely to be portable and multi-functional. They are usually associated with high-altitude groups who use a great deal of logistical mobility (Binford 1980). Other tool strategies have been identified. These include *versatile* and *flexible* ones (Nelson 1992). The first refers to generalized, multifunctional implements meant to address a variety of needs (Shott 1986), while the other refers to tools easily reconfigured to meet a variety of needs. Either kind of simple, portable multifunctional tool is desirable where resources are unpredictable but continuously available and mobility is high (Shott 1986). Collectors in risky situations, on the other hand tend toward more specialized, complex, reliable designs (Torrence 1983). This tendency is also found in high-risk hunting circumstances.

In reality, though it may be useful to recall a distinction between *maintainability* and *reliability*, applying these concepts to specific artifacts or assemblages is dicey at times, since most situations have aspects of both (Odell et al. 1996:378). Nobody ever said archaeology was for the faint-hearted or intellectually glib. For example, Bleed (1986) relates unpredictable hunting to maintainable tools, because they can be repaired and reused. Myers (1989), however, suggests that Mesolithic hunters adjusted to an increasingly unpredictable presence of game animals by designing reliable projectiles with reliable multiple microlith tips that work when needed. In fact, ascertaining the strategy implied by one sort of tool or the other may be a result of circuitous reasoning or circumstantial evidence, and therefore acutely subjective.

Another problem with using ideas derived from hypothetical studies lies in our appreciation of hafted lithic technologies using backed blades and microliths during the African Middle and Later Stone Age. When dealing with the archaeological remains of composite tool technology in which implements are made up of many parts, the archaeologist never has a whole tool. The *tool* by design is a composition of bits of sharpened stone, wood, or reed and organic bindings of sinew or fiber bound by some sort of adhesive or another, making up the working edge, the haft, and other parts of the tool. In addition, there is the likelihood of a projectile thrower, or bow, as well as some other accessory, and the application of idiosyncratic decoration (Odell 1994). All this must be implied from the discovery of bits of shaped stone or a core capable of producing the right kind of stone element. It should come as no surprise that hunting peoples make less than 11 percent of the component parts of their tools out of stone (Shott 1986:36). To apply theories of technological design, then, one must accept the highly speculative task of inferring the likely form of the complete tool from a small fraction of its original components. This is a task akin to inferring the existence of Niagara Falls from a drop of water.

Now we arrive at the task of demonstrating intent behind the design of an artifact. We can stipulate that this is not the same as describing its potential virtues or even the way it was used. Shott (1986) suggested that the number of worn areas on a tool could measure its versatility. Though such a measure provides clues as to the way it was used, it does not affirm that its design was an intentionally flexible one. Consider how many screwdrivers one has used as a pry bar, a hammer, or a stirrer! Simply observing that a tool was used in different ways does not necessarily signify that multifunctionality was an important consideration in its design (Kuhn 1994). This is not to argue that technological design studies are useless. They have been particularly successful when considering how the quality of raw material and its relative abundance affect the manufacture of formal tools as opposed to expedient ones. Andrevsky (1994) pointed out the necessary relationship between high-quality raw materials and formal tool designs. Middle Paleolithic hominids in Mongolia working with poor-quality stone chose the best pieces for a prepared core; otherwise, they used blanks with inclusions and other imperfections for simple expedient tools (Brantingham et al. 2000). The intent is clearly evident.

As much as we may wish to establish hard-and-fast rules, a direct relationship of raw material to technology, or mobility to technology, is unlikely to hold in all cases. Studies of technological intent often take a deductive bent, relying on circumstances and context. That is, particular cases are understood through the application of general, often opposing, principles, such as curation versus expediency and residential versus logistical mobility. Throughout prehistory, as far as we know, similar technological strategies were used time and again in similar behavioral contexts. This is the rationale for much of our analytical reasoning. For example, bipolar core reduction is handy for making tools on the spot: a strategy useful for mobile people, especially when raw material quality might permit little else. Recognition of this recurrent habit lets us speculate on the maker's economic strategy, site use and mobility pattern, and much else. Similarly, a broad relationship seems to exist between curated tools and highly mobile strategies. Thus, identifying any part of the pattern logically permits us to take the rest for granted. At least it works that way in theory.

Reality can be harsher, since variation in resources, human skills and knowledge creates exceptions. As we have seen, bipolar core reduction is a common manifestation of expedient production, the hallmark of residential mobility. However, bipolar flaking is also a way to minimize use of rare raw materials and so counter the theory that some highly mobile hunter-gatherers seem to have used curated technologies (Kelly and Todd 1988:239). In the light of such exceptions, the general models must be qualified. Another approach to stone tools that contrasts with the curated/expedient approach reverts to examining specific cases and applying theoretical models from behavioral ecology.

Torrence (1989), Metcalfe and Barlow (1992), and Bousman (1993) examined some of the models of optimal foraging theory as a way of ascertaining how humans make decisions about procuring, manufacturing, and transporting tools and faunal remains. These models may apply the strategies of curation and expedience and discuss implications of design decisions and tool formality, but they also factor in foraging models, the dietary spectrum, and estimates of the costs and benefits of hunter-gatherer technologies. For example, the dietary breadth model suggests that hunter-gatherers procure foods in order of their profitability until their handling costs exceed the benefits of the resources. That is, they will search for foods opportunistically but always select high-ranking foods whenever they encounter them. The least costly mode is a broad spectrum, diverse collecting strategy. This strategy is reflected in the toolkit, as well, as diverse diets are usually associated with low-cost extractive tools. As a result, broad-spectrum forage is profitable when technological costs, such as acquisition and repair costs, are low (Bousman 1993). Only as people narrow their dietary choices will they need expensive and specialized tools. Farming is an obvious example, but the toolkits and ancillary equipment of intensive collectors of the North American woodlands or Mesolithic Europe should be ample evidence of the costs of managing an intensive, high yield, narrow spectrum diet. As people broaden their dietary choices to achieve lower costs, they also regulate their material procurement procedures with respect to the cost of acquiring and handling the different lithic raw materials available to them.

Although human behavioral ecology models are generally highly quantitative, they can be applied to archaeology. For example, in applying the diet breadth model to stone-tool technologies, one could rank different lithic raw material by the costs of their acquisition and subsequent working (Minichillo 1999). These costs would be offset against the benefit of different flaking characteristics and any economic benefit achieved from the finished implement. Craftsmen had to reckon the distance to sources of lithic raw material, the cost of acquiring it, the technological strategies pertaining to each kind of raw material, as well as the function of the finished implements and the possibilities of markets further afield. Later, it would be necessary to ameliorate costs through recycling, reuse, and repair, and sometimes to absorb the cost of a lost tool. In other words, the cost-benefit accounting in even the least complex kind of economies is very involved. Throughout the progression from raw stone to meat on the table, for example, many key decisions or choices must be made and settled upon. It is the residue of this sometimes esoteric process that we try to recapture in archaeology.

Summing Up

The very first stone tools gave hominids access to crucially important food resources, even if they were originally procured at the behest of more successful carnivores. Over time, humans became better hunters, and improved technologies were a major part of this process, to which the increasing complexity of the *chaîne opératoire* bears witness. At first, they made generalized multipurpose tools, but, in time, they created more specialized implements, as well the means to make other tools. They developed the craft of stoneworking, comprehending the varied inherent properties of different kinds of crystalline rock, and ways to carefully apply force into it, flaking off just the right amount of stone. In time, mastery of this craft led to fabrication of compound implements, permitting even greater economies of stone and effort.

The history of stone technology is one interlinked with the rise of hunting and gathering as an effective lifeway. Stone tools permitted the butchery of large animal carcasses, the preparation of plant foods, and later the craft of weaponry. Heavy stone tools opened the forests of Central Africa to hunters and collectors. Later, smaller microlithic tools accompanied people on their annual rounds throughout these same areas. The first hunter-gatherers to venture off the continent carried stone tools, implements they would take to the ends of the Earth. All this came about in response to clever early Pleistocene hominids, who not only broke rocks but also saw a virtue in continuing to do so.

Over the past century or so, archaeology has attempted to reconstruct these times and the behavior of the people who lived in them. Progressing from formal classification of artifact types and descriptions of the modes of production, prehistorians have come to understand that artifacts and the ways they are manufactured tell subtle tales about their makers. The types and kinds of sites as well as the tools made to exploit one opportunity or another fit into the pattern of daily life of early hunter-gathering communities, leaving a dim palimpsest for the archaeologist to read. Archaeological debate, as we have seen, is over how we read the clues, finding a clear message beneath layers of analysis subject to changing academic fashion. We have seen academic debates resolve themselves in distinctions with little difference, while opening up our eyes to new ways to view the past. Whether the argument is over style versus function, or the correct interpretation of curated strategies, the outcome is an evaluation of behavior, behavioral patterns that shaped economic effort or delineated an "ethnic" population. The latter is a social, perhaps even a psychological, distinction, but it is one revealed from the close scrutiny of the remains of some past technological endeavor. There are many objectives in the maze of analysis. The problem is one of defining our goal and finding the correct pathway.

In that light, we need to consider more than the types and kinds of artifact made and the manufacturing process. That only answers a descriptive purpose. We need to express the different steps in the manufacturing process, from garnering the stone to the final destination of the finished product. This process required adherence to culturally ordained formats and training in specific techniques. Stoneworking is an orderly process. Understanding where in the sequence some flake or the other fell offers clues, not only to the knapping process but also to questions of acquisition and transport as well as use. In all our attempts to refine the analyses of lithic technology, we have tried to get nearer to the original intent of the makers and their attempts to reconcile the quests for food, flakeable stone, water, firewood, and—just as important—for contact with other humans. Ascertaining the final destination of a completed piece often brings us face to face with allied people and webs of social involvement.

4

Hunters, Gatherers, and a Social Universe

African environments offered humans a varied mosaic of economic opportunity. Human communities in the guise of tool makers explored that countryside, carving out ecological niches for themselves. Unlike the other animals resident there, theirs was a cultural landscape: a human dynamic engineered to effect ecological relationships, imposing human ingenuity upon nature. As nascent hunter-gatherers, mobile people moved out onto the vacant land, settling first one region and then another. As their number grew, moving from place to place, they had commerce with others like themselves, colleagues on much the same quest. Fellow rovers were met, people with access to prime hunting, sources of vegetable foods, water, stone, or mates to exchange.

No individuals or groups live very far from social contact. All are involved somehow with someone else. Not only human society but also human survival demands it. Interaction between individuals obviously occurs in all living things. Humans achieved something else: relationships of cooperation, mating, and child rearing that were expressed in communities and bound by culturally defined normative behaviors. As members of societies, tool-making hominids were prepared to take on the world.

Technological systems are cultural creations that fit humans into environmental circumstances. That is, they are part of humanity's way of solving problems posed by their surroundings, part of humanity's survival strategy to establish favorable ecological relationships. In order to consider the role of human interaction, we can first consider the social relationships that regulate the uses of technology.

We reflected on human interaction when we speculated on the formation of the first groups and their material circulation. Now we can look at some specific aspects of interaction in the lives of hunting-gathering people.

Almost any conceivable form of social behavior may be called interaction. It is behavior directed toward another, who expects some gesture in return. Some interactions are person-to-person, others are nation-to-nation, but the kind of interaction most relevant to hunter-gatherer situations is called *permission granting* (Kelly 1995:164). These are behaviors, such as sharing, exchange, and land usage, which stake claims, by warranting others access to a wide universe of resources, whether of implements, kinship, friendship, mates, or valuable possessions. The medium is good will, sharing, with the intention of encouraging a level return. This sort of behavior occurs in every conceivable kind of human relationship and is essential to most forms of communication between people.

Sharing and Exchange

Giving and sharing are some of the most important modes of social interaction among hunter-gatherers. Ever since Mauss ([1924] 1990), anthropologists have recognized the role of gifts in creating or affirming the responsibilities and obligations of social bonds. The value transferred may be insignificant, but the relationship is just as binding. It is a lasting social bond sanctioning access to hospitality, resources, or labor. The bond is its own justification, giving meaning to the gesture. Other social bonds are forged by birthright, kinship, or the mutual observance of ritual. Sharing is similar to the latter, though it occurs between relatives as well as strangers. In every case, its objective is the formation of an interaction sphere, an arena organizing strategic exchanges of both materials and information.

It should come as no surprise that socially regulated transfers of value are a critical element of hunter-gatherer economies. Sharing and exchange is not only an expedient way to transfer value in noncapital economies. It also redistributes risk. It ensures that any discrepancy in individual payoffs is minimal and that all participants in material circulation get a share (Cashdan 1985; Winterhalder 1986). Arrangements of this sort are critical to survival strategies of those dependent upon scattered or seasonal foodstuffs, distant sources of raw materials, small work parties, or whatever constitutes risk.

Several kinds of "transfer of value" are implied in a sharing relationship. These include *tolerated theft*, when value is transferred when the costs of defending it exceed its benefits; *reciprocity*, when value is transferred in expectation of future return; *trade*, when value is exchanged in a mutually beneficial transaction; and *cooperative acquisition*, when value is acquired collectively, then divvied up among the procurers (Kelly 1995:174). Sharing transactions are critical to sustaining the hunter-gatherer's lifeway. They are often complex and multipurposed (Winterhalder 2001b). Hunter-gatherer sharing is not an expression of altruism. The otherwise "community of equals" finds its divisions based on gender, age, kinship relationship, hunting success, or religious knowledge, revealed at the "dinner table" (Speth 1990).

A Web of Symbols

One enters into permission-granting relationships with a reasonable expectation of return. Regulation of stable reciprocal relationships requires ability to detect "cheaters," who do not fulfill the expected transaction. In small groups, social familiarity is usually enough to discourage cheating (Deacon, T. 1997:398). This is particularly so when the cost of being named a cheat significantly outweighs any benefit of cheating. The social disgrace inherent in failure to reciprocate, ensures adherence to the rules, and ongoing trust in systems of reciprocity (Smith, E. A. 1988:240). The system, licensing the social compact, is weighted to succeed, since failure carries with it the threat of exclusion. The sanction is material, but the injunction is symbolic.

The regulated nature of sharing behavior is symbolic. It is embedded in a symbolic awareness of what the relationship entails, and the obligations and responsibilities undertaken. The compact to continue exchanges passes from generation to generation, dissipating anxiety or conflict, regulating behavior, and ameliorating antagonistic confrontations. The sharing compact provides customary regulation to often complex, nonliterate societies. In fact, it is the uniquely symbolic aspect inherent in exchanges that interests us. It leads us to humanity's unique capacity to devise, organize, and use abstraction. Before systems of sharing could even be devised, some hominids were able to conceptualize future happenings, and eventually sanction them.

This scenario presupposes ways of representing the world quite different from those of other animals, including the higher primates (Deacon, T. 1997). Humans not only view the world differently, they articulate their perception differently as well. Most animal calls are responsive to immediate stimuli. A predator call is indeed a way of representing an immediate danger as a particular vocalization, as the call "Fire!" might also be. However, the representations that other animals make have, for the most part, some kind of similarity or correlation with the things they represent. They are called iconic or indexical representations. In human language, on the other hand, words and other units of language are arbitrary in form relative to what is represented. Humans have the capacity to disassociate words or other symbols from the things or concepts that the words refer to, so that the symbols can be invoked independently. We can enunciate the word "jaguar" signifying, in most cases, the idea of a large dangerous cat, rather than the immediate presence, or peril, of the actual animal. This is the genius of human speech, the capability to encode arbitrary abstractions, encapsulating a wealth of information economically as symbols. Individual symbols have meaning when they are connected within a web of other symbols. The word "jaguar" by itself has little meaning without other words, syntax, and grammar that embed it in a meaningful sentence.

Rather than an innate, limited set of vocalizations animals use to communicate, human speech involves a repertoire of sounds that can be joined together into language. Language is an information-bearing system, bound by implicit rules for forming sounds into words arranged and combined to yield a meaning. It is supposed that the flexibility and creativity given humans by language allows them their hallmark creativity and innovative capacity. Only humans express ideas and store information, and transmit it from person to person and generation to generation. Our ability to form and share thoughts has given us an extraordinary evolutionary advantage. It was within this web of mutually agreed upon symbols that the human cognitive process wove disparate individuals into the shared fabric of society.

The Role of Interaction
in the Evolution of Symbol

The paradox we face in coming to grips with the origins of this uniquely human cognitive process is that it is embedded in our own biologically ordained way of representing the world (Bednarik 1994:169). Many attempting to understand language precursors and the origins of language have grappled with this hurdle. Bickerton (1992), drawing upon studies of human toddler language, conceived of a simple "protolanguage" with limited expression of conditional and future tenses. Deacon (1997) considered the transition to symbolic modes of representation to have taken place in a social context among early hominids needing means to regulate sharing relationships. He associates the beginnings of this with the appearance of *Homo ergaster*, the first dedicated terrestrial hominid, around 1.8 million years ago.

The australopithecines, with quite different feeding habits, predated *Homo ergaster*. Sound evidence of early hominid diet is scarce and somewhat ambiguous (Sillen et al. 1995); nevertheless, models of early australopithecine diet suggest they were adapted to the understory of forested areas. They ate small animals, fungi, insects, fruit, and the like (Lovejoy 1993). About 2.5 million years ago, however, an increasingly dry climate made such habitats scarce. Later tool-using hominids preferred a variety of habitats but always near lakes and streams like the Olduvai and Turkana Basins (Rogers et al. 1994; Plummer and Bishop 1994). It is tempting to suggest that these early forms were less mobile.

Homo ergaster, on the other hand, had a different foraging and social system. They represent our earliest evidence of residential mobility and flexibility of habitat use. In this respect, they resemble the habits of modern hunter-gatherers (Walker and Leakey 1993). These early members of our genus were larger than the australopithecines, with larger brains and longer limbs, well adapted for walking. The difference in body size between females and males, found in other sorts of early hominid, were greatly reduced (Cachel and Harris 1996; Rogers et al. 1994). Skeletal remains of this species were the first to show not only limb proportions similar to those of modern humans, but also a larger brain and the narrow pelvis of upright walkers.

The narrower pelvis caused an "obstetrical dilemma," since the heads of matured infants were unable to pass through the pelvic opening. The young of *Homo ergaster*—like us—were born with immature nervous systems and brains still growing during their first year of life. Maturing infants, once weaned, still required provisioning. They could not forage on their own. The metabolic and social expense of increased brain size required a steady supply of nutrients to infants and their mothers, as well as more involved forms of social nurturing.

Slightly later, technological and social changes also appear. The Acheulian Industrial Complex, with its large symmetrical and bifacial cutting tools, replaced the Oldowan Industrial Complex (Clark,

J. D. 1994). Archaeological evidence shows that sites dating to this time are larger and denser, and found in more varied habitats than earlier ones. Stone tools were transported over longer distances. These symbols of greater mobility fit well with the skeletal evidence of a terrestrial species capable of a more mobile existence, enjoying the fruits of a variety of habitats (Cachel and Harris 1996). Monahan (1996) has shown that the Olduvai Gorge hominids, at sites like BK and MNK in Bed II, not only consumed the meat of larger animals but also had early access to the meaty portions, an improved efficiency in attaining meat.

Whatever the selection pressure, these hominids developed larger brains needed for maintaining effective mental maps of large territories and widely dispersed resources. If less mature infants required a predictable and high-quality food, these folk with more capable mental abilities were able to meet the challenge. To meet these needs several approaches were available. Some investigators have asserted a role for carnivory among *Homo ergaster* as a way of getting high-quality food in an arid grassland (Cachel and Harris 1996). Others have suggested the significance and reliability of plant foods, which they associate with an increased importance of female economic roles (O'Connell, Hawkes, and Blurton Jones 1999). At the same time, more intensive parenting emphasized lengthening of female life spans, even into the postreproductive phase (Hawkes et al. 1997). Effective congregations of humans of more than a generation or two were needed and became feasible. The building blocks of the hunter-gatherer "band" were coming together; the first "societies" were given life.

It appears, then, that sometime around 1.8 million years ago *Homo ergaster* was doing something new (Brooks 1996). This "something new" included a more expansive use of an exclusively terrestrial habitat and the more efficient procurement of meat. The reduction of the strong sexual dimorphism found among the australopithecines also hints at intriguing changes in social structure—among other primates, sexual equality of body size is associated with pair-bonded mating (McHenry and Coffing 2000). In any case, the human social pattern, combining pair bonding and cooperative groups, is unique among primates. Ultimately, such a social system can work only if access to a mate can be guaranteed (Lovejoy 1993). Symbolic representation marked exclusive pair bonds and sharing relationships with a prescription for future behaviors, the expectation of fidelity and reciprocity.

According to Deacon, the need to provision infants with high-quality foods led *Homo ergaster* to become more carnivorous. In his scheme, males hunted exclusively. Females engaged in parenting more vulnerable, fast growing babies. At the same time, they may have improved the proficiency of their gathering, with the cooperation of related females and aid in childcare from postreproductive women (O'Connell, Hawkes, and Blurton Jones 1999). At any rate, a sharing of provisions would have supported a parenting couple and assured males of benefiting their own offspring.

Deacon's emphasis on female provisioning, which is also a part of Lovejoy's (1993) explanation of societal origins, may be challenged. Female hunter-gatherers get much of their own food. Hunters often take the most nutritious parts, portions that may be forbidden to women. This proscription causes them to experience greater nutritional stress than do compatriot men (Jenike 2001). Although such disparities are not universal and derived from ethnographic studies, they suggest that male provisioning is not always the most important source of food for hominid females. Furthermore, males hunt to feed their children, but also for other reasons (Bird 1999).

Nonetheless, it is still likely that sharing relationships among closely connected people were the first symbolically constituted human social relationships—and that they entailed great expectations. There was a compact greater than that between two individuals that included the others in the group, as well. As such relationships became more critical, the need to organize rules of sharing became equally crucial. These social contracts provided moral constraints on cheaters, making reciprocity more stable and in turn stabilizing society as a whole.

The arrival of a symbolic capacity and regulated societies was a self-reinforcing phenomenon. They arose from a need to create shared concepts of social obligation. Although this scenario can be challenged, it acknowledged that no single factor caused the changes described. The increasingly arid conditions stressed prevailing food-getting regimens, emphasizing in turn those best able to imagine and retain elaborate cognitive maps of increasingly extensive foraging ranges. Those most capable of the necessary cognition required a long period of postnatal care, necessitating a different kind of social arrangement, conducive to a sexual division of labor and social responsibility.

The information encoded in language forms a body of passed-down knowledge that can be added to in each generation, a cumulative process called the *rachet effect* (Tomasello 2001). The body of knowledge encodes critical information on how to make a living (Sugiyama 2001). Yet, the benefits of language go beyond its ability to encode information or regulate sharing or other social relationships. The arbitrary web of symbols, as a system of interrelated meanings, may incur rapid and frequent change. The web of symbols is learned and passed on from generation to generation. From time to time and place to place, transmission of cultural acumen is a so-so process, carelessly learned, or learned in such a way that the meaning is misunderstood, altered, or embellished. Unlike biological reproduction, which is a kind of copying process, cultural learning is a creative one, in which learners individually and corporately create meaning and understanding. They bring to the learning process their own prior experience and knowledge. Because of the creative processes involved, languages, rather than a single primal language, developed, each the property of diverse groups seeking to communicate between themselves. Language differences acted as "ethnic" boundaries separating those likely to reciprocate from those less likely to do so (Nettle and Dunbar 1997). The symbolic interactions within groups defined expected permission-granting behaviors, affirming and maintaining social identity. At the same time, symbolic concepts of ethnicity provided a social distance that reduced the likelihood of interaction with less trustworthy individuals (Nettle and Dunbar 1997:95). Language, by marking those reliable enough to invest ones future survival, provided a new foundation for social interaction.

The Evolution of Symbol

Ultimately, then, human interaction is based on symbolic relationships. Unfortunately, neither symbolic representation nor language is preserved archaeologically. However, archaeologists have sought to infer the presence of symbolic capacity through its material correlates, citing representational art as unequivocal evidence of symbolic representation. However, things we can identify as representational are limited to the last 50,000 years or so. As a result, some have inferred a cognitive leap at that time, accounting for the invention of art as a way of externalizing human ideas of reality and communicating an awareness of perceived reality (Klein 1999:572, 590).

Since, however, the relationship between the symbol and what it signifies is an arbitrary one, the symbolic nature of any material expression can only be known by the members of the group who created it. Representational art is at the very least an iconic, not a symbolic, representation of its referent. Nonrepresentational art is more likely to have symbolic content (Bednarik 1994). Though we detect a persistent pattern of "art" during the past 50,000 years, there are earlier candidates for that distinction. Early forms of symbolic art are construed from patterned scratches on bone found at Bilzingsleben, a 300,000-year old site occupied by *Homo erectus* (Bednarik 1994). However, demonstrations of the symbolic content of the marks on such artifacts remain unconvincing.

Others attempted to find symbolism in archaeological evidence of ritual behavior, such as cannibalism, deliberate burial or grave goods, in the production of artifacts of adornment, or signs of aesthetic sense, for example, the curation of unusual objects or use of ochre (Barham 2002). For the period before the origin of biologically modern humans, however, most if not all of these claims are questionable. Others have sought evidence of symbolic capacity and even language in stone artifacts. However, the influence of tool use on the evolution of other human behaviors, like language, is debatable. Some believe that the need for verbal instruction and standardization of tool-making methods created a selective pressure for speech (Guilmet 1977; Holloway 1968). Others have seen correlates between language and speech in critical technological processes, since all are governed by strict rules (Isaac 1976) or a series of sequences (Frost 1980; Hewes 1973). Toth (1985), suggesting a causal link between stone tools and language, speculated that early hominids displayed handedness and brain lateralization. However, the proposal that early hominids preferred one hand to the other has been questioned (Pobiner 1999). Though many posit that the complexity of a toolkit indicates linguistic or cognitive complexity (Isaac 1986), there is no necessary link between language and tool manipulation, since very different cognitive processes govern them (Wynn 1993b).

Another approach claims that the complexity of typology indicates systems of categorization, such as language. That is, standardized stone tool types imply a symbolic concept of the individual tool forms indicating the use of language (Wurz 2000). However, matching a mental template to an external form does not require a symbolic mode of representation. Archaeological signs of shared, imposed arbitrary forms begin with Acheulian handaxes and cleavers, tools that changed little over their 1.5 million-year long history. Even if cultures have standard mental templates of tools, they would still not require symbolical modes of thought to use them. Finally, Mellars's theory of standardization overlooks the by-play of archaeological analysis. Archaeologists put together typologies to answer specific purposes, quite apart from anything intended by their long dead makers. This debate over the reality of created types has a long history in archaeology. We will not solve it here, beyond noting that any classification made by archaeologists is sure to be more elaborate than the typologies of the tool maker.

A more informed approach to stylistic evolution begins with Lemmonier's idea that technology is embedded in social meaning. Every artifact is linked to a myriad of arbitrary meanings regarding its functional and other informational·domains. All this is arbitrary, in that the cognitive sense of anything is a cultural artifact, to be interpreted differently by different people, generations, or circumstances. These meanings and their interrelationships are in constant flux, due to the inherent unreliability of human learning. This flux in a culture's symbolic systems may be reflected in relatively rapid differences in the type of conventional stone artifacts a people make from place to place and time to time (Byers 1994). Technological change over time is perhaps the most important marker of the presence of symbolic capacity. Dynamic technological systems are based on innovation, training, and creativity.

Technology is embedded in social arrangements. Since these arrangements change frequently, so can technological expression. Since we presume that artifacts at any one time or place have a practical function, changes in their form or frequency must imply a deeper cause, relating to changes in operational procedures, intuition, or perceived need. People do not change proven habits for arbitrary reasons. For example, Klein (1999:535) links the rapid changes in successive Upper Paleolithic cultures—time-restricted variability—to the first appearance of the human innovative capacity. Signs of time-restrictive patterning, art, and adornment are also hints of symbolic capacity. Humans evolved a capacity for symbolic representation, easing the transition to formalized kinds of society. Social relationships became encapsulated in symbolic packets. However, the ultimate symbol in their lives was their mental picture of the land, its bounty and seasonality, and people's claims upon them.

The Web of Earth

On the face of it hunter-gatherers should have little interest in landholding. A piece of ground either has a seasonally available resource, or it does not. If it is an abundant one, like the rabbits hunted by the Washo, many bands need to come together to harvest them. If provisions are scant, the flexibility of band structures reduces the number of mouths to be fed. The extra people search elsewhere. The value of territories seems to be more political than economic. People use their putative "ownership" as a bargaining chip in a greater game, the forging of interaction.

Land-tenure systems delegate land use through implied ownership. Though such ideas usually apply to sedentary landholders, hunter-gatherers, too, need to order and reconcile access to necessities. Some of these systems are referred to as territoriality, a narrower term that denotes resource defense, restricting access to resources. In the case of farmers, it limits use to those who prepared the land, whereas hunter-gatherers claim only entry to seasonal resources. However, resource defense is only one means of regulating land use. Usually, there are social rules setting forth its use. These range from cases of flexible and negotiated consent to very strict control by kin groups. Many classic hunter-gatherers use flexible rules, in that local groups do not always have exclusive rights (Lee and DeVore 1968b:12). Variations in food supply create a fluid situation, requiring not only flexible social organizations, but also ones that facilitate movement of people from one area to another, leading to reciprocal arrangements where "the hosts of one season are the guests in another" (Lee and DeVore 1968b:12).

This is a system of shared rights, or a common property regime (Lee and Daly 1999). It acknowledges descent group claims of "ownership" of a particular area, but it also assigns foraging privileges to others (Lee and Daly 1999:4). Consequently, many groups have claims to many different territories, ensuring access to requirements, when and wherever they may come about. Individual descent groups are "owners" of a waterhole and its surrounding territory, called *n!ore* among the Ju/'hoansi (Lee 1979:334). They can even inherit rights to two or more *n!ore*. Proprietorship places them in an advantageous position. Trading partners or kin ask for temporary usage rights, which are seldom, if ever, denied. Permission is given in the expectation of making a later claim that cannot be refused. The result is a secure system bound by commonly understood rules, and a format of shifting bands and highly flexible patterns of interaction with necessary resources (Yellen and Harpending 1972).

Another example comes from the Pintupi or the Pitandjara of the Western Desert of Australia, who form associations of waterhole "owners" that qualify them as "one countrymen" (Myers 1986). Though usually hereditary, membership can be gained by participation in sacred rituals, the usual substitute for legitimate kinship. The resultant alliance sanctions access to a vital resource in circumstances where refusal would create conflict, limiting future access elsewhere. Such arrangements notwithstanding, there are conventions meant to protect the rights of kith and kin. Among Kalahari hunter-gatherers, marriage to second or third cousins ensures retention of land rights within the descent group, protecting the undivided inheritance of descent group property (Wilmsen 1989). It is fair to infer that these are not contrary behaviors. Each upholds proprietorship and supports a vital *entrée* to critical exchange networks.

For the same reason, a group diminished through emigration or death will actively seek marriage alliances in order to gain access to land and resources. The result is the same, a sound base of responsible alliances and reciprocal obligations (Wilmsen 1989). Having spent a lifetime building this coalition of mutual involvement, one transfers it to one's children. The web of interaction is woven with many threads—birthright, friendship, kinship, and membership in sodalities or other groups.

In the Kalahari, another way to create such alliances is by gift exchange, called *hxaro* among the !Kung San, or *//ai* among the Nharo. *Hxaro* alliances can exist between partners as far as 200-km apart. After several exchanges, the relationship is considered firm (Wiessner 1982a). In practice, the larger one's *hxaro* network, the better the marriage chances for one's children, the relationship providing one with working keys to long-term benefit. In the Kalahari, where peril can arise from drought, plant failures, or scarcity of game, as well as sickness and disease, fictive kinship, friendships, and *hxaro* partnerships promoting advantageous social bonds are the surest alternative means to provisions and minimized risk.

The negotiation of strategic marriages is predicated on the intention of stabilizing ecological arrangements. Hunter-gatherers travel from place to place on seasonally scheduled rounds, entering and using various territories. Some places they visit by right as descent group property, and others are entered by social arrangement. In interviews, hunter-gatherers claim social reason for their mobility. They seem to be justifying their actions, claiming that social, rather then ecological, reasons are foremost on their minds. Visits and mate seeking are the primary reasons given by Hadza individuals for traveling (Mabulla 1996). What does one look for in an ideal mate? The answer has ecological overtones. A spouse, her families' connections, and the resources they command ought to come neither from one's own neighborhood nor from a location so remote that exchange and alliance are difficult to maintain (Wobst 1978; Mandryk 1993; MacDonald and Hewlett 1999). Few people look more than 40-km away, a comfortable distance to easily include in one's annual round, with nearby in-laws to call upon in times of distress. The marriage rules of hunter-gathering people often seem cumbersome, until seen as a pattern for extensive self-supporting kindred. A combination of favorable marriages, *hxaro*-like alliances, and a finely textured social network justify the energy expended competing successfully for marriage partners. All these many ties forge a secure and lasting ecological situation, predicated on politics of resources, landholding, proprietorship, and the accession of permission.

Territoriality and Society

Emerging out of marriage, visiting, and gift exchanges, the land tenure system takes shape. Territories and their potentials shape the structure of hunter-gatherer society, as the only real asset they possess.

Ecological ideas of territoriality suggest that animals create and defend territories when resources are predictable and plentiful; that is, ones that are relatively economical to defend (Brown 1964; Davies 1978). Such territories tend to be compact and easily "patrolled." However, when resources are less predictable, transient, or mobile, territories become larger and less convenient to protect. The extra effort needed to secure a large territory exceeds the benefits of maintaining it. In marginal environments with few resources, territorial behavior is unlikely (Dyson-Hudson and Smith 1978). Dyson-Hudson and Smith actually describe four different kinds of human territoriality based on resource structure and the idea of territorial defensibility (Figure 4.1). Where both density and predictability of resources are low, groups are dispersed and mobile and lack territorial boundaries.

Obviously, where resources are abundant and dense, hunter-gatherers are likely to maintain and protect their rights in relatively small territories. Among the Mbuti of Congo's Ituri forest, bands lived in territories ample for their needs and avoided hunting near their boundary if the neighboring band was in the vicinity; trespass was rare (Turnbull 1965). The Ju/'hoansi and the people of the Australian Western Desert, however, living in areas of unpredictable, but plentiful, resources—the stands of *mongongo* nuts frequented by Ju/'hoansi, for example—utilize systems of shifting and overlapping territories and the kinds of social claims to land use we have described. Even the Mbuti incorporate this type of social risk-pooling in a much richer environment: "since a claim of kinship is sufficient to grant at least temporary admission to any hunting band, every Mbuti has a wide choice of bands and territories that he or she can join at will, at any time" (Turnbull 1983). To Dyson-Hudson and Smith, Mbuti resource sharing

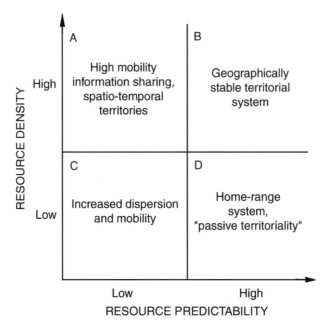

Figure 4.1. *Dyson-Hudson and Smith's model of human territoriality in four different types of resource structures.*

is a response to some measure of unpredictability in their forest environment.

Variations in the settlement patterns of Ju/'hoansi, G/wi, Nharo, and !Xõ San of the Kalahari elucidate Dyson-Hudson and Smith's approach with groups living in generally similar circumstances. The !Kung have the most fruitful environment, with high rainfall and some year-round pans, and groves of *marula* and *mongongo* nuts. The Nharo experience a similar high rainfall and access to the Ghanzi, a limestone ridge that holds water during the dry season (Barnard 1992:134). The G/wi live in an area of less rainfall, without permanent water sources, and only a few occurrences of melons and cucumbers to provide water during the drier times. Similar sources must satisfy the !Xõ, whose territory is driest of all (Barnard 1992:64). As would be expected the environments with the least rainfall have the fewest plants and animals (Cashdan 1983:52).

Two levels of social organization are recognized among these groups, the family and the band. Bands vary in size from 7 to 167 persons (Hitchcock and Ebert 1989:55). They move across highly variable, often overlapping territories of anywhere from 800 to 4,000-km^2 (Hitchcock and Ebert 1989). Whatever the band size, their settlement pattern is linked to available surface water. Ju/'hoansi and Nharo bands travel about the landscape, separately during the wet season, when water is plentiful, and aggregating during dry season, forming groups of several bands around the permanent water sources. The G/wi, however, due to lack of surface water, affected smaller groups. Family bands traveled from place to place during the dry season, feeding on the *tsamma* melon, cucumber, or water from animal stomachs. The family groups came together to form composite bands around the waterholes in the wet season. These aggregations are highly ephemeral, however, and only last for about three weeks (Hitchcock and Ebert 1989; Barnard 1992:101–102). Among all these groups, band membership is fluid, individual movement is high, and band territories overlap; kinship groups are spread over wide areas in a scattered pattern (Yellen and Harpending 1972). The maintenance of common property regimes allows them to manage access to very large territories, without incurring the additional costs inherent in large domains, because band size varies to accommodate resource availability.

The !Xõ are unique among Kalahari hunter-gatherers because, in addition to the family and the band, they organize into a third unit, the band cluster (Heinz 1979; Barnard 1992:66–67). These clusters form a distinct category of land and kinship demarcation (Barnard 1992). They mark language variants, speakers of different dialects forming the primary interaction sphere. They do not overlap the range of other groups, but are segregated by strips of unoccupied no-man's-land. Band proprietorship is acknowledged; land is not foraged exclusively by any one band, but visited, with permission, by other bands within the cluster. The clusters tend toward cluster endogamy in that social contact, including marriage, with a neighboring cluster is rare. However, people will intermarry with other clusters if there are no eligible women in their own (Heinz 1979:472–473). But, the chief social allegiance is to the cluster. When the !Xõ aggregate at water sources on the southern edge of their territory, they gather together as a single cluster (Heinz 1979). People from other clusters come alone or with their immediate families. Though principally the "property" of one cluster or another, the boundaries between cluster territories are occasionally crossed. In times of extreme local scarcity, the !Xõ *prefer* to forage the land of a neighboring band belonging to their cluster, though they may be forced, by extreme circumstances, to *seek permission* from the "most esteemed headman" of a neighboring, unrelated one (Heinz 1979:473).

Cashdan (1983) contends that the Kalahari examples do not fit Dyson-Hudson and Smith's model. The !Xõ, living in the harshest environment, are significantly more "territorial" than are the other groups. They maintain an exclusive area restricted to the resident's use (Cashdan 1983:47). Similarly, Barnard (1992) notes that territoriality is least developed with Ju/'hoansi and Nharo, but greatest among the G/wi and especially the !Xõ (Barnard 1992:234; Cashdan 1983). The !Xõ and G/wi do illustrate Dyson-Hudson and Smith's model, however, as examples of extremely dispersed and mobile groups where resource density and predictability are low (Kelly 1995). In areas of large scale, regional scarcity, and very sparse populations, the effort necessary to maintain a system of sharing is not worth the meager returns. Therefore, exchange is only practiced by the Ju/'hoansi and Nharo, groups with spatially concentrated resources (Barnard 1992). Instead of cultivating social alliances across space like the Ju/'hoansi, the !Xõ erect difficult to penetrate social boundaries around their territories. These social boundaries guarantee their exclusive access, but it does not rise to the level of the defended territoriality envisioned by Dyson-Hudson and Smith (1978). They have only drawn their interaction sphere smaller than the others. Ideas of landholding among hunter-gatherers are more a mechanism enforcing alliances rather than one of restricting access at all costs. By acting as the proprietors of sets of resources, they cede permission to utilize others.

Ethnicity and Interaction

Permission is most commonly granted to members of one's own cultural or ethnic group. Common heritage and language are major aids to building understanding and trust (Nettle and Dunbar 1997). One feels comfortable with "friends." With one's kith and kin there is a sense of shared values, expressed in a common ideology, ritual, and cooperative ventures. One often has recourse to a common corps of ancestors to warrant social transactions. All this is lacking with "strangers." When reciprocities exist across ethnic boundaries, they are often uneasy ones: a balance of theft, conflict, or competition. The Ju/'hoansi and !Xõ, for example, rarely interact and regard each other with suspicion (Wiessner 1983). This is understandable. They have little in common. Interaction networks are built for purposes of ensuring certain access to necessary things, intricately woven from social relations that span generations. They are critical to ensuring survival. The presence of different ethnic groups in near proximity may set other processes in motion.

There are at least two ways of explaining the interaction of self-acknowledged "ethnic" communities. One emphasizes the difficulties of interregional interaction and the creation of boundaries reinforcing ethnic differences. In this case, the participants find virtue in their differences and emphasize them. In contrast, another explanation posits that interaction gives groups in prolonged contact an impetus to homogenize their cultural expressions, artistic styles, rituals, and languages by forming interaction spheres. That is, they come to share vital cultural information. In both cases, however, the local "ethnic" character remains distinct, the information transferred to and assimilated in an interaction sphere usually refers to new kinds of organization, not disruption of extant patterns.

Barth (1969) turned common sense on its head, writing that cultural diversity was a by-product of interaction, not of isolation: that ethnic boundaries persist despite movement of people and information across them, entailing dualities of familiarity and difference, exclusion, and incorporation. The specification of an ethnic awareness is a product of its members believing themselves distinct, possessing a universe of shared behaviors, values, and goals. They are comfortable with the label; outsiders recognize the conceit, though it is a self-ascribed distinctness (Barth 1969:11). This opinion has had some influence in African anthropology and archaeology, suggesting that ethnic identity has less to do with cultural content than with the signaling of negotiable distinctions. In many cases, competing ethnic groups interact in different ways, but always in support of the conceit of ethnic difference. In so doing, people create boundaries, separating themselves from others.

Knutsson (1969) points up the intricacies of group interaction, its ecological basis, proving Barth's idea that the most intense interactions entail among the most ethnically distinct groups, while groups who are the most similar interact far less. At the same time, we can describe, at least, four different outcomes of interethnic contact. The first case is the symbiotic one, where the groups develop a mutually beneficial relationship, the next is one of conflict, where the parties contest claims to a resource. The third is avoidance, where one of the parties moves away to avoid both competition and cooperation. Finally, we see a condition of segmentary opposition, where closely related but competing groups erect strong cultural boundaries in order to prevent interaction. We have some examples of these effects in the history of interaction in Ethiopia. Though not directly illustrative of hunter-gatherer affairs, they lay bare the ecological parameters of cultural boundaries.

The Arsi and Laki of the Ethiopian Highlands were pastoralists and cultivators, respectively. Although there was conflict in their past over land, and the Arsi succeeded in driving the Laki onto islands in Lake Zwai, by the late 1960s they developed the kind of symbiotic interrelation to be expected of groups occupying distinct ecological niches (Knutsson 1969:91). The two exchange fish and cloth for milk products, grain, or meat.

However, the Arsi and the Highland Amhara and Shoa Galla agriculturists do not have an ecologically complementary relationship, but one based on competition over land use. Open conflict between them is common, causing the Arsi to divide into two groups. One practices agriculture, in the shadow of the Amhara and Shoa Galla, ensuring conflict. The others moved to the lowlands, where they practice low-yield pastoralism. Although the high-altitude Arsi are similar, economically, to the Amhara and Galla, they maintain a strong ethnic boundary through adherence to Islam. They maintain cultural boundaries in spite of similar economic pursuits.

The relationship of the Arsi to the Jille represents another kind of relationship. These two groups belonging to the large Galla group speak similar languages and live on the Ethiopian Rift floor, where they practice mixed pastoralism. However, their ethnic boundary is well marked. They live apart, on either side of the Awash and Maki Rivers, and they do not engage in market exchange, because of their similar economies. The relationship here is one of segmentary opposition between groups striving to control the same ecological niche. Rivalry over land contributes to a mutual hostility and carefully maintained frontiers.

Another way of examining culture process stresses congruity rather than difference as a long-term outcome of regional interaction. The idea of the interaction sphere (Braun 1986) frames a mechanism explaining similar sorts of manifestation in disparate cultures, otherwise describable as autochthonous localized patterns. That is, they shared a broad range of regional phenomena and coordinate change. In theory, critical long-term contact encouraged the exchange of ecological information, solutions to common kinds of problems, in order to facilitate interaction. That is, they transferred ideas, ritual behavior, or significant regalia in order to legitimate material circulations between otherwise distinct "ethnicities." The regional interaction sphere is a melting pot, summoning together a collective native genius and pooling a "symbolic reservoir" (MacEachern, 1994). Summoned forth are new institutions, as well as a common ethos validating interaction. Moreover, the interaction sphere, like Barth's mode of interaction, is multileveled. Different people participate in it differently. Some are involved in broader contacts and others are the recipients of other's contacts.

The differences between Barth's idea and that concept of interaction spheres may not be as profound as they seem at first reading. Barth's idea, in principle, describes an interaction sphere, albeit on a smaller scale and more temporally limited than others propose (Renfrew and Cherry 1986, as well as many others). Self-reified interactive ethnicity is, in reality, an interaction sphere, a coalition of shared values. It explains the existence of territorially bound ethnicities and at another level explains coordinated regional change. They are quite different, but not necessarily dichotomous uses of the same principle.

Ethnicity and Style

The study of ethnic interaction is dependent on identification of style. Yet, we have no consensus on the value of observations of style, and many doubt that stylistic variables can be reliably discerned at all. Most simply put, style can be defined as a way of doing something. Finished products manufactured through different processes usually leave traces of their different styles; learned procedures unconsciously embedded in cultural traditions, conforming to a format determined to be the right way to do things. But how do we discern that format? This is a question that has vexed archaeologists for fifty years or more. Wobst (1977) thought artifact "style" an expression of boundary maintenance separating contiguous ethnic groups. Consequently, such behavior could be considered common and obvious in situations where ethnic interactions and contact were intense. That is, there was a need to constantly be reminded of one's ethnic identity in much the same way that folk of different ages or social class will identify themselves by distinctive dress. Wiessner (1984) suggested that hunter-gatherers imbue artifacts with meaning on two levels: *assertive style* allowed artisans to give artifacts individual signatures; *emblemic style* is the group signature or ethnic marker.

Sackett (1982) countered that emblemic style was largely unconscious and a result of the artisan's adoption of style from his cultural milieu in the context of ethnic traditions, which may mean little more than that artisans conform to an ethnic ideal. This parallels Lemonnier's (1992) comment that technological style is a way of doing something. The something done is learned behavior, a cultural artifact itself. Nevertheless, identity of style is often the only hint archaeology has of interregional circulation.

An Archaeology of
Hunter-Gatherer Interaction

We have seen in the foregoing discussions that hunter-gatherers, as do all people, interact with others, some similar to themselves, some very different. Sometimes, new ideas are transferred from one group to another, while at other times the transfer is reciprocal, as in an interaction sphere. The archaeology of hunter-gatherer lifeways tends to neglect social interaction. Much effort has been expended in measuring their economic and ecological dimensions. Yet social intercourse is the crux of their lifeway, expressing the politics of groups and individuals, boundary maintenance, authority, power relationships, risk minimization, exchange, and ritual (Nelson 1992). Though much attention has been paid to mobility's influence on toolkits, social influences, though sometimes recognized, are more likely to be overlooked (Gould and Saggers 1985). Given the importance of interaction, an archaeology that pays attention to intersite patterning, artifact style, and sourcing seems a good way to approach the social dimension of interaction and permission granting, as well as some more arcane aspects of extinct societies.

For example, distinctive kinds of artifact are often found in exclusive times and places. The question is how they got there. They may move from place to place as a result of hunter-gatherers carrying them about in the pursuit of economic tasks (Binford 1980), or they may have been involved in an exchange, with people transferring them from place to place in fulfillment of sundry goals, intrinsically economic, but vested with social value (Wiessner 1982b, 1983). Sampson (1988) criticized the hunter-gatherer settlement pattern reconstructions we have examined that attempt to identify residential bases, task group camps, and other site types based on ecological and technological dimensions but ignore the importance of ethnic group boundaries in influencing human settlement patterns. These are critical questions that go to the heart of the hunter-gatherer lifeway; they are not epiphenomenal to the concerns of site function and subsistence (Wiessner 1982b).

Archaeologists examine intersite patterning, as well as that within settlements, as evidence of social interaction. In campsites, simple things like the number of hearths are suggestive of the number of family units within each community. Their size, location, proximity to one another or to an activity area may all be vital clues to the social significance or value of individuals, families, and their livelihoods. The distributions of artifacts, ranged by function or value, are equally important traces of the domestic and ritual life of a settlement.

If a goal of archaeology is to observe the behavior of the long-dead and the way that they interacted with others, then we must scrutinize our data more closely, eking out all the information we can. Extending our observations to a variety of related sites—the interacting socially bound territory—is a way to track people through their annual round, observing what was done when, with what, and by whom. At the same time, introducing materials, finished work, or personnel from outside the bounded territory reflects on other sorts of social intercourse, maintenance of social links with others, their resources, and so forth. Detecting the presence of "strangers" returns us to questions of ethnicity and style.

The study of exchange systems requires an understanding of both distinctive materials, artifacts and the social mechanism by which people transfer things from place to place. That is, we must learn to distinguish styles in order to pinpoint sources and material circulations—what is produced where, where does it end up and how does it get there? We have already noted the importance of self-defined ethnicities. People tend to have distinctive "ethnic" styles as ways to distinguish them from others. These conform to cultural prescription identifying one group from another. Since raw material sources may be pinpointed in the landscape, material culture has proven a valuable source of information, implying the mapping of ethnic and linguistic boundaries (Ericson and Earle 1982; Renfrew and Cherry 1986, and many others). Mapping the geography of circulation, we gain insight into territories, ranges, and social interaction, as well as ethnic or social frontiers within which exchange took place, suggesting what was exchanged and with whom, and whether one did so directly or through a system of intermediaries. In other words, do the things found far from home denote passage of the "maker," casual exchanges within a chain of "owners," or formal entrepreneurial exchange networks? Do ritual centers or places of seasonal assembly serve as places where trades or sharing partnership are negotiated? Who fixes value or arbitrates differences in opinion? If the institution of circulation networks is filled with questions, identifying them is equally difficult.

Circulation networks are recognized by the identification of distinctive artifact styles. Even questions relating to detecting style lead to questions of residence. Was the object carried from one group to another or did the artisan leave home to take up residence elsewhere, as woman potters are apt to do? As should be obvious, identifying regional circulation patterns is very difficult. Explaining the way they work even more so. Even such basic things as the identification of "style" are fraught with debatable attitudes. I have already alluded to whether the "style" we perceive is congruent with that of the maker or not; and whether what we define as "ethnic" is truly group-specific. If defining style creates problems for us, how much more thorny is the separation of style from function? Can we archaeologically define and truly discern "ethnic zones" of regional interactions when the zones themselves are often fluid? Can regional interaction be studied for the extremely low-density hunter-gatherer groups with large territories that often populated Africa without spending decades in survey? Yet, these are the kinds of inquiry we need to make, testing our observations, while pondering technical and theoretical pitfalls.

Exchanged or Transported: A Case of Stone Tools and Beads

We take a special interest in lithic raw material or other artifacts because unlike "mental templates," trace elements can be discerned, material sources found, and their distribution mapped. In this way, we are able to construe the range of prehistoric groups, or at least the dispersion of distinctive artifacts (Clark, J. D. 1980b:54). Of course, these two things may not always be the same. In some cases, objects are taken to cultural contexts, places, and times far outside the milieu of the makers. These are usually easily discernible. In other more ordinary instances, analyses of lithic raw material can identify transported materials and give an indication of material circulations and the distances embraced. Plotting finds and ethnic zones offers an opportunity to detect social contact.

Archaeologists generally agree that the distances artifacts travel is somehow indicative of the mobility range, territorial limits, the extent of trade or other exchange (Wilmsen 1973). The distance artifacts are transported or the proportions of material from different sources in an assemblage are also thought to shed light on varied aspects of mobility or exchange (Ambrose 2001). This is based on the simple proposition that one tends to find less and less of some material or another as one gets farther and farther from its source. This is a mark of the range of a particular material circulation and its strength, if not its organization. Any material found far from its place of origin may be deemed valuable, and more apt to be curated and passed on through exchanges. Frequency of a particular sort of find may be indicative of the possible reach of a network overlapping other circulations in touch with places and people.

High frequencies of more locally available raw materials probably indicate more ordinary things. These artifacts are the common coin of a group's technology. Residential shifts or the range of a group may be detectable from a survey of these sorts of material, but many other factors also determine the proportions of these lithic raw materials in archaeological assemblages. The timing of tool discard and replenishment all affect the basic composition of a deposit (Ingbar 1994). The number and timing of these, as a toolkit's owners moved in a regular pattern through a series of sites, alters the proportions of raw material found, regardless of the owner's mobility pattern. At most stages, signs of only a few of the sources visited by or accessible to the group are present, suggesting that calculating raw material ratios by themselves reveal little about home range size or mobility patterns (Ingbar 1994:51). By the same token, those needing imported material may procure it indirectly without ever visiting the sources themselves.

In any case, the types, kinds, and relative proportions of different materials in sites are the product of a much more complex set of circumstances and decisions than the simple proposition that hunters go about regularly losing bits of worked stone hauled from one place or another. Many factors enter the equation, including arranging acquisition of the stone, its quality, and core reduction techniques. The sort of debris left behind is affected by the frequency of refreshing edges, tool reuse and recycling, as well as the decision to discard—a decision that may depend of the value of the stone as much as the condition of the implement. The stone may even have a social value. All these factors affect the makeup of archaeological assemblages we wish to identify with the fluid membership of hunter-gatherer bands.

Stone is a reliable asset to archaeological investigation, but its interpretation may be dodgy at times. It is plentiful, amenable to knapping technologies, and so useful that it sometimes passes over long distances, is used and recycled or lost in ways that baffle our models. It is possible, however, to use items with a specialized function in exchange to delineate boundaries.

Based on ethnographic analogy with the San case, the archaeological distribution of ostrich eggshell beads and marine shells can reveal integral social regions, abrupt dips in their numbers signifying frontiers (Mitchell 1996). That is, coherent distributions of hallmark items suggest a discrete orbit of circulation. The numbers of hallmark items will decrease as one draws away from this interaction sphere. Mitchell identifies four interaction spheres in southeastern South Africa—in the Thukela River basin, southeastern KwaZulu-Natal and eastern Lesotho, the northeastern Cape Province, and the eastern Free State. For the past two millennia at least, the dispersal of marine shell and ostrich eggshell, as well as some kinds of stone, seems to lie inside what may be construed as linguistic or socioterritorial precincts.

The ultimate sourcing and attendant technological procedures on distinctive artifacts can furnish important clues to material circulations, particularly with objects less obviously associated with exchange. To this end, many have introduced physical and chemical analyses as a way to pinpoint sources. Others stress the characterization of manufacturing procedures to determine cultural sources. These approaches have been usefully applied to pottery (Mercader et al. 2000), iron artifacts (Kusimba, Killick, and Creswell 1994) as well as stone (Merrick and Brown 1984). By scrupulously ascertaining the ultimate source areas of stone and clay and the identity of makers, archaeologists are able to map material circulations accurately. If we are correct in assuming that social distance is a factor in exchange relationships, we can estimate levels and kinds of social structuring as well. Exchange is an important part of the hunter-gatherer lifeway. Techniques devoted to comprehending it should comprise an equally important part of the archaeological repertoire.

Hunters, Gatherers, and Food Producers

We have seen in the foregoing discussions that hunter-gatherers, as do all people, interact with others, some similar to themselves, some very different. Sometimes, new ideas are transferred from one group to another, while at other times the transfer is reciprocal, as in the operation of an interaction sphere. Most of the group interaction relating to the social and economic life of hunter-gatherers is with other foraging groups, negotiating access to resources or arranging strategic alliances through marriage or common ritual practices. For most of history, hunter-gatherer groups were the only human groups around—we have seen the complexities of interaction among foragers themselves. Some other interactions important in their lives involve hunter-gatherer coexistence and interaction with food producers. These have been going on since the origins of agriculture (Wilmsen and Denbow 1990). Though one is apt to consider these different groups in conflict over strategic resources, cooperation is often the case ethnographically. There are many hunter-gatherers for whom this interaction and resultant exchanges influence their livelihoods and their identities. These include, to name just a few, the Agta and Batak in the Philippines (Peterson 1978), the Efe and Mbuti of the Democratic Republic of Congo (Turnbull 1965; Bailey 1991), the Okiek of Kenya (Blackburn 1982; Kratz 1981), and the Birhor of India (Fox 1969).

Such interactions provide hunter-gatherers with many strategic options. On the one hand, they may opt to develop long-term complementary relationships with the food producers, what Barth (1969) calls *symbiosis*. In these cases, one might expect long-term stability in hunter-gatherer–food producer interactions. An example of such a strategy comes from the Congo Basin. Here, the Mbuti and Efe hunter-gatherers have lived with food producers for the last 2,500 years (Clist 1999), providing them with labor and forest products in return for cultivated foods.

Marriage, ritual, and information also passed across this boundary. The result was a meld of societies with mixed economies and technologies, providing a successful and stable lifeway (Mercader et al. 2000). In some cases, the hunter-gatherer ethnic boundary dissolved as they absorbed the language, culture, and eventually the economy of neighbors. The Batwa peoples, widespread throughout Bantu Africa, especially in Zambia's Bangweulu swamps and on East Africa's Great Lakes, are erstwhile hunter-gatherers now almost indiscernible from their agriculturist neighbors (Schadeberg 1999). The Okiek of Kenya have clan names, age sets, circumcision ritual, and a patrilineal system of resource management, probably adopted from their pastoralist Masai and Nandi neighbors (Kratz 1981). At the same time, they harvest honey to exchange with nearby pastoralists, establishing an economic relationship effecting Okiek ideas of property. Although this arrangement entails considerable risk of assimilation (Cronk 1989), some Okiek have so far been able to maintain their ethnic identity.

Paradoxically, people opt for change when it allows them to continue some basic cultural pattern. This is an essential corollary of all discussions of culture change, but is worth restating. Sometimes, it is of benefit for hunter-gatherers to acknowledge the economic power and society of food producers as a source of protection, food, and trade goods (Bailey 1988; Smith 1998). This is not as simple a transaction as we might think. Most African descent groups are extensive landholding corporations, and marriages are contracts between the descent groups requiring guarantors in the form of negotiated material transfers, usually termed bride price, that, in reality, acknowledges the social and economic value of the alliance (Kuper 1982). A male hunter-gatherer trying to enter this system would be a stranger, without the wherewithal necessary to negotiating a marriage—no cattle, real property, or influential connections. A woman, however, could marry into a patrilineal community in the same way as any woman from another agricultural community. Her "bride price" would be minimal. On the other hand, she would, of course, have difficulty attaining access to the matrilineal societies in Central Africa, having no economic value in the form of farmland, and her children would lack "uncles" to educate them, among other cultural obstacles (Holy 1986).

Farmers in a hunter-gatherer's vicinity are more likely to disrupt free exercise of aggregation and dispersal than marry eligible bachelors (Moore 1981). The two groups may live in close proximity and in a comfortable relationship, if they are not competitors for land or resources and are able to supply one another with necessaries. Long-term "frontiers" may result (Thorp 1996). A third case posits neither coexistence nor assimilation, but an alternate course where hunters become integrated into a herding or farming community for a while, while retaining the option to return to the hunter-gatherer lifeway. Such a situation describes 1,500 years of interaction between hunter-gatherers and herders in South Africa (Deacon and Deacon 1999). Except for obvious cultural differences, these are the same people, sharing a common biological heritage and related languages. Even their material culture is similar (Bollong, Sampson, and Smith 1997). How and who adopted pastoralism is murky and vigorously debated (Sadr 1998). Nevertheless, it is an illustration of hunter-gatherer folk adapting, in part, to a different lifeway. It was never vitally necessary for hunter-gatherers to interact with their farming neighbors. But it did take place. Sometimes it was as face-to-face contact between individuals. At other times, more esoteric transactions connected distant trading partners. In most cases, it was the relationships between one hunter-gatherer and another that took precedence.

A Summing Up

In the foregoing, I have suggested an idea of the hunter-gatherer lifeway that goes beyond a description of economy or a simple social order. We have seen how these folk use the interplay of environment, technology, and social interaction to operate in a real world, a world of opportunity and considerable risk. Early hominid communities subsisted primarily on the proceeds of reaping naturally occurring food sources and used learned behaviors like tool use to expand their food-getting abilities. They were still, however, a long way from the hunter-gatherers of today. The first true hunter-gatherers, by contrast, learned to represent the world around them symbolically. This allowed them to exchange, disseminate, and store information about their surroundings and to create dynamic and flexible technologies to extract sustenance from them. It gave them enormous evolutionary advantage.

The intricacies of symbolic representation may well have been mastered as human communities elaborated sets of invented rules regulating interaction and determining correct patterns of social behavior. Most likely, basic human concerns like parenting responsibilities were involved in the creation of these first symbolic social relationships, but very early on the imputed rights and responsibilities of these relationships were also applied to issues of group identity and access to resources. Succinctly put, they created premeditated sanction, the act of getting, giving, or withholding permission. These social rules govern not only those in daily face-to-face contact but also the manner and mode of meeting others.

Intergroup interaction, and the enlisting of allies through the medium of common ethnic identity, forms a vital part of the survival strategy of most hunter-gatherers. These meetings with others form the crux of the hunter-gatherer lifeway, permitting access to critically needed resources, mates, or labor. As a result, hunter-gatherers weave for themselves an intricate network of alliances, obligations, and commitments. This is a strategy that allows them to cope with a variety of situations, secure in a social safety net.

When did the first true hunter-gatherers emerge? It may have been the Middle Stone Age.

5

The Emergence of the Hunter-Gatherer

During the Middle Pleistocene, humankind engaged in a further series of experiments, testing the efficacy of technology and moving from *façonnage* to prepared core reduction. In one place or another, people began an appreciation of the seasonal nature of their food sources, organizing their lives in an annual round, seeking out geographically dispersed raw materials and seasonally available foodstuffs. In other words, the rudiments of a hunter-gatherer lifeway were invented, adapting humans and their new behaviors to a variety of environments.

As we have seen, *Homo ergaster* was the first hominid to possess singularly human traits like full terrestriality, most likely a basically monogamous social structure, greater reliance on meat, more helpless infants, and sophisticated childcare as well as gathering skills. In many ways, this species utilized the primary building blocks of the hunter-gatherer lifeway (Brooks 1996). However, as we have seen, hunting and gathering as we know it is based on far more than these basic human characteristics. Other crucial components of hunter-gathering include dynamic technological systems based on innovation, training and creativity, and permission-granting behaviors granting access to the sharing of resources. The era of the Acheulian Industrial Complex, which begins around the time of *Homo ergaster* and ends around 250,000 years ago, seems a long way from a modern human condition.

Our available evidence is fraught with poor dating and uncertain geological contexts, and in Africa is based on less than fifty sites, such that "nontrivial behavioral inferences are mostly tentative" (Klein 1999:343). Nevertheless, some features of the Acheulian are informative in their differences from patterns of the archaeology of modern people. The pace of technological evolution was remarkably slow. Acheulian Industrial Complex sites are spread throughout the Old World following soon after the spread of *Homo ergaster* out of East Africa. In spite of the wide geographic spread of Middle Pleistocene hominids, there is little evidence of regional differentiation, or technological style, save a wide-spread duality of patterning in which some assemblages and sites contain large handaxes, cleavers, and knives, while others possess only the chopper-flake toolkit perfected by the earliest stone tool makers (Clark, J. D. 1994). Certainly, technology was not as dynamic as among modern people, but was a rather stereotyped behavior.

In eastern Africa, we find the traces of the annual round at reliable water sources, with the economic activities at each place marked by diverse kinds of toolkit. At Kalambo Falls, high above Lake Tanganyika, camps were used year after year, their successive fire pits built one atop the other (Figure 5.1; Clark, J. D. 1974). At Torralba and Ambrona in the Pyrenees, *Homo heidelbergensis* gathered seasonally to kill or butcher large mammals periodically passing thorough the mountain passes (Freeman 1994). They hunted large mammals with sophisticated javelin-like spears of hardened wood (Theime 1997). Climates experienced many fluctuations and mankind flourished in many different biomes. Other archaic forms such as *Homo erectus* adapted to tropical and temperate areas of Eastern Asia. Around 250,000 years ago, the Acheulian Industrial Complex ended and new people and cultures replaced them under circumstances we do not fully understand.

During the subsequent Middle Stone Age, hominids in Africa developed more specific adaptations to particular biomes. Greater regional differentiation exists, suggesting greater diversity in lifeways and an increased flexibility in adaptation. Middle Stone Age hunter-gatherers delved into new food choices and food-getting technologies. Contemporaneous *Homo neanderthalensis* lived in Europe and Western Asia, successfully using Middle Paleolithic prepared core technologies, hunting, and becoming "the original caring society" (Gamble 1999:267), burying their dead and nursing the injured and sick.

Over the past decades, understanding these immediate predecessors to those like ourselves has been one of the biggest challenges to anthropology. On the one hand, to some the Neanderthals "lacked some fundamental behavioral capabilities of living people, probably because their brains were differently organized" (Klein 1999:367). To Hayden (1993), on the other hand, their "capacities of planning, forethought, abstraction, kinesthetic coordination, (and) learning appear well developed." The argument over contemporaneous Middle Stone Age culture in Africa has stressed similar themes (Klein 1989; Deacon and Deacon 1999). During the Acheulian, human culture was marked

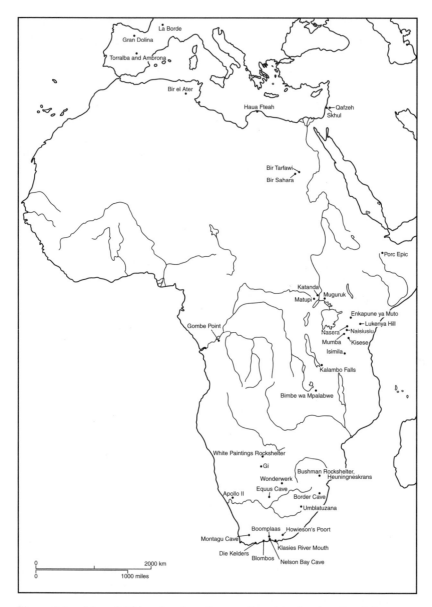

La Borde
Gran Dolina
Torralba and Ambrona
Bir el Ater
Haua Fteah
Qafzeh
Skhul
Bir Tarfawi
Bir Sahara
Porc Epic
Katanda
Muguruk
Matupi
Enkapune ya Muto
Lukenya Hill
Nasera
Naisiusiu
Mumba
Kisese
Isimila
Kalambo Falls
Gombe Point
Bimbe wa Mpalabwe
White Paintings Rockshelter
Gi
Bushman Rockshelter,
Heuningneskrans
Wonderwerk
Apollo II
Equus Cave
Border Cave
Umblatuzana
Boomplaas
Howieson's Poort
Montagu Cave
Klasies River Mouth
Die Kelders
Blombos
Nelson Bay Cave

0   2000 km
0   1000 miles

Figure 5.1.   Map of Africa showing sites mentioned in chapters 5 and 6.

by the appearance of handaxes and cleavers throughout much of the Old World. In the Middle Stone Age, for the first time, the modern pattern of heterogeneous cultural inventories shows up. Distinctive assemblage and unique modes of manufacture and subsistence activities mark different regions (Clark, J. D. 1988). These may be the signs of the first modern hunter-gatherers staking their claim through a rachet effect of accumulated knowledge we recognize archaeologically as regional traditions. On the one hand, there is much of the story of modern hunter-gatherers that is missing from the Middle Stone Age game plan—symbolic artifacts and evidence of exchange are important lacunae. On the other hand, some of this evidence of modern behavior could become more common with time within the 200,000-year long course of the Middle Stone Age. To understand why this debate is so important and why it is connected to the Neanderthal question, a bit of background is necessary.

The Development of Modern Human Behavior

Over the past decade, two scenarios explaining the origins of modern humanity have commanded our attention. The first, the *Recent African Origin* theory, argues that the first fully modern people evolved in Africa around 200,000 years ago. Some then left Africa, absorbing or replacing Eurasian archaic humans such as Neanderthals (Relethford 1998). The second theory, the *Multiregional Hypothesis*, claims that modern humans evolved in Africa and Eurasia at more or less the same time. Subsequently, genetic intermingling allowed the far-flung African, European, and Asian populations to assume a common genetic makeup (Wolpoff et al. 1994). Recently discovered genetic, archaeological, and paleontological data supports the African origin of modern humanity. However, the evidence is often murky, and there are detractors (Relethford 1995; Templeton 1997, 1998).

According to the human skeletal evidence, people similar to us appear earlier in Africa than in Eurasia, where Neanderthals survived as a distinct type until about 30,000 years ago (Rightmire and Deacon 1991). However, skeletal markers of modernity in the African fossil specimens are subtle (Smith 1993; Lam, Pearson, and Smith 1996), and some sources of evidence have been disputed. At Border Cave, for example, the grave of a modern human child with a shell pendant, incontrovertible evidence of symbolic behavior, was found to be intrusive from a higher level (Sillen and Morris 1996).

Perhaps the best evidence of the modernity of African morphology comes not from Africa itself but from the caves of Skhul and Quafzeh on Mt. Carmel in Israel, dated to about 90,000 years ago. The skeletons of more than twenty individuals, similar to present-day people morphologically, were found that retained some archaic features, such as brow ridges and retromolar spaces, but on the whole are considered *Homo sapiens sapiens*. These people have limb proportions consonant with tropical origins. They have long arms and legs, characteristic of tropical people today. This body type is thought an adaptation to hot weather, because it efficiently dissipates heat (Pearson 2000). They first appear in the Near East accompanied by African faunas. This suggests an extension of an African ecozone into the upper reaches of the Rift valleys and the passage out of Africa, at this time, by another type of human with novel ideas of tool making (Brooks 1996; Lahr and Foley 1994).

In Iberia, the disappearance of Neanderthals occurred nearly 15,000 years later than it did in the Near East. This suggests to some that modern humans, the authors of the innovative material culture, arrived in Europe from the Near East and possibly Africa, and that they replaced Neanderthal purveyors of Middle Paleolithic toolkits by numerically swamping them (Gamble 1999; but see d'Errico et al. 1998). Genetic evidence suggests that African populations are older and more variable than elsewhere. Though this conclusion is controversial, it would suggest that African populations stand a good chance of being the forebears of modern Eurasians (Relethford 1995, 1998). This would imply that within the matrix of African Middle Stone Age cultures lie clues to, if not the actual origin of, modern hunter-gathering culture.

While a consensus may be forming to support the Recent African Origin theory, we still understand little about the behaviors and way of life of the earliest biologically modern humans. Many questions need to be answered. Was their intellectual capacity fully modern? Did they have the cultural features and adaptability of modern hunter-gatherers? We know that they were adept at fitting themselves into a well-rehearsed ecological niche. However, were their technologies dynamic? Did they possess permission-granting systems? Were African Middle Stone Age people the first to possess a modern cultural repertoire?

The Transition to Modern Hunter-Gatherers

Just as there are two ways at looking at the arrival of modern humanity on the stage of history, there are two points of view explaining how and when modern hunter-gatherer cultures developed. The first might be termed the *revolution hypothesis*. In this scenario, fully modern human beings evolved biologically and culturally in a recent and sudden evolutionary event. This, according to Klein (1999), was a fortuitous change or mutation that enabled the human brain to represent the world symbolically. This, in turn, allowed them to encrypt their world and use their superior cognitive capabilities to expand out from somewhere in Africa to colonize the rest of the Old World. As they moved from their place of origin, perhaps around 50,000 years ago (Klein 1999:512), they out-competed or absorbed other more archaic peoples they met. The possessors of an enhanced ability to cogitate symbolically, and thus realize a more versatile technological and social repertoire, won out.

The contrasting idea might be called a *gradual cultural evolution hypothesis* (McBrearty and Brooks 2000). This also places the origin of modern humans in Africa, but makes the point that biological and cultural modernity evolved together and gradually over the Middle Stone Age period. The modern hunter-gatherer repertoire is thus the sum of changes begun more than 300,000 years ago, when the large core-based industries of Acheulian mode were being replaced by ones based on the manufacture of flake tools from prepared discoidal cores; from the beginning, however, there were several different techniques for doing this (Tryon and McBrearty 2002). This transition seems to be coterminous with the appearance of modern forms of *Homo sapiens* (McBrearty and Brooks 2000). According to this idea, the better part of the cultural experience found in modern human cultures was accumulated gradually and expressed intermittently from the Middle Stone Age onward.

The revolution hypothesis seems to fit the facts of European prehistory and the gradual cultural evolution of the events in Africa. Asia, unfortunately, remains little discussed. In sum, it may be fair to say that neither is a fully satisfactory explanation for every circumstance. The idea of a revolutionary new population possessing superior toolkits fits well with the sudden appearance of highly advanced hunter-gatherer culture in Europe. The European archaeological record shows no evidence of fully modern hunter-gatherers as we understand them until the Upper Paleolithic, around 40,000 years ago. The archaeological record in Europe is a complex one, but a brief summary will serve to illustrate the discontinuity observable in the passage from Middle to Upper Paleolithic cultures.

The Transition from European Middle to Upper Paleolithic

As we have suggested, a close association between hominid physical type and industry marks the Eurasian Middle to Upper Paleolithic replacement. Upper Paleolithic fully modern humans, not unlike us, replaced Middle Paleolithic Neanderthals (Klein 2000). This has occasioned the idea of rapid replacement or absorption of the earlier populations by immigrant groups of modern humans. Some time around 30,000 years ago, Neanderthals no longer form a significant population in Eurasia and soon thereafter cease to make any showing at all in European deposits. The picture is one of a world once inhabited by Neanderthals, invaded by better-equipped and somehow brighter humans, who take possession of their lands and begin to dominate human history.

The European Paleolithic record is traditionally divisible into three parts (Sackett 2000). The Lower Paleolithic includes Oldowan-derivatives and Acheulian industries, associated in Europe with archaic hominids like *Homo ergaster*, *Homo heidelbergensis* from Heidelberg, Germany, and *Homo antecessor* from Gran Dolina, Spain. It lasted from at least 1.4 million years ago until around 250,000 years ago. At this time, the Middle Paleolithic stone industries appear. These are linked to the Middle Pleistocene *Homo sapiens* species, the *Neanderthals—Homo neanderthalensis*. The associated stone industries emphasize the manufacture and reduction of prepared cores. Prepared core technology originated in the Acheulian as a method of making cores that could be used to produce a set of usable and retouchable flake blanks of predetermined shape and size. Prepared cores were now used to produce flakes, blades, and "points." The people of the Middle Paleolithic used these differently shaped blanks to create scraping tools and spear points (Shea, Davis, and Brown 2001), as well as a variety of other tools by retouching along the edges.

The use of prepared cores clearly reflects a desire to replicate consistent usable blanks of particular size and shape, often maximizing the breadth and length of these blanks. The production of handaxes, cleavers, and knives with reference to shared mental templates is our earliest hint of indexical representation. However, Acheulian light-duty or small tools exhibit less attention to standardized tool shape. The makers of these implements seem to be concentrating on the production of the working edge, rather than conforming to a predetermined idea of what an implement should look like (Clark, J. D. 1994). During the Middle Paleolithic, by contrast, small shaped flakes are made to consistent formats, in order to facilitate their use in hafts (Clark, J. D. 1988). In other words, some implements, rather than being hand-held, were fastened into wooden handles, using sinews, mastics, and other adhesives. In spite of differences in available raw material and environment across much of Eurasia, there is a broad uniformity in Middle Paleolithic methods of core reduction and tool manufacture. Such differences that occur can be attributed to the effects of working different raw kinds of stone, or differences in function (Dibble 1987).

In Europe, Middle Paleolithic modes of stone working were replaced by new industries of the Upper Paleolithic over a period of 20,000 years (Gamble 1999:268). Often, however, the changes appear abrupt when individual sequences are considered. They were based upon the production of narrow flakes, which are called blades or bladelets when they are small. These blades were an efficient and economical use of raw stone. Once the core was prepared, many blades would be struck off with little waste and the core could be more completely reduced than in the case of Middle Paleolithic core reduction (Boeda 1988). Upper Paleolithic people routinely used bone and antler tools and made composite tools with ivory, stone, and bone components. An increased emphasis on hafting is associated with greater standardization of tools. Middle Paleolithic people, by contrast, made fewer distinct tool types and almost never used bone tools (Villa and d'Errico 2001). Toolkits included new kinds of tools, like shaft straighteners, burins, grinders, and so forth, suggesting both novel tool forms and a new range of activities. Upper Paleolithic settlements are often activity-specific. Most have specialized activity areas and much more elaborate site architecture.

For the first time in the European archaeological sequence there is substantial evidence of crafts that go beyond making the implements of subsistence. Upper Paleolithic craftsmen made textiles (Soffer et al. 2000), as well as beads of ivory, soapstone, tooth, and bone (White, R. 1985). They used ochre and colored pigments, exploring artistic expression. Their art included mobile as well as parietal art. Even early Upper Paleolithic people had a mature art that exhibits great diversity from place to place and time to time. Upper Paleolithic artists vividly imbued their real world, especially large animals like rhinoceros, lion, and mammoth, with imagination and ideology (Clottes 1996).

The other material manifestations of the successive cultures of this epoch vary from time to time and place to place as well, dividing the Upper Paleolithic into distinct regional as well as temporal manifestations. This pattern shows a degree of "ethnicization" and a degree of time-restrictive patterning (Byers 1994) not noted heretofore. These "ethnic zones" are characterized by the presence of tool types specific to certain times and places. Furthermore, though earlier people participated in material circulation, later ones seem more far-reaching. Upper Paleolithic camps contain imported objects, such as marine shells, from as much as 500-km away, signaling extensive exchange networks. The people of the Upper Paleolithic seem less conservative, culturally, and more apt to innovate than the people they replaced. Their many different regionally and temporally distinct stone tool industries suggest a sense of ethnicity (White 1985). Acheulian industries, throughout their distribution, were essentially unchanged over hundreds of thousands of years. Those of the more volatile Upper Paleolithic barely endure for periods counted in tens of centuries. This is in sharp contrast with the apparent homogeneity of the Middle Paleolithic (Gamble 1999:415). The world of the Upper Paleolithic seems a richer, more dynamic one than that of the Neanderthals.

There is no sign of cultural antecedents in the Middle Paleolithic to the behavior of the later stages of the Paleolithic. In sum, the appearance of so much cultural difference in such a short period of time seems a revolution, a quantum leap in culture change.

The African Middle Stone Age

Both the revolution and evolution perspectives recognize that sometime during the last 100,000 years similar cultural developments were going on among African hunter-gatherers. New stone-working industries were replacing long-lived prepared core tools. However, where it was once thought that the Middle Stone Age was roughly contemporary with the European Upper Paleolithic, many now view the African case as broadly analogous to the earlier Middle Paleolithic. This is in large part because of the high incidence of prepared core blank production in African industries. The identity of the makers of the African material is a thornier question. Human remains from the Middle Stone Age are few and difficult to classify (Smith, F. H. 1993). However, they include specimens of early modern human types from Florisbad, Klasies River, Mumba, Omo 1, Die Kelders, and Equus Cave.

These individuals have smaller, less prognathic faces and smaller teeth and brow ridges than larger, contemporaneous Neanderthals of Eurasia, and also have canine fossas like people today (Stringer 1995).

Nevertheless, according to the revolution hypothesis, Middle Paleolithic in Europe and Middle Stone Age in Africa are, for the most part, similar, contemporaneous industries produced by different kinds of people. It is apparent that in Africa humans were biologically evolving in the modern direction, beginning at least 100,000 years ago, almost 40,000 years before the shift from Middle to Later Stone Age. According to the gradual evolution hypothesis, the African Middle Stone Age actually shows a unique development of modern human behavior.

Middle Stone Age
Expansion and Diversification

Beginning nearly 300,000 years ago, the Middle Stone Age spanned glacial as well as interglacial periods. We believe that it ended about 50,000 years ago (Klein 1999). Over that long period of climatic flux, two patterns emerge in Middle Stone Age use of the environment. For the first time humans achieved a greater geographic and environmental range than did any of their predecessors. From time to time, they occupied marginal areas in the extreme north and south of the continent. Second, there is increasing geographical variation in Middle Stone Age material culture, evidence of specialized adaptation to differing conditions. An earlier colonization of tropical rain forest in the Late Acheulian was a cold period refuge (Clark 1994). Otherwise, the earliest occupations in large parts of West Africa are Middle Stone Age (Cornellissen 1997). The reach of humans into these areas represents a newfound ability to utilize the environs of tropical forest, represented by a large tool sequence from the Lupemban to Tshitolian industries, which spans the Middle to Upper Pleistocene. At this time, the number of humans on Earth was increasing, producing added personnel necessary to colonizing these new habitats. In Central Africa, places like Kamoa and Gombe Point in the D. R. Congo and Kalambo Falls in Zambia display signs of recurrent use, as traveling bands returned year after year to favored campsites. All these places display heavy tool technologies useful in forested environments. East of the rain forest, but still on the Equator, Mumba and Nasera shelters in Tanzania exhibit long-term adaptation to arid grassland (Mehlman 1989).

In areas less than perfect for human habitation, such as the more arid northern and southern extremes of the continent, the ebb and flow of human presence coincides with environmental shifts. Many South African Middle Stone Age sites, such as Border Cave, Klasies River Mouth, and Boomplaas, were only used at the beginning of the last interglacial, around 133,000 years ago. Many were abandoned around 60,000 years ago, as it became increasing colder and drier. Many Middle Stone Age campsites are located on the milder coasts, rather than more seasonally arid inland areas, where resources were often hard to find (Avery 1995). Water was the key to settling the desert regions. The first occupations of the Sahara occurred late in the Acheulian. They are found in playa, lake, and stream deposits of an interglacial (Wendorf and Schild 1998). Later ones occurred during subsequent interglacial periods also associated with long since dried-up water sources. During the last interglacial, the Western Desert of Egypt, which today receives no effective precipitation, received 500 mm of rain a year. At that time, there were permanent lakes, springs, and streams. The area was a bushland with large game animals such as extinct buffalo, camel, giraffe, antelope, and gazelles. During this period, the Aterian, a Middle Stone Age industry associated with the hunting of this desert fauna, spread throughout the Saharan Maghreb as far as the Nile Valley (Wendorf and Schild 1992).

Clark (1970:126) emphasized the geographical diversity of Middle Stone Age industries, since worked stone tool types vary greatly across major geographical zones. At the same time, the lithic reduction sequences form an overall technological unity. In East Africa, the Middle Stone Age features unifacial and bifacial "points" and scrapers made from discoidal cores. The post-Acheulian Sangoan Industry had large heavy-duty picks and core axes (McBrearty 1986; Mehlman 1989; Merrick 1975). These are found throughout West, Central, and southcentral Africa, loosely associated with forest-based woodworking (Clark and Brown 2001). Large blades typify many South African Middle Stone Age assemblages (Figure 5.2), but interleave with deposits including Stillbay Industry bifacially worked tools and Howieson's Poort backed blades (Figure 5.3). Because of this regional patterning, Clark (1970, 1988) credited to the Middle Stone Age "the beginnings of regional identity."

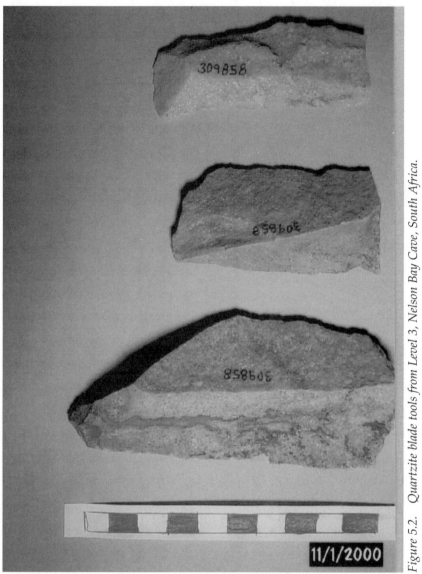

Figure 5.2. Quartzite blade tools from Level 3, Nelson Bay Cave, South Africa.

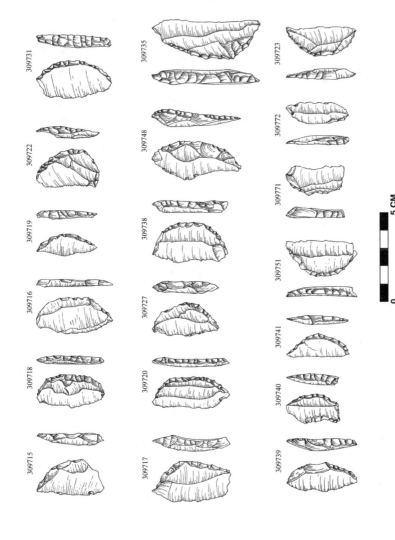

Figure 5.3. Quartzite-backed blades from Level 1, Nelson Bay Cave, South Africa.

Middle Stone Age Technology and Diets

In articulating the gradual evolution hypothesis, McBrearty and Brooks (2000) argue that the Middle Stone Age shows the gradual accumulation of the modern hunter-gatherer repertoire. They argue that several features of the Middle Stone Age are well-advanced over the contemporary Middle Paleolithic culture of European Neanderthals. They use several features of the Middle Stone Age to argue this pattern. First, pointed stone artifacts of various styles, thought to be armatures for spears or arrowheads, are found throughout the African continent. Many of these, like the tanged Aterian points, were obviously hafted. However, these have been interpreted as spear points and considered too bulky to have been used on arrows (Clark, J. D. 1989:572). Second, some Middle Stone Age assemblages include backed microliths, a technology that does not appear in Europe until much later. The small, razor blade–like inserts are parts of multicomponent tools, which become standard equipment in the Later Stone Age. The development of microliths, an elaboration of hafting, permits the manufacture of multicomponent tools, where several inserted parts are fastened into a haft with plant glues, bitumen, or sinews. Third, unlike in the Middle Paleolithic, bone tools were also manufactured. At Katanda in the Congo and White Paintings Rockshelter in Botswana, symmetrical barbed and engraved bone points may be as much as 80,000 years old (Brooks et al. 1995). Bone points from Blombos Cave were found in Middle Stone Age levels also dated to 70,000 to 80,000 years in age. The site yielded twenty-eight shaped and polished bone tools and engraved ochre pieces (Balter 2002; Henshilwood et al. 2001), implying that Middle Stone Age people worked and used bone to a much greater extent than did contemporary Europeans (McBrearty and Brooks 2000).

Fourth, the cooperative hunting of dangerous animals is demonstrated at sites like ≠Gi in Botswana and Klasies Rivers. At Klasies River, eland may have been driven over cliffs (Klein and Cruz-Uribe 1996; Milo 1998). At GvJm46, bones of an extinct alcelaphine, *Damaliscus ageuleaius*, accumulated at the base of a cliff-like drop (Marean 1997). Fifth, the Middle Stone Age exploitation of fish, plant foods, and other small resources suggests significantly greater dietary breadth than heretofore. The consumption of fish is documented at Bir Tafawi in Egypt; Blombos Cave in South Africa; and White Paintings Rockshelter, Botswana. Evidence of plant use includes charred vegetal material at Klasies River and grindstones at Mumbwa, Zambia; Katanda, Congo; and ≠Gi, Botswana. At the same time mollusks were eaten at Haua Fteah, Libya, and other North African sites as well as at Klasies River, Die Kelders, and other sites in South Africa. Accumulations of land snail remains at Lake Eyasi in Tanzania do reveal some use of smaller-scale resources (McBrearty and Brooks 2000). Much later on, increasing use of such foodstuffs is evidence of a start toward economic intensification. It certainly heralds a diversified pattern of eating. The shift in dietary choices from large, terrestrial fauna to smaller ones, plants, and fish is a complex one, requiring both new technologies and social mechanisms through which increasingly sedentary groups maintain their material and information flows.

Middle Stone Age Interaction

Sixth, some argue that Middle Stone Age people practiced a new land-use pattern of alternating dispersals and aggregations practiced by most modern hunter-gatherers. In South Africa, both Middle and Later Stone Age people left behind circular fire-hardened hearths and middens of food waste. Their trash, production debitage, and well-marked fire pits are all indications of foraging parties involved in patterns of aggregation and dispersal like those of modern hunter-gatherers. The stratigraphy characteristic of Middle and Later Stone Age sites, alternating human occupations with sterile periods, when the shelter was unoccupied, imply the episodic reoccupation typical of an annual round (Deacon and Deacon 1999:128–129). It is suggested that the bands split into smaller parties for part of the year and came together at other times. Hearths and post moulds associated with these activities show construction of shelters in the Middle Stone Age horizons of Mumbwa Cave, Zambia. Nevertheless, in South Africa at least, Acheulian nomads preferred to camp outdoors near water, but Middle and Later Stone Age groups in southern Africa lodged in rockshelters and caves, as well as in the open. The changeover from open-air to rockshelter use may signal an increased control of fire. For modern hunter-gatherers, aggregation and dispersal modes assume strong social bonds of interaction. The practice of patterned aggregation and dispersal probably arose from more cause than territorial restriction, including broader economic and social reasons. The social causes were, undoubtedly, compelling ones. The substance of their social behavior is evident in other practices, as well. Middle Stone Age people took care of the sick and infirm, if we may judge from deformed Salé and Singa crania (McBrearty and Brooks 2000), a further indication of attitudes we associate with modern populations.

Seventh, McBrearty and Brooks (2000) argue for the presence of long-distance exchange networks in the Middle Stone Age. Obsidian from the central Kenyan Rift Valley was transported to the west and south as many as 320-km to Nasera and Mumba Shelters in northern Tanzania (Merrick and Brown 1984; Merrick, Brown, and Connelly 1990). Other places to which it traveled were Pundo Makwar, in western Kenya, nearly 190-km from its source, and Lukenya Hill over 165-km away.

Eighth is the evidence of symbolic behavior in the Middle Stone Age. Although the web of symbols underlies almost everything humans do, the only incontrovertible archaeological signs of symbolic behavior are objects of art and adornment. Bone and shell pendants are found at North African Aterian sites, dating to between 130,000 and 40,000 years ago. Perforated objects were found with the early modern humans at Qafzeh, in Israel, possibly meaning an extension of African influences, including humans, into the Near East (Bar-Yosef and Vendermeersch 1993). In an early LSA, ostrich eggshell beads have been found at Enkapune ya Muto, in Kenya, and dated to 39,000 years ago, at White Paintings Rockshelter, in Botswana, dated to at least 26,000 years ago, and at Mumba and Kisese II Rockshelters in Tanzania, where they date to 35,000–45,000 years ago (Ambrose 1998; Klein 1999:513; Robbins 1999; Robbins et al. 2000).

Another intriguing sign of symbolic behavior in the Middle Stone Age comes from mounting evidence of nonutilitarian use of ochre pigmentation. Middle Stone Age artifacts from Lion Cavern in Swaziland, South Africa, and a variety of other sites in southeastern Africa suggest the mining of hematite and other pigments (Barham 2002). Hundreds of bits of ochre were found at Klasies River (Singer and Wymer 1982:117; Wurz 2000:110). Ochre is deeply scored to extract powder, ochre lumps, and pencils, and ochre-stained grinders were found at Blombos Cave (Henshilwood et al. 2001), and Border Cave, Porc Epic, ≠Gi, Florisbad, and Enkapune ya Muto (McBrearty and Brooks 2000).

Ochre had a variety of uses. It was used for medicinal properties, in hafting, and in treating hides, as well as for its symbolic use as a pigment applied to art objects and the body. At Blombos Cave, large quantities, including an engraved piece, were recovered cached on man-made shelves in the cave walls. However, it is very difficult to discern the function of all the ochre found in any particular context and whether it was used in a ritual or symbolic act.

Around the above eight points, a case can be made that the period of the African Middle Stone Age demonstrates a gradual accumulation of traits typical of the archaeological records of modern hunter-gatherers (McBrearty and Brooks 2000). Some say that humans during the Middle and Later Stone Ages, having assembled this repertoire of modern human cultural abilities, experienced population increases due to their increased food-getting abilities (Klein 1999). These modern humans increased their numbers and extended their range. Migrating out of Africa, they met the archaic peoples of Eurasia. As we posited, their excellent repertoire of adaptive behaviors allowed them to either successfully compete with or simply outnumber others like Neanderthals. The *Homo sapiens sapiens* who launched the last phases of the Middle Stone Age were near-modern in their physical characteristics. The question archaeology asks is whether these people, and their behaviors, were the first modern hunter-gatherers.

Evidence of Modernity in the Middle Stone Age

When evaluating McBrearty and Brooks's eight points, one approach might be to compare Middle Stone Age Africa with Middle Paleolithic Europe. In order for the gradual evolution hypothesis to hold water, the Middle Stone Age must have behaviors not found in the Middle Paleolithic. This would establish, based on the available evidence, the trend toward modernity in the Middle Stone Age. Such a comparison seems to yield different results for the eight features compared.

Hunting Points

The geographic diversity of pointed tool forms across Africa suggests different technologies adapted to different environments, but also suggests that "different ways to skin a zebra" developed within evolving technological traditions. As compared to the European Middle Paleolithic, one could argue for considerably more regional diversity. However, the area covered by Neanderthals was smaller than the African continent, and African hunting tools' greater stylistic diversity may merely be coincident with its greater size as well as differences in raw materials, environments, and resources. Furthermore, hafted points used as spears are not only found in Africa. Neanderthals made them as well in several sites (Shea, Davis, and Brown 2001). More than anything, hunting points appear to be a basic component of life over both Eurasia and Africa at this time.

Effective Hunting

Middle Stone Age people were clearly effective hunters, but their game choices are different from those of Later Stone Age people and the reasons for their contrasting food choices are often poorly understood. The faunal remains from Die Kelders and Klasies River suggest that African Middle Stone Age hunters took on less dangerous game, hunting throughout the year rather than just seasonally and preferring the docile eland to the dangerous buffalo. On the other hand, some of these differences may be due to the larger size of Later Stone Age populations or even the methodologies of analysts. In any case, Neanderthals and even the preceding *Homo heidelbergensis* were effective hunters; at La Borde (Jaubert et al. 1990), for example, Neanderthals hunted prime-aged adult aurochs, as *H. heidelbergensis* did horses at Schöningen (Theime 1997). It is hard to evaluate hunting "success" across varying contexts, species hunted, diets, and environments—there is no question that, again, by this general time period, hunting success is evidenced in both Europe and Africa.

Small Resource Procurement

Numerous sites, especially in Botswana and Central Africa, demonstrate a very early economic dependence on fish, which went hand in hand with the development of bone harpoons (Robbins et al. 1994, 1996, 2000). However, small resource use is also evidenced by coastal Neanderthals, who ate shellfish at Gibraltar (Barton et al. 1999). Furthermore, it is often assumed that Later Stone Age people had wider diet breadths than Middle Stone Age people, largely because they had specialized technologies for plant food processing, fishing, and so on. Marean and Assefa (1999) have argued that the greater diet breadth of Later Stone Age people was a response to higher population densities, not the signature of greater technological sophistication. In this case, an inability to distinguish behavioral capacity from its material manifestations plagues us. We are unable to decide whether the behavioral differences we observe are due to variance in inherent behavioral potential, technological evolution, tradition, or choice. Although evidence of small-scale resource use is intriguing, it was only occasionally practiced in limited regions and was still incipient when compared to the Later Stone Age. Neanderthals also ate small foods like turtles, nuts, and shellfish in good measure (Barton et al. 1999; Stiner 1993).

Changes in Site Use

Documenting settlement patterns is one of the most challenging of archaeological tasks and often requires survey data, poorly available for the African Middle Stone Age. The shift from an Acheulian pattern of open-air camps, often in watercourses and wadis, to the Middle Stone Age/Later Stone Age pattern of repeated use of cave sites suggests that humans attained the abilities to defend caves from predators and to repeatedly visit them. That their visits were assisted by controlled fire is evident. It is fair to point out, however, that evidence is perhaps equally good that *Homo heidelbergensis* engaged in somewhat similar habits, returning many times to well-used palimpsests like Kalambo Falls, where they left horizons of superimposed hearths, or at the stratified artifact lenses at Isimila (Phillipson 1993:47) or possibly Terra Amata in France, where post holes were also found, and Bilzingsleben in Germany (Gamble 1999:114). Evaluating changes in land-use patterns between the Acheulian, Middle Stone Age, and Later Stone Age will eventually require wide-scale survey data.

Long-Distance Trade

In one form or another social interaction existed from the beginnings of human society. It is the symbolic nature of this interaction as encoding systems of permission granting that seems to mark the better-orchestrated hunter-gatherer lifeway. If trade is a correlate of social interaction, however, one would have to concede that the Middle Stone Age never rises to levels seen much later and is only marginally better off than the Acheulian that preceded it.

Middle Stone Age people transported obsidian from the Central Rift to western Kenya. However, the numbers of these are very small, at most only 2 percent of the stone used at Lukenya Hill and even less at sites like Muguruk (Merrick, Brown, and Connelly 1990). In the Lukenya Hill sequence, Later Stone Age assemblages show dramatic increases in nonlocal obsidian compared to Middle Stone Age ones (Barut 1996). These pieces of imported stone seemingly arrived at western Kenyan Middle Stone Age camps by chance or indirect trade. There seems to be little evidence of enduring, culturally sanctioned interaction during the Middle Stone Age. Among Later Stone Age foragers, by contrast, stable, reliable trade networks brought consistent streams of necessities and information from near and far (Merrick and Brown 1984). The evidence for such widespread interaction is scant, and we cannot attribute high-quality organized material circulation to the Middle Stone Age. Indeed, one striking feature of the Later Stone Age as opposed to the Middle Stone Age is the increase in use of nonlocal material (Ambrose 2001; Gang 2001; Mehlman 1989).

Backed Blades

Although widespread in Europe by the Mesolithic, Middle Stone Age blade tools are unique to a few sites in Africa. Blade tools and hafted blades are also found in the Eurasian Middle Paleolithic (Kuhn and Bar-Yosef 1999), but they are not backed like the Middle Stone Age examples from Howieson's Poort sites in South Africa and from the Mumba site in Tanzania. Although they are not widespread, Middle Stone Age blade tools are common enough to constitute a significant "modern" part of the African Middle Stone Age.

Furthermore, some of them are small enough to be called microliths. Microliths are essentially splinters of stone, dull on one edge and sharp on another. They are easily manufactured through snapping and backing blades with pressure. They are easy to produce and carry, allowing a hunter in the field the opportunity to re-edge his weapon. They are used to produce composite tools, allowing both efficient use of raw material and a lightweight stock of replacement parts, and they can be components of a tremendous variety of composite tools, even shredding boards (Clark, J. D. 1969). As Clark (1975:191) pointed out, "The early appearance of backed blade forms and burins in the Middle Stone Age in sub-Saharan Africa—well before 35,000 years ago—appears to anticipate, rather than follow, from the appearance of the Upper Paleolithic in Europe."

Bone Tools

The later stages of the Stone Age sequences in Europe and Africa used materials other than stone to make tools. Wood was used by

Neanderthals and long before them. But, in contrast to wood, bone was plentiful and easily fashioned to a cutting or piercing edge. Bone was always found at kill sites, and lying about camp. It was a low-cost asset to the manufacture of multicomponent implements. However, for whatever reason, Neanderthals almost never worked bone, and worked bone is not widespread in the Middle Stone Age itself except for the series of points from Blombos. The spotty occurrence of worked bone in Middle Stone Age Africa could reflect the lack of locally available hardwoods.

Evidence of Symbol

Ochre, beads, and pendants are categories of objects with little utilitarian value. They may indicate aesthetic or symbolic sensibilities. The ochre in South African Middle Stone Age sites may indicate some kind of symbolic use. However, it is more commonly found in site levels with backed microliths, where it may have been a hafting material (Singer and Wymer 1982). Nevertheless, the quantity of ochre found in the South African Middle Stone Age sites is greater than that associated with the contemporary Mousterian sites. Scored objects are also much more common in the Middle Stone Age.

Based on the nothing more than format analogy, the Aterian pendants and Later Stone Age ostrich eggshell beads from Mumba, Kisese, White Paintings Rockshelter, and Enkapune ya Muto may be our earliest signs of this sort of symbolic behavior, as well as the evidence of *hxaro*-like exchange networks (Wadley 1993). No similar beadwork exists in the Middle Paleolithic. Nor are perforated objects found, although they exist in the Middle Stone Age. In fact, Middle Stone Age beads appear to be either around the same age as Upper Paleolithic Aurignacian beads, or perhaps somewhat older, especially those from Mumba and Kisese II. Again, if such evidence of African modern behavior could be reliably pinpointed to the Middle Stone Age, it would support the theory that such behaviors in fact evolved in Africa.

In summary, then, the evidence for Middle Stone Age behavior we would accept as modern varies in quality. Only the early appearance of backed microliths and ostrich eggshell beads in the African Middle Stone Age stands out as a most intriguing hint of modernity. Often, however, it is difficult for archaeologists to explain observed differences between Middle and Later Stone Age behavior. We are unable to decide whether the behavioral differences are due to variance in inherent behavioral potential, technological evolution, culture, or behavioral choice.

Summing Up

By the end of the Early Stone Age, post-Acheulian populations had learned the basics of the hunter-gatherer lifeway and demonstrated hunting competency (Stiner 1993). In Africa, family bands explored a variety of new ecozones. They put together specialized toolkits based on prepared core reduction and meant to ease work in these varied environments. The new flake-based tools were the working ends of tools with hafts, permitting a greater use of smaller, sometimes imperfect material found close at hand. Though there are earlier signs of the pattern of band dispersal and aggregation at open-air camps, caves now seem a favored spot for their recurrent encampments. Judging from the preferred use of local lithic raw materials, Middle Stone Age people foraged in smaller territories for resources close at hand, and using tools made to suit the opportunities available. Middle Stone Age people settled into cozy social contexts, with only scant signs of interaction beyond that expected between kith and kin. They were born into their family bands, lived out their lives in one or another gender-specific roles, undertook obligations to share, engaged in communal ritual and decision making, became parents, trained their offspring, aged, and may have buried their dead with ritual observance. Over time, Middle Stone Age people evolved physically toward the modern type we are today.

We can easily comprehend the success of new behaviors and culture traits that emerge toward the end of the Middle Stone Age. Less comprehensible is their origins. As we saw, opinion is divided between those who wish to view these happenings as a sudden and revolutionary biological event and those who see physical and cultural evolution as a gradual unfolding of human potentials. The gradual cultural evolution model is a compelling one, explaining the origins of modern human behavior in a parsimonious fashion. It draws the inference that human behavior gradually adapted, accumulating new kinds of information and ways of reacting to its circumstances. It does not require us to imagine the sudden appearance of novel kinds of human, replete with new ways of doing things. It supposes a gradual sharpening of the human genius. This model also requires that earlier behavior carry the seeds of this "modern" way of doing things. However, much is still lacking in our ability to recognize the rudiments of human culture, which appears to us today only in its complete form. However, there are hints of "modernity" to be found in the Middle Paleolithic, and even greater portents exist in the Middle Stone Age as well.

In contrast, the revolution perspective claims that the African Middle Stone Age and the Middle Paleolithic of Europe are not only contemporaneous but also predate anything we would consider modern human behavior. Supporters of this hypothesis point to the lack of art or adornment, a form of symbolic behavior that may be associated with language. Middle Stone Age people certainly communicated. The quality of that communication is hard to determine. Language is generally regarded an important expression of the complexities of modern lifeways, but there is no evidence of its material correlate until 40,000 years ago. Klein (1999) explained the origins of art as a result of changes in the workings of the brain. This fortuitous mutation caused language to develop. However, Deacon (1997) likens explanations for evolutionary change that hinge on fortuitous, chance events a kind of "hopeful monster" theory, and considers it unlikely that symbolic thinking, so profoundly embedded in the human brain, emerged in one pivotal event. On the other hand, it accords well with the European evidence of radical change in late Pleistocene cultural repertoires, innovative technologies, the colonization of new environments, and the first art. As far as the African record is concerned, on the other hand, the apparent set of rapid changes may be a fiction created by our methodologies. As Deacon writes (1997:36–37): "paleontological finds can appear irregular for many other reasons, not least of which is our predisposition to organize the evidence in categorical terms."

The question remains whether we can find evidence of the use of symbols in Middle Stone Age or Middle Paleolithic contexts. Neither Europe nor Africa has produced signs of an established and ongoing esthetic tradition of symbolic representation. If art is a precursor, or at least a companion, of language, then there is no strong evidence of symbolic usage during the middle stages of the Stone Age—with the exception of the later parts of the African Middle Stone Age.

There are differences in behavior between African Middle Stone Age hunters and their European counterparts. For example, hafted projectiles were used by Eurasian and African hunters by 100,000 years ago or so. On the other hand, certain technologies, such as backed pieces or the Blombos bone tools, are unique to the Middle Stone Age. Whatever similarities may seem to link the middle stages of the Eurasian Paleolithic with the contemporary industries of Africa, it is apparent that the two traditions were developing separately.

The emerging picture suggests that in Africa the transition from the Middle to the Later Stone Age was less a replacement of an obsolete behavioral package than an autochthonous development of modernized behavioral patterns. The diverse expressions of the African Middle Stone Age ought not surprise us. Having invented the foraging lifeway on the pleasant highlands of East Africa, mankind left its nest to master diverse environments. The palimpsest they left often puzzles us. The Blombos Cave Industry contains twenty-eight bone artifacts, while the nearby Klasies River has only one. Elsewhere, bone tools are equally rare. The people at Blombos obviously preferred bone or settled for it instead of something else. We may never know. The distinctive Katanda points are only found at a single site. The Howieson's Poort-like backed blade industries are found south of the Limpopo and at Mumba in Tanzania, some distance away. Could these instances suggest a burgeoning localization of tool-making traditions, similar to the hallmark regional or ethical manifestations of the later stages of the Stone Age? Regionally distinct expressions seem to signify the introduction of something akin to modern social relations (White 1985), such as the interaction of bands traveling through well-known landscapes and the recurrent meetings of kith, kin, and sometimes strangers. On the other hand, could the distinct regional expressions of the Middle Stone Age mean that these people lacked the interactions so basic to modern hunter-gatherers (Yellen 1998)?

The Middle Stone Age may appear superficially to be a constellation of disparate cultural expressions. However, each can be rationalized as an attempt to fit organized societies into diverse and distant environments. Whatever circulation occurred outside their home areas, for most hunter-gatherers of that time the paramount interaction sphere was the tight circle of kith and kin. As we will see, Later Stone Age people had wider spheres of interaction.

What we seem able to distill from this welter of data embedded in a piecemeal pattern is the gradual assembling of the modern package. In any case, it is sure that the behaviors of "ante-moderns" in Africa over the past 200,000 years or so must be examined as a single ongoing phenomenon. The autochthonous behaviors cultivated in the Middle Stone Age continue to illuminate the affairs of later populations.

Hints of this continuity of cultural expression appear in many deeply stratified sites. There the transition from Middle to Later Stone Age is expressed as a gradual reduction in tool type size. This is seen quite clearly in the Central African forest traditions (Cornellissen 1997). Across this Middle to Later Stone Age transition on the grassland and woodland of eastern to southern Africa, microlithic industries become more and more common (Brooks and Robertshaw 1990). Microlithic tools may indicate the evolution of lighter hunting weapons like the bow and arrow (Clark, J. D. 1975:191). "Leptolithic" technologies also allowed a wider range of finished tools to be created using microlithic blade inserts and allowed more economy in their use of stone. This gradual microlithic development begun in the Middle Stone Age must have had significant design ideals behind it, although reliability, flexibility, and maintainability (Nelson 1992) have all been attributed to microlithic tools. In any case, Howieson's Poort, which we will explore next, rather than being an anomaly, seems to be one of many isolated instances of the invention and utilization of a microlithic technology during the period of the Middle Stone Age. Whatever calendars and classificatory conformity may imply, Howieson's Poort is an industry seemingly out of step with its contemporaries. Appearing to preview the technologies of the Later Stone Age, it nevertheless epitomizes the variety of technical expression during the Middle Stone Age.

Whether modern styles of lifeway began in the Middle Stone Age or not is more than a difficult question to answer. It is a difficult one to frame, since we have no sure way to reconstruct an "original" human society. We have ideas, but little consensus. The observable differences in hunter-gatherers were probably there from the beginning. We have no reason to believe otherwise. Humans adapt here and there to meet the challenges environments pose. The earliest humans evolved in Africa bearing a comprehensive cultural repertoire. It was not graven on stone, but the product of generations of experience. We should expect diversity. It is the common heritage of all of us.

6

Microlithic Episodes: Nelson Bay Cave and Lukenya Hill

In this chapter, we compare two very different contexts for the early appearance of backed microliths and examine the implications of these different sites and contexts for validating the "modernity" of hunter-gatherers during the Middle and Later Stone Age. At Nelson Bay Cave, backed microliths are associated with the Howieson's Poort facies of the Middle Stone Age dating to about 65,000–70,000 years ago. They appear as an addition to a basic package of typically Middle Stone Age technology and were made and used for perhaps 10,000 years (H. Deacon, personal communication). Then, they disappear from Middle Stone Age toolkits. Lukenya Hill, a large inselberg in south-central Kenya, is one of the largest repositories of Later Stone Age assemblages and settlements. The first appearance of backed tools, if compared to other dated sequences, seems to be somewhat later, perhaps around 40,000 years ago. These backed tools, however, remain in the hunter's tool inventory to become even more common in subsequent assemblages. They are associated with permanent changes in hunter-gatherer land-use patterns, a consistent demonstration of highly refined stone working, and the sorts of interaction that become widespread in Africa by, at the very latest, 20,000 years ago (Brooks and Robertshaw 1990).

The Enigma of Howieson's Poort

Howieson's Poort is a distinctive, unusual, and difficult to interpret manifestation of the Middle Stone Age. There are many hypotheses to explain its occurrence at more than eighteen cave sites south of the Limpopo characterized by fine-grained chert, silcrete, and calcedony raw materials used to manufacture backed bladelets and other microliths. Named for the type-site near Grahamstown, South Africa, the industry consists of crescent and trapezoidal-shaped tools, blunted on one edge with steep retouch (see chapter 5, Figure 5.2). These short bladelets are narrow parallel-edged flakes struck sequentially from cylindrical cores, in a process sometimes called unrolling the core. Microliths are often little more than splinters of stone struck from cores and used as is, dulled on an edge, or shaped with fine pressure-flaked backing. In the Later Stone Age, of course, blade-based tool making is sometimes important. Consequently, to many observers Middle Stone Age microliths seem out of place, or even oxymoronic. Nevertheless, in the Howieson's Poort Middle Stone Age microliths appear in the same assemblages with large, facetted-platformed flakes from prepared cores (Figure 6.1, 309775, 309777, 309778, 309769), large blades struck from prepared cores (Figure 6.2, 309946, 309947, 309945, and Figure 6.3, 309949, 309948), and rare retouched pieces such as denticulates (Figure 6.1, 309779; Figure 6.2, 309732). In other words, in most Howieson's Poort assemblages the majority of artifacts have uncontestable Middle Stone Age credentials.

Furthermore, the Howieson's Poort occurs in cave deposits, interleaved between cultural horizons lacking microliths altogether. Taken out of its stratigraphic context, Howieson's Poort could be characterized as a much later industry. An alternative interpretation of its context believes it may in fact be transitional to the Later Stone Age where it might typologically be more at home (Parkington 1990), although most people believe it is significantly older than the early Later Stone Age. It should be said, though, that contemporary-backed blade industries found together with Middle Stone Age tools are also known from Mumba Cave in Tanzania, Enkapune ya Muto in Kenya, and other sites (Ambrose 1998; Brooks 1996). Howieson's Poort may not be as isolated a phenomenon as once thought.

The South African Howieson's Poort Industry includes the large flake-based implements typical of the Middle Stone Age, it also includes backed blade tools from bladelet cores using silicious raw materials like chert and silcrete, which are generally smoother and easier to flake. In Europe, similar technologies only became common during the much later Mesolithic. In southern Africa, rather than act-

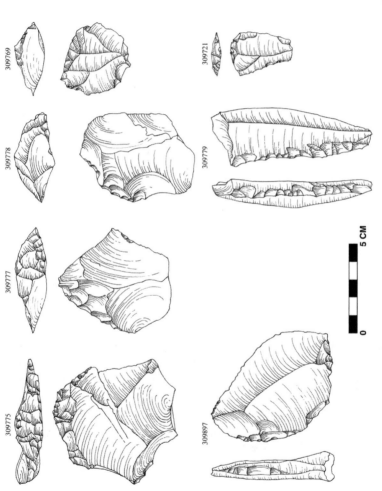

Figure 6.1. Quartzite artifacts from Level 2, Nelson Bay Cave, South Africa. 309775, 309777, 309778, 309769, 309897, facetted-platformed flakes from prepared cores; 309779, denticulate; 309721, small flake.

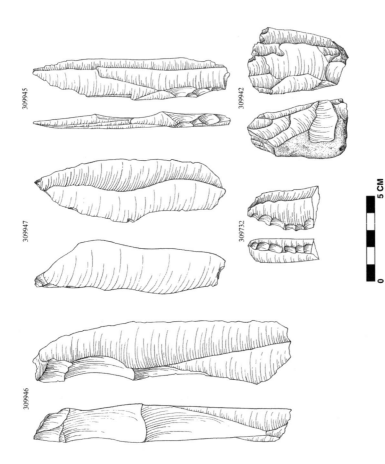

Figure 6.2. Artifacts from Nelson Bay Cave, South Africa 309946, 309947, 309945, quartzite blades, Level 2; 309732, quartzite denticulate, Level 3; 309942, chert double-platformed core, Level 5.

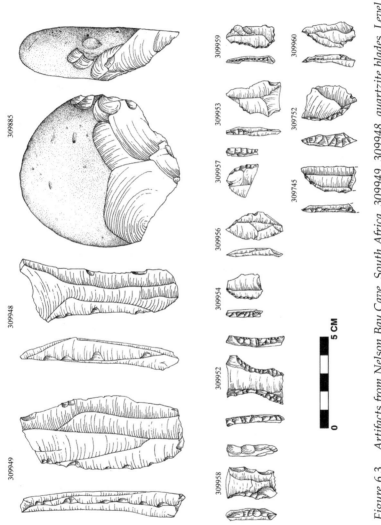

Figure 6.3.   Artifacts from Nelson Bay Cave, South Africa, 309949, 309948, quartzite blades, Level 1; 309885, silcrete core on cobble, Level 2; 309958, 309952, 309954, 309956, 309957, 309953, 309959, 309745, 309752, 309960, silcrete-, calcedony-, and chert-backed blades, Levels 5 and 6.

ing as an antecedent to Later Stone Age expressions, Howieson's Poort disappears, replaced by other typical South African Middle Stone Age practices. All in all, Howieson's Poort, in terms of raw material usage, typology, and technique, is quite distinct from all Middle Stone Age phenomena. Except for this "enigmatic" instance, common Middle Stone Age practice was to use local quartzite to produce triangular, rectangular, or irregularly shaped flakes or blades (Figures 5.2, 6.1, 6.4) struck from discoidal and prepared cores. In the prepared core method, the core was crafted to preshape the flake blank, and the end result was a very precisely struck flake to a predetermined form.

The Discovery of Howieson's Poort

John Hewitt originally reported the type-site in 1925. The assemblage, thought to reflect the Middle Stone Age Stillbay, associated with Howieson's Poort trapezoidal microliths, microlithic segments, and burins, led Goodwin to consider it a transitional industry, part of the terminal Middle Stone Age, and a precursor of the Later Stone Age (Goodwin and van Riet Lowe 1929). This would be consonant with our usual expectations of the trend of evolutionary change in worked stone technology as an orderly progression from core to flake to blade and microlithic industries. The type-site was a single-component one. This lack of associated, contrasting industries ensured that the collection was uncontaminated by later material, as would be the case of a disturbed multicomponent situation. However, the lack of stratigraphic succession at the site contributed to the uncertainty of the industry's relationships with other ways of stone making. It was difficult to agree on its place in the stratigraphic succession, although the cultural stratigraphy implied a fairly late position in the local chronology. Goodwin, in 1935, reported that Howieson's Poort levels were found interleaved between typically Middle Stone Age ones at Cape St. Blaize. In 1948, Jolly confirmed this stratigraphy at Skildergat Cave, where the Middle Stone Age horizons occurred both before and after the Howieson's Poort ones. It was not a precursor of the Later Stone Age. Subsequent work at Klasies River main site in 1967 verified the stratigraphy (Singer and Wymer 1982).

Figure 6.4.   Quartzite-pointed blades, Level 2, Nelson Bay Cave.

While its seemingly advanced character accorded it a status as a contemporaneous, if pale, reflection of the Upper Paleolithic, its standing in the stratigraphic succession suggested a much earlier cultural episode (Clark, J. D. 1975). Consequently, early investigators of the Howieson's Poort did not know what to make of it. In the beginning there was no apparent problem; the South African Middle Stone Age was thought to be contemporaneous with the European Upper Paleolithic. From this point of view, the Later Stone Age–like aspects of Howieson's Poort were to be expected, and it wasn't considered irregular at all. After revision of radiocarbon dating in the early 1970s established that the Middle Stone Age was, in fact, a contemporary of Europe's Middle Paleolithic, Howieson's Poort Industry became an anomaly, its backed blades seemingly out of place for those assuming parallelism in development on the two continents. At the same time, if the European revolution model was applied to the African succession, it implied that the Early and Middle Stone Ages, like the European Early and Middle Paleolithic, were party to more primitive, less modern behavior. The revolution model, so convenient to explaining the European succession, could fit the Middle Stone Age even if it forced a few uncomfortable anomalies like the Howieson's Poort.

The revolution view of the African Stone Age succession was challenged again when examination of human fossils showed morphology significantly more modern than that of contemporary Neanderthals (Brauer 1992). Biochemical studies of DNA suggested that essentially modern forms of humanity lived in Africa at this time (see chapter 5). More specifically, modern humans on all continents appeared to be descended from a recent African ancestor. This conclusion was supported by modern human skeletal material from Border Cave (but see Sillen and Morris 1996) and Klasies River Mouth. Almost-modern humans were not an uncomfortable fit with premodern behaviors presumed for the Middle Stone Age, since the same moderns made Middle Paleolithic tools in the Levant. The Middle Stone Age could then be considered a product of premodern *Homo* types, while the transition to Later Stone Age modes, in Africa as well as in Europe, was thought to be a relatively rapid one involving either purely behavioral alterations (Soffer 1989) or biological changes along with modifications in brain function (Klein 1989). In any case, the neat scheme linking premodern tools and premodern cultures in the South African Middle Stone Age was undone. These new perspectives require us to reanalyze supposed "anomalies" such as the Howieson's Poort.

The Status of Howieson's Poort

From the foregoing, it is obvious that Howieson's Poort is not a typical sort of African Middle Stone Age representative, and its backed blade and bladelet industry is tens of thousands of years older than those of Europe. It has no immediately apparent local precursor in eastern or southern Africa, nor an obvious successor, although some other African Middle Stone Age people made microliths.

At one time or another, it has been thought a product of the migration of a distant ethnic group utilizing a backed microblade-insert mode of tool fabrication (Singer and Wymer 1982). At other times, it has been relegated to a period of population disruption caused by an arid climate and less abundant, more widely spaced foodstuffs (Ambrose and Lorenz 1990). It has even been cited as evidence of intergroup exchange patterns (Deacon and Deacon 1999; Wurz 1999). For the moment, we can leave aside questions of origins and meaning and briefly describe the industry itself.

Howieson's Poort was originally identified by the presence in Middle Stone Age assemblages of crescents and trapeze-shaped backed blades and bladelets and single or double platform blade cores. These are frequently made of nonquartzite stones, such as milky or rose quartz, indurated shale, silcrete, chalcedony, and other cryptocrystalline silicates (Deacon and Wurz 1996). It also includes more typical Middle Stone Age artifacts like large blades, flakes, points from discoidal cores, and prepared cores. Stratigraphically, it occurs between conventional Middle Stone Age assemblages. It has been identified at eighteen sites, including Border Cave, Klasies River, Boomplaas, Apollo 11, and Rose Cottage Cave among others (Wurz 1999). At some of these, it is preceded and succeeded by typically Middle Stone Age assemblages. Its "sandwiched" position within the Middle Stone Age is well established (but see Parkington 1990).

Different techniques have been used to date it (oxygen isotope dating of shell in Butzer 1982 and Deacon, Talma, and Vogel 1988; ESR in Grun, Shackleton, and Deacon 1990; and amino acid racemization in Miller, Beaumont, and Johnson 1992 and Miller et al. 1999). The first age-determinations of the Howieson's Poort assemblages at Klasies River suggested a florescence around 80,000 to 70,000 years ago, during an episode of cooler and drier conditions and sea-level regression. An emerging consensus, based on different dating techniques that do not always agree, accepts an age of around 60,000 to 70,000 years ago. That is a period coincident with the start of the last glacial. Much of the South African Middle

Stone Age dates to this glacial period, a time of colder, wetter climates, for the most part, when much of the hinterland would have been forested (Avery 1995; Wurz 1999). Around Border Cave, today in the Highveld Grassland, there was moist *miombo* woodland, with nearly twice today's rainfall, or around 1,600-mm. The different Howieson's Poort localities date to an early period of this glacial, when climate was probably colder than now. The successor Middle Stone Age industries resume around 60,000 years ago when a somewhat warmer period returned.

The Howieson's Poort from Nelson Bay Cave, Western Cape Province

Nelson Bay Cave, is located on the Robberg Peninsula at Plettenberg Bay, approximately 530-km east of Cape Town, on a cliff looking over the coastal plain (Figure 6.5). Though dwarfed by the Cape Fold Mountains, which separate the Great Karoo basin and interior plateau from the coastal plain and the coast, the mountains and deep valleys create an environmental mosaic valuable to foraging populations (Inskeep 1987).

Nelson Bay Cave was chosen for investigation, even though the deposits appeared to be disturbed, because of its accessibility and proximity to Cape Town. Inskeep had in mind gaining experience before turning to the apparently undisturbed Klasies River sites, only 50-km to the east and also on the seashore (Inskeep 1987:1). His test cuttings in 1964 revealed more than six feet of deposits. The first four feet or so uncovered burned and comminuted shell, as well as stone artifacts and large animal bones (Inskeep 1987:5). Below his level seventeen were another two feet of loam, with stone artifacts and smaller bones (Inskeep 1987:5). His investigations and those of R. Klein in 1970 and 1979 concentrated on Later Stone Age deposits near the cave mouth (Figure 6.6). His 1970–1971 excavations discovered a long sequence of Later Stone Age cultural deposits These collections form the basis for a cultural stratigraphy of the Robberg, Albany, and Wilton industries found over much of Africa south of the Limpopo River (Klein 1972; Deacon, J. 1978; Volman 1981; Wadley 1993).

Klein continued excavations there in 1970 and 1971 in order to sample Middle and Later Stone Age–related fauna, but he found no analyzable preserved bone older than 18,000 years. The recovered fauna, in levels dated to 18,000 to 12,000 years ago, included at least two extinct types, a giant buffalo and a very large alcelaphine, a bovid adapted to open grasslands. Springbok and several alcelaphine antelopes, as well as

Figure 6.5.   Mouth of Nelson Bay Cave.

Figure 6.6. Nelson Bay Cave during excavation.

quagga, were found. These discoveries are consistent with other evidence from the Cape suggesting that in Pleistocene times, the area was open grassland, about 80-km from the sea. Nelson Bay Cave's Holocene fauna, on the other hand, is consistent with the closed evergreen forest found in the area today. Marine shells and seals, as well as eland, bush pig, and bushbuck, were found in Holocene levels, documenting a heavier vegetation and seashore location. This would be expected on the Cape coast during the last interglacial, which was so like today (Klein 1972).

Two meters of cave deposit containing Middle Stone Age artifacts but no faunal remains lay beneath one-half meter of rubble. Volman (1981) attributed most of the material to the Howieson's Poort. Butzer's study of sediments together with analysis of oxygen isotope composition of shells by N. J. Shackleton suggested an age of 70,000 to 80,000 years ago. However, other methods, as we have seen, suggest a date somewhere closer to the transition to the last glacial episode, or around 65,000 to 70,000 years ago. Apparently, the diet of the inhabitants was a rich and varied one. Though no food bone or plant remains were preserved in the Middle Stone Age at Nelson Bay Cave, the nearby Klasies River site had a wide variety of faunal remains (Klein 1989; Klein and Cruz-Uribe 1996). It preserved evidence that small antelope like the grysbok were hunted, as well as medium to large bovids, an extinct giant buffalo, eland, and Cape Buffalo. Seals were captured offshore, and shellfish gathered along it. Large kitchen middens formed from their remains; carbonized material found there seems to be food plant residue, possibly from corm tunics piled up near cooking fires, that were burnt and preserved (Deacon 1993).

Stone workers at Nelson Bay Cave used hard quartzite cobbles. The stone was formed by nearby wave action and therefore immediately available around the cave mouth. Some artifacts display characteristic cobble or pebble cortex, and others were quarried directly from local outcrops. Small quantities of cryptocrystalline silicate rocks, such as silcrete, hornfels, chert, and chalcedony, and indurate shale, were acquired as pebbles or cobbles from riverbeds. A silcrete cobble from Nelson Bay Cave 40-cm long may represent the maximum size of cobble used (Figure 6.3, 309885). Although the infrequently used nonquartzite stones are often characterized as imports, their provenience is unknown. Much of it was easily obtainable, though. The nearest silcrete source at the Langkloof is little more than 20-km away, relatively local, by itinerant hunter-gatherer standards (Wurz 2000). An examination of cores suggests that the nonquartzite material is consistently smaller than the quartzite and easily transported. Other lithic raw materials found at Nelson Bay Cave may have come from the South African interior, hundreds of kilometers away (Sampson, personal communication 2001).

The Nelson Bay Cave Assemblages: Typology and Variability

MSA levels at Nelson Bay Cave were excavated in a series of arbitrary levels numbered down 1 to 10. In his original analysis of the material, Volman (1981) attributed most of the levels to the Howieson's Poort, with the last three being attributed to the Middle Stone Age I and II, as identified at nearby Klasies River Mouth. More formally, we can assign Levels 1 to 6 at Nelson Bay Cave as representative of the Howieson's Poort Industry and Level 7 as transitional, intervening between the Middle Stone Age and Howieson's Poort. Levels 8 to 10 represent the Middle Stone Age (Table 6.1; Volman 1981). Based on lithic raw material proportions and the types of tools produced, the assemblages from Nelson Bay can be grouped into three types. One type of assemblage, in Levels 1, 2, and 7, contains many backed pieces, but very little of the nonquartzite stone. The second type, in Levels 3, 4, 5, and 6, has backed pieces and a much larger proportion of nonquartzite stone. Levels 8 to 10 seem to be a more typical Middle Stone Age assemblage (Tables 6.1, 6.2). Table 6.3 shows that Levels 1, 2, and 7 are distinguished by large proportions of quartzite-backed pieces. In Levels 5 and 6, the preference of silcrete for making these tool types is clear.

The arbitrary levels of the Nelson Bay Cave deposit vary not only in material used to manufacture backed pieces but also in the kinds of

Level		Industry Type (Volman 1981)
1	mostly quartzite; many quartzite-backed pieces	Howieson's Poort
2	mostly quartzite; fewer backed pieces of quartzite	Howieson's Poort
3	mostly quartzite, few backed pieces	Howieson's Poort
4–6	• diverse raw materials; only 83% quartzite • 25–75% of shaped pieces are backed pieces, usually on chert and silcrete but up to 50% of them are quartzite • importation of fine-grained cores	Howieson's Poort
7	mostly quartzite, with some backed pieces, 70% of quartzite	Transition
8–10	mostly quartzite, few backed pieces of quartzite	Middle Stone Age I/II

Table 6.1. Assemblage Types at Nelson Bay Cave, South Africa

Level	Industry Type (Volman 1981)	(%) Quartzite	Backed Pieces (% of shaped tools)	Backed Pieces as Quartzite (%)	% of Cores of Nonquartzite Materials
1	Howieson's Poort	95	52	91	3
2	Howieson's Poort	99	22	82	3
3	Howieson's Poort	96	11	25	9
4	Howieson's Poort	88	24	50	36
5	Howieson's Poort	83	59	0	35
6	Howieson's Poort	83	73	26	29
7	Transition	98	47	72	6
8	Middle Stone Age	98	4	100	0
9	Middle Stone Age	99	0	–	0
10	Middle Stone Age	98	16	100	0

Table 6.2.   Differences in Typology and Raw Material Composition in the Nelson Bay Cave Deposit

Level	Quartz Scrapers	Quartz-Backed Pieces	Silcrete Scrapers	Silcrete-Backed Pieces
1	38	70	9	7
2	33	10	0	2
3	5	1	3	3
4	4	2	1	2
5	1	0	6	13
6	1	5	2	14
7	30	23	2	9
8	20	1	2	0
9	9	0	0	0
10	5	1	0	0

Table 6.3. Number of Quartz and Silcrete (and Other Cryptocrystalline Silica) Scrapers and Backed Tools in the Nelson Bay Cave Assemblages

backed pieces made. In Levels 1 and 2, the backed pieces are finely shaped crescents (Figures 5.2 and 6.7). In the other Howieson's Poort group, they are oblique truncations, miscellaneously backed pieces, and curiously notched and strangled blades (Table 6.4; Figure 6.3, 309958, 309952, 309954, 309956, 309957, 309953, 309959, 309745, 309752, 309960; Figure 6.8; and Figure 6.9). These could be characterized as microliths lacking true backing, but with microscarring typical of woodworking (Wurz 2000:89). The quartzite and nonquartzite-backed pieces are not only different in form, but in size, by every measure, in their length, thickness and weight, the backed quartzite pieces are significantly larger and heavier (Table 6.5). These backed pieces show differences in design that go beyond those determined by raw material alone. They were specifically designed to be different tools.

Levels 4 through 6 have most of the features we think of as typically Howieson's Poort. They have a larger proportion of nonquartzite raw materials and an increased tendency toward the production of backed pieces. Level 6 contains the highest proportion of backed pieces (73 percent of all tools there, but only a quarter of them are made of quartzite). The large amount of debitage of nonquartzite stone and the presence of chert cores in these levels (Figure 6.10 and Figure 6.2, 309942) suggests the greatest access to fine-grained raw materials was in these levels, and that core reduction and the manufacture of blanks, or at least core discard, occurred at the site itself. Other Howieson's Poort levels do not have cores of the fine-grained materials, with the exception of the large core from Level 2 (Figure 6.3, 309942). Instead, in Levels 1, 2, and 7, the local quartzite was skillfully employed for blade core reduction (Figure 6.11). In Level 1, quartzite cores include small single and double platform blade cores, in place of the chert and silcrete blade cores of Levels 5 and 6, as well as larger Levallois and discoidal cores on which the more typical Middle Stone Age blades were produced. Clearly, quartzite raw material was not a significant impediment to the production of backed pieces.

As we can see from the foregoing characterizations, the seven Howieson's Poort levels at Nelson Bay Cave show considerable variability in typology, raw materials, and selection of raw material for specific tool types. It is tempting to infer that this is in fact not a single industry but a succession of different ones "linked by a superficial sharing of backed elements" (Parkington 1990:49). In effect, it's possible that the Howieson's Poort has been too briefly and broadly characterized to be an internally consistent lithic industry (Wadley and Harper 1989). Before we can so cavalierly dismiss it, we should note some patterns that do emerge.

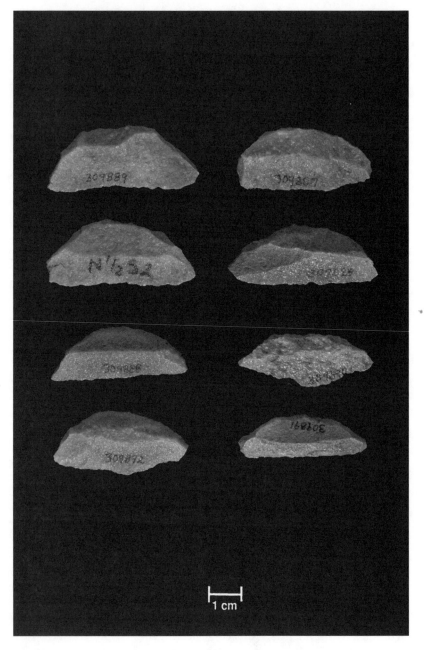

Figure 6.7.   Quartzite crescents, Level 2, Nelson Bay Cave, South Africa.

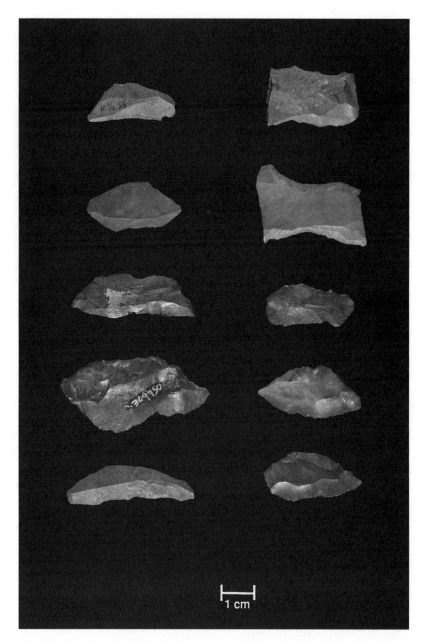

Figure 6.8.   Silcrete- and calcedony-backed blades, Level 6, Nelson Bay Cave, South Africa.

Figure 6.9. Silcrete- and calcedony-backed and strangled blades, Nelson Bay Cave, South Africa.

Tool Type	Level 1	Level 5	Level 6	Total
Crescent	38	2	2	42
Backed fragment	8	2	4	14
Backed piece—miscellaneous	5	6	4	15
Backed blade	4	1		5
Crescent and notch	3		1	4
Oblique truncation	7	15	5	27
Trapeze	2		1	3
Double notch	1			1
Double truncation	1	1		2
Orthogonal truncation		1		1
Retouched blade			1	1
Notched strangled blade		4		3
Grand Total	69	31	18	118

Table 6.4.   Typology of Backed Pieces and Microliths in Levels 1, 5, and 6 at Nelson Bay Cave

Figure 6.10.   Silcrete cores, Levels 5 and 6, Nelson Bay Cave, South Africa.

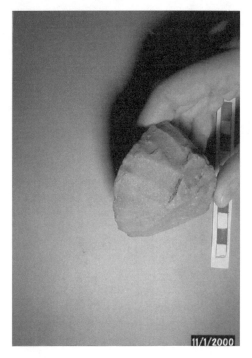

Figure 6.11.   Quartzite blade core, Level 2, Nelson Bay Cave, South Africa.

	Number	Mean Length	Standard Error, Length	Mean Width	Standard Error, Width	Mean Thickness	Standard Error, Thickness
Level 1	24	42.34	9.31	19.00	4.56	9.68	1.12
Levels 5 and 6	22	32.52	8.13	16.64	3.64	5.26	0.60
p value for t-test			Length <.01		Width >1.0		Thickness <.001

Table 6.5. Size of Backed Pieces from Level 1 and Levels 5 and 6 and t-tests of the Differences.

To me, the most striking features of the Nelson Bay Cave series are the inconsistent use of nonquartzite stone for the manufacture of backed blades, and the typological diversity of the microliths and backed tools. In the early Level 7 assemblages with backed pieces and the later Levels 1 and 2 assemblages, these tools are made mostly of quartzite. In the middle levels, however, they are made on non-quartzite stone. In other words, although Howieson's Poort is usually characterized as a Middle Stone Age flake-based industry with backed segments made on fine-grained siliceous raw materials, this is not always the case. There are several explanations that could cover this; that the successive "Howieson's Poort" lenses are not the recurrent occupations of the same groups, that fashion changed for a time, or that sources of the fine-grained siliceous stone were used up. So enigmatic is this sequence that you can take your choice or propose alternative explanations.

The backed pieces of the Howieson's Poort Levels 1, 2, and 7 are mostly finely backed crescents on the one hand, and in the Howieson's Poort Levels 5 and 6 the backed pieces include oblique truncations, miscellaneously backed pieces, and irregularly notched strangled blades (Table 6.4). Quartzite- and nonquartzite-backed pieces vary in form and size. One reason for the differences in the form of the backed pieces in the different levels may be, of course, the different core size and differing flaking characteristics of quartzite and the other raw materials. The size and shape variations suggest differences in the design of composite hafts and handles that the quartzite- and nonquartzite-backed tools were a part of. We might also consider different functions for the implements, such as the notched tools that Wurz (2000) suggests could have been for woodworking. Projectile armatures are usually light in weight, weighing less than 10 g. The much heavier quartzite microliths found in Levels 1, 2, and 7 suggest that they were not projectile armatures (McBrearty and Brooks 2000). Some were probably fitted to other implements, hafted into cutting tools, or simply held in the hand. The harder, less brittle quartzite probably lent itself to many different uses, probably on harder materials like wood.

How important was the selection of the different types of lithic raw material to the manufacture of typical Middle Stone Age and blade tools? Is the Nelson Bay Cave pattern merely a local phenomenon? Apparently not—it seems very similar to that of nearby Klasies River. At this site, we find few nonquartzite pieces at the beginning of the sequence, though they increase in number in upper levels of the deposit (Wurz 1999, 2000). Silcrete and other raw materials are used for backed pieces in the earlier levels. In the upper levels, there are fewer silcrete artifacts, while quartzite was the preferred stone for crescents and similar shapes (Wurz personal communication 2001). At both Nelson Bay Cave and Klasies River, then, the earliest and the latest Howieson's Poort levels include backed pieces made on nonlocal quartzite, whereas the middle levels emphasize other raw materials (Singer and Wymer 1982:98–99).

It is clear that over time, local craftsmen changed their stone preference along with their choice of finished product. However, whether we are faced with a conscious choice, a change in supply, the availability of more suitable stone, or whatever, is difficult to determine. Could the Cape Coastal pattern of Howieson's Poort variation be found in other Howieson's Poort sequences? Unfortunately, many of these sequences are only cursorily published. It would seem, though, that the Klasies River and Nelson Bay Cave occupants used more quartzite than did those of any other Howieson's Poort site (Wurz 2000:59). Wurz attributes the use of quartzite in the area to a lack of other suitable rocks in the vicinity. In sites near the silcrete sources of the Cape Fold Mountains, for example at Montagu Cave and the type-site, the backed tools were made mostly on nonquartzite material (Wurz 2000). It would appear that Howieson's Poort craftsmen sought out and used stone close to hand.

If not a question of supply, why then did prehistoric people change their material choices through time? The first reason is that sources of available stone were changing through time. In the Nelson Bay Cave sequence, most of the nonquartzite tools were made from secondary sources—that is, pebbles of silcrete and other materials that eroded out of primary mountainous sources and made their way downstream in riverbeds (Shelley 1993). Such sources are subject to the vagaries of erosion and doubtless are changeable in their location and abundance. Changing natural distributions, of course, affect the procurement choices of mobile hunter-gatherers.

Another alternative explanation is that human settlement patterns varied as the environment changed, affecting the acquisition of preferred lithic raw materials. One approach along these lines is based on the assumption that the nonquartzite raw materials were more distant from sites like Nelson Bay or Klasies River (Ambrose and Lorenz 1990). Similar approaches view proportions of locally acquired versus exotic stone in archaeological horizons as an index of hunter-gatherer mobility, since stone procurement may be largely incidental to the food quest (Binford 1979). According to this scenario, then, raw material choice, rather than novel-backed microlith tool type, is the more important phenomenon of the Howieson's Poort. According to this view, the Howieson's Poort is a period of greater mobility corresponding to a more arid phase, when resources became more widely distributed and foragers became more mobile in pursuing them, procuring the nonquartz material on these wider foraging paths. Following this point further, one might surmise that microliths were invented when knappers developed an appreciation of the design and flaking potentials of the new raw materials. Indeed, more formal tools are usually made on finer-grained, more workable raw materials (Brantingham et al. 2000).

The mobility hypothesis is intriguing and raises two questions. As we have seen, proportions of stone raw materials and their source distances from sites are a way to estimate hunter-gatherer mobility (Andrevsky 1994). However, this method is best applied when stone sources are well known. In the case of Nelson Bay Cave, most of the worked stone was acquired in the near vicinity of the cave, where there are quartz veins and shale beds (Marean personal communication 2001; Inskeep 1987:30). Silcrete was obtainable about 20-km away in the Cape Fold Mountains. However, it may have been brought into the site area by river action. This would affect its availability over time. Other stone, such as opaline silica, is found only 100-km away (Sampson personal communication 2001). Given the secondary source nature of the nonquartzite materials, they may have been just as widely *distributed* as the quartz, but somewhat *rarer*. This availability pattern suggests that procurement might be more fruitfully modeled as an optimal foraging exercise (Minichillo 1999).

We presently have no way of ascertaining the exact loci of these different materials, nor the extent to which the availability of preferred kinds of stone varied over the period of the Middle Stone Age. We do know that erosion and sea-level changes do affect material availability. Differing proportions of one kind of stone to another is not prima facie evidence of a high level of residential mobility. We have already seen that many factors other than mobility have an effect on the look of a cultural deposit and the proportions of different stone or artifacts found there. In the simplest case, the duration of a tool's use and the frequency of reworking or delayed discard can cause more of one kind of stone to be found than another type. In other words, when mobile hunter-gatherers discard tools frequently, or discard them close to their source, they mimic the sort of debris likely in assemblages produced by less mobile folk (Ingbar 1994).

Second, the relationship between raw material procurement decisions and typological change is far from clear-cut at either the Nelson Bay Cave or Klasies River sequences. At Nelson Bay Cave, at least, technological shift precedes rather than follows raw material shift. The

162 / Chapter 6

first backed tools appear in Level 8, where a single crescent is made of quartz. In Level 7, the numbers of backed pieces increase markedly, although most are made of quartzite. The focus on backed tool production declines in Levels 3 and 4, when nonquartzite raw materials again become scarce. However, backed crescents are again abundant in Levels 2 and 1, but made almost entirely on quartzite (Table 6.3). In other words, a shift to nonlocal raw materials may in fact be related to their greater appropriateness in the production of backed tools, especially the lighter, smaller tools of Levels 5 and 6. However, the silicious raw material was not selected for all backed tool manufacture. Although increased mobility may explain the increase in nonquartzite tools in some of the Howieson's Poort levels, it cannot explain the manufacture of backed tools, which seem to have taken place independent of the availability of chert and silcrete.

In any event, within the acknowledged Howieson's Poort sequence at Nelson Bay Cave, there is ample evidence to suggest two or more variants of the microlith theme—the presence, at different times, of tool makers with two somewhat different ideas of the acceptable form of microlithic tools. How these variant behaviors came about is presently hidden from us, since the processes of innovation or change are not apparent at Nelson Bay Cave. Any intermediate stages, if there be any, are no more evident than are those that produced Howieson's Poort in the first place.

Interaction and Symbolic Behavior

Another opinion about the Howieson's Poort holds that its trademark nonquartzite raw materials are evidence of evolutionarily "modern" behavior. It has been posited that the use of nonquartzite raw material in Howieson's Poort–backed blades added to their social value (Deacon 1997; Wurz 1999). Wurz suggests that since backed pieces in both quartzite and nonquartzite stone were manufactured, that those using the scarce, imported material were made as exchange items. The comparative rarity of the nonquartzite raw material added an extrinsic value to pieces made from it, since it needed to be traded from afar; it had, therefore, an accrued value. Kalahari hunter-gatherers frequently exchanged arrows in *hxaro* systems, where they were likely imbued with social value, a personal emblemic style (Wiessner 1983). Since Wurz detected little size difference between the quartzite- and nonquartzite-backed pieces, she contended that the choice of raw material was not a functional, but a stylistic one. This argument holds that when these artifacts lost their extrinsic social aura production was stopped, since stone preference had no functional value.

Most stylistic explanations in stone tool studies are usually countered from a "function" point of view. Sackett (1982) and others make a case for the priority of functional explanations over stylistic ones; in other words, as far as stone tools are concerned, variability usually arises from differences in function. The Level 1–backed pieces are heavier and thicker than those of Levels 5 and 6. It may be that they were hafted as knives or even hand-held for cutting, while the Level 5– and 6–backed tools could have been armatures. The weight and thickness differences between the quartzite- and nonquartzite-backed pieces suggest they were made for different purposes. This would favor functional rather than stylistic explanations for the variations noted at Nelson Bay Cave, which may have coexisted with shifting raw material distributions and settlement patterns. (Analysis of edge wear might clarify this issue; unfortunately, quartzite often retains no traces of use wear.)

From a technological design perspective, however, the variations noted between the various strata at Nelson Bay Cave probably incorporated aspects of both function and tool design—for example, they might be a function of increasing standardization of hafts or the modification and redesign of complex implements of which the backed blades were but one component. Changes in lithic raw material choice are but one part of the chain of technological decisions that go into designing and making tools.

Punch-Struck Blades in the Howieson's Poort Industry

The Howieson's Poort assemblages have long been considered technically exceptional. Original interpretation of technique suggested that silcrete blades were punch-struck, since they had diffuse bulbs of percussion and small platform areas (Clark, J. D. 1970; Wurz 1999). However, it has also been suggested that these characteristics are more consistent with soft-hammer usage, rather than punch-struck techniques (Pelegrin 1993; Inizan, Roche, and Tixier 1992; Wurz 1999). At Nelson Bay Cave, the nonquartzite blades were almost exclusively manufactured using a hard-hammer technique, although some use of soft-hammer percussion is apparent (Figures 6.12 and 6.13; Table 6.6).

Figure 6.12. Calcedony blade, Level 6, dorsal surface, Nelson Bay Cave, South Africa.

Figure 6.13. Calcedony blade, Level 6, ventral surface showing diffuse bulb of percussion, Nelson Bay Cave, South Africa.

Level	Raw Material	Hard Hammer	Soft Hammer	Total
5	Cryptocrystalline silica	34	3	37
5	Silcrete	142	10	152
6	Silcrete	81	8	89
6	Cryptocrystalline silica	101	4	105

Table 6.6. Number of Cryptocrystalline Silicates and Silcrete Non-retouched Blades Manufactured through Hard-Hammer and Soft-Hammer Technique from Nelson Bay Cave Levels 5 and 6

It is possible that the South African Middle Stone Age contains more variability than the present sample shows. When one considers the variation not just within a single site, or among many diverse, supposedly related ones, it is clear that the industry termed Howieson's Poort incorporates many difference styles of manufacture. At Die Kelders, Lower Level 4/5, though only 5 percent of the worked stone is silcrete, more than one-fifth of the flake blades are of silcrete. This may suggest that there never was a Howieson's Poort "tradition" or industry, but perhaps one or two specific tool or haft designs that were passed from hand to hand within southern African interaction spheres. To sum up, then, changes in technological style, changing radii of interaction spheres, and changing raw material distributions may all help to explain variation within assemblages called "Howieson's Poort."

Much of the interest in Howieson's Poort arose from its sudden appearance. It then vanished from the scene just as suddenly. The backed pieces that characterized it did not reappear again until the Later Stone Age. What was going on? Horizons containing it were securely interleaved with those of typical Middle Stone Age facies. Its makers seem to have occupied this part of the coast while still making typical Middle Stone Age tools. If it existed, as we construe it, its closest counterpart, in time and modus operandi, is the microlith-based industries of the Later Stone Age, beginning some 20,000 years later. Perhaps its appearance and change through time can be related to changing mobility patterns, the scarcity of stone, a form of exchange relationship, or even a set of unique hafted tools that disappeared along with their makers. Certainly, human populations at this time were small, dispersed, and vulnerable to extinction (Klein 1989). This is a true conundrum. However, we can show cultural affinities with other "advanced" assemblages of the Middle Stone Age, such as the Mumba Industry of northern Tanzania, which also includes large, backed pieces, often on chert, together with an essentially Middle Stone Age industry of Levallois and discoidal reduction of quartz, and perhaps the sequence at Umhlatuzana rockshelter in KwaZulu-Natal where backed blades are "added on" to a Middle Stone Age industry (McBrearty and Brooks 2000). The Howieson's Poort craftsmen were not alone.

Lukenya Hill

Like hunter-gatherers of the South African Robberg, the Later Stone Age occupants of rockshelters and open-air sites at Lukenya Hill hunted migratory herbivores on Kenya's Athi Plains (Figures 6.14 and 6.15). Lukenya Hill is one of the richest Pleistocene Later Stone Age sites in East Africa. It is located on the Athi Plains of southcentral Kenya. To the southeast are the wooded Mua Hills. The hill contains extensive signs of Later Stone Age occupation on its southeastern side, where many rockshelter sites have formed (Figure 6.16). These sites, some of which are contiguous in part, include GvJm16 (Merrick 1975), GvJm19 (Nelson and Mengich 1984), GvJm22 (Gramly 1976; Gramly and Rightmire 1973), GvJm46 (Miller 1979), and GvJm62 (Kusimba, S. 1999), which a group of archaeologists and I dug in 1993 and 1994 (Figure 6.17), respectively. Our purpose was to determine how the transition to microlithic technologies and composite tools influenced land-use patterns (Kusimba, S. 1999).

GvJm62 was discovered by Stanley Ambrose and originally described as an open-air site at the base of an alluvial fan surrounding the rocky cliffs of the southeastern side of Lukenya. To the east of the site, the hill apron slopes downward to the Athi Plains. To the south is a large gully approximately 60-m wide by 100-m long and 30-m deep; it is one of many gullies around the hill's apron. The stratigraphy suggests that originally the site extended into the area now dissected by the gully.

Obsidian, chert, and quartz were worked. Obsidian bombs and lapilli were handily available on top of, weathering out of, and embedded within a welded tuff that outcrops over several kilometers on the Athi Plains, about 5-km to the east. Most of these bombs are small, between 1- and 2-cm in diameter (Figure 6.18). Secondary sources of chert nodules are, like the Nelson Bay silcretes, scattered

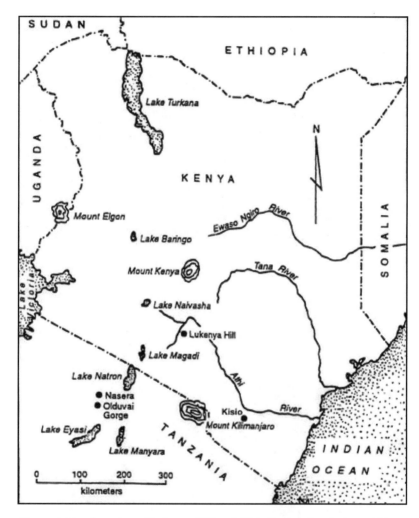

Figure 6.14. Location of Lukenya Hill and Kisio Rockshelter in East Africa.

Figure 6.15.   Giraffe on the Athi Plains west of Lukenya Hill.

Figure 6.16.   View of the rocky vertical slopes of the southeastern side of Lukenya Hill, which contain numerous rockshelter and open-air sites.

Figure 6.17.   Lukenya Hill site GvJm62 during excavation.

Figure 6.18.   Obsidian bombs from Lukenya Hill.

widely in riverbeds throughout the Athi Plains. The nearest chert source is the dry bed of the Stony Athi River, 5-km from GvJm62, although chert sources could be found in the riverbeds around the Athi Plains. The chert nodules are between 2- and 4-cm in diameter.

Large quartz veins are found in the inselberg bedrock adjacent to GvJm62 and GvJm46. Lukenya Hill vein quartz appears as rounded cobbles or angular fragments varying in uniformity and grain size, and even include quartz crystal. Chemical analyses demonstrated that some of the Lukenya obsidians came from the large flow outcrops around Lake Naivasha in Kenya's Central Rift Valley, 150-km northwest (Figure 6.19), or from the Kedong Escarpment, 65-km west (Merrick and Brown 1984). These outcrops produced pieces larger than the local bombs, and they are easier to flake into a wider variety of tools.

The Lukenya Hill Assemblages

Two early Later Stone Age assemblages at Lukenya Hill are relevant to our discussion of the impact of microlithic tools. The Lukenya Hill 1 industry is found at sites GvJm 46 and GvJm 62. It may date to 40,000 years ago or more (Ambrose 1998). This industry contains a large proportion of scrapers (around 60 percent of shaped tools) and very few microliths—around 12 percent of shaped tools in both assemblages (Table 6.7). The obsidian microliths are small and short, probably because they were often made on the local bombs (Figure 6.20, top row). At both sites, "fan" scrapers and convex scrapers were the most common types of chert scrapers and steep scrapers the most common quartz scrapers (Figure 6.21). In other ways, the tool inventories at these sites' are different. GvJm46 is unique in having denticulate scrapers, while GvJm62 has notched blades and three invasively retouched bifacial points. In both industries, though, prehistoric people made abundant use of the local quartz and especially preferred bipolar core reduction for working the local quartz. Their use of local quartz fit the classic expedient strategy model: Very few formal tools were made and cores were worked briefly, such that a wide range of sizes is revealed in the lithic assemblage. Their rare chert and obsidian cores, on the other hand, were reduced mostly through freehand core reduction.

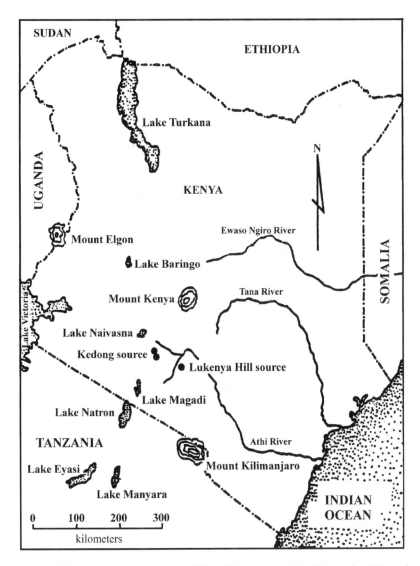

Figure 6.19.   Location of Lukenya Hill, Kedong, and Lake Naivasha (Central Rift) obsidian source localities in Kenya.

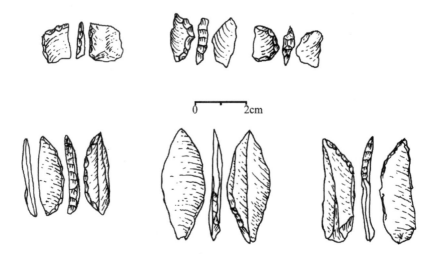

Figure 6.20. Backed blades from the Lukenya Hill sites. Top row, miscellaneous backed piece and crescents, obsidian, GvJm46.

The Lukenya Hill 2 industries, found at sites GvJm16 and GvJm22, are substantially younger than Lukenya Hill 1. Bone radiocarbon dates, although not very reliable, indicate these assemblages may be 20,000 years or so younger than the Lukenya Hill 1 assemblages. Lukenya Hill 2 assemblages are similar to those from Naisiusiu at Olduvai Gorge, which has been radiocarbon dated to around 40,000 years ago (Manega 1993). More dating of Later Stone Age residues in eastern Africa is needed to resolve the presently unsure chronology of the Lukenya Hill 1 and Lukenya Hill 2 industries,

Artifact Type	LH1		LH2	
	GvJm46	GvJm62	GvJm22	GvJm16
Scrapers	163	223	82	67
Backed pieces	36	42	193	179
Bipolar cores	108	237	35	50
Freehand cores	147	171	314	230
Proportion of quartz	98	91	86	74
Proportion of chert	2	6	10	19
Proportion of obsidian	>1	1	3	6

Table 6.7. Artifact Types in the Lukenya Hill Assemblages

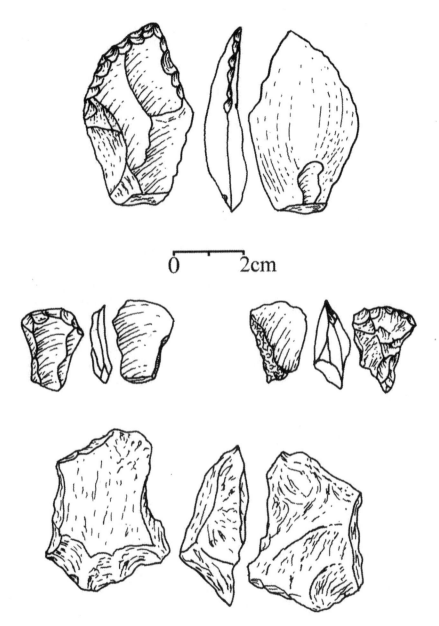

Figure 6.21. Scraper types in the Lukenya Hill 1 assemblages. Top row, chert scraper; middle row, chert "fan" scrapers; bottom row, quartz steep scraper.

which even among themselves are not wholly contemporaneous. In any case, Lukenya Hill 2 is different from Lukenya Hill 1 in many ways. First, Lukenya Hill 2 has a much larger proportion of microliths, which make up 43 percent and 60 percent of the shaped tools at the two Lukenya Hill 2 sites (Figure 6.19, bottom row). Obsidian microliths in particular tend to be larger than the microliths in Lukenya Hill. Second, the Lukenya Hill 2 sites contain much more chert and obsidian. Core-reduction techniques are the inverse of those in the Lukenya Hill 1 assemblages: freehand core reduction predominates over bipolar core reduction. Bipolar reduction, when practiced, was in fact used mostly on the nonlocal obsidian and chert: a conservationist strategy that was employed as cores became too small to work freehand (Kusimba, S. 1999). Rather than working the local quartz in an expedient fashion, the cores were worked more formally and more completely and were significantly smaller than in the Lukenya Hill 1 assemblages (Tables 6.8 and 6.9).

The raw material economy differs between Lukenya Hill 1 and Lukenya Hill 2 sites. In the Lukenya Hill 1 assemblages, quartz artifacts showed several indicators of expedient technological strategies (Nelson 1992). That is, local quartz was procured, used, and discarded on the spot (Kusimba, S. 1999). Such expedient practices are associated with more stable residential patterns (Andrevsky 1994; Parry and Kelly 1987; Shott 1989). At the same time, Lukenya Hill 1 groups maximized use life of their chert and obsidian tools through bipolar flaking and greater reduction of chert tools (Kusimba, S. 1999; Figure 6.20). The economical use of the rarer chert and obsidian would also suggest that Lukenya Hill 1 groups stayed at Lukenya Hill longer and traveled less, importing the small amounts of Central Rift obsidian they needed, manufacturing long use–life blades.

In the Lukenya Hill 2 assemblages, by contrast, chert and obsidian raw material were more accessible and less conserved. Chert and obsidian artifacts are more numerous and cores, tools, and flakes are larger. Even the abundant, local quartz was not treated expediently, but in fact its economy was similar to that of chert and obsidian, as shown by the small size of quartz cores at GvJm16 and GvJm22. The Lukenya Hill 2 groups were more mobile, stayed at Lukenya Hill for shorter periods, and had more contact with the rarer chert and obsidian sources, especially in the Central Rift.

Raw Material	Group	Site	N	Mean Length (mm)	St. Dev.	Coefficient of Variation	Range
Quartz	LH 1	GvJm46	40	39.40	13.87	.35	17.50–66.30
		GvJm62	54	39.20	22.00	.56	13.40–93.00
	LH 2	GvJm22	10	17.60	2.70	.15	12.00–22.00
		GvJm16	33	22.22	9.00	.41	7.00–44.00

Table 6.8. Size Ranges for Quartz Freehand Cores in the Lukenya Hill 1 and Lukenya Hill 2 Assemblages. Data from GvJm16 and GvJm22 (Merrick 1975)

Source	Sum of Squares	df	Mean Square	F
Between groups	43985.97	4	10996.49	121.67
Within groups	18437.81	204	90.38	
Total	62423.78			
p < .001				

Table 6.9. Results of an ANOVA Analysis of Quartz Core Length Data from Table 6.7.

In other words, the dramatic increase in microlithic technology at Lukenya Hill is accompanied by a complete reworking of the organization of lithic technology. Although the poor dating of the assemblages, as in the case of the Howieson's Poort, somewhat hinders our understanding of the contexts of these changes, we can speculate nonetheless on the impact of microlithic tools; in both the Lukenya Hill 1 and Howieson's Poort, they are a significant but never a major portion of the retouched toolkit; in Lukenya Hill 2, they dominate.

The structure of nonlocal tool transport and use is another striking feature of the Lukenya Hill 1 and Lukenya Hill 2 sites. It helps us understand something of the land-use patterns in which this single point on the landscape was but one node. Chemical analysis of obsidian artifacts from the Lukenya Hill 1 and Lukenya Hill 2 sites firmly establishes that the amount of nonlocal obsidian is much greater in the Lukenya Hill 2 assemblages. In Lukenya Hill 1 sites, about 30 percent of the obsidian is from the Central Rift Valley; in Lukenya Hill 2 assemblages, this number increases to 46 percent and 73 percent of the obsidian coming from the Central Rift (Barut 1996). Since the 100- to 150-km distance between Lukenya Hill and the Central Rift is well within a hunter-gatherer's range (Hitchcock and Ebert 1989), the Central Rift material probably was obtained directly, rather than through exchange, perhaps via person-to-person transactions, given the frequent movement of individual and anucleate band membership of tropical hunter-gatherers. However, one will need to increase the numbers of investigated sites in order to fully understand the means of transport of Later Stone Age obsidian to sites like Lukenya Hill.

More important, the form of transported material also changes. At GvJm62, obsidian was imported as cores, but also as large blades and blade segments that could be segmented into smaller tools (Figure 6.22;

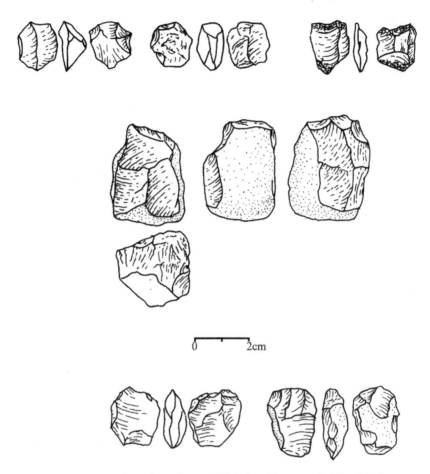

Figure 6.22. *Cores from the Lukenya Hill 1 sites. Top row, obsidian bipolar cores on obsidian bombs and lapilli; middle row, chert freehand core; bottom row, chert bipolar cores.*

Kusimba, S. 1999). In other words, there was a balance between provisioning *places* (core transport) and provisioning *people* (transport of tools, blades, and blade segments; Kuhn 1995:22). The greater abundance of obsidian cores in the Lukenya Hill 2 industries shows that, with the transition from Lukenya Hill 1 to Lukenya Hill 2, the provisioning *place* strategy came to predominate. Could the Lukenya Hill 2 occupations of Lukenya Hill have been more "planned" and less opportunistic? Did human population densities increase, such that a tighter web of exchanges facilitated the transport of greater amounts of obsidian? Did people move over larger ranges of territory, thus increasing their contact with the Central Rift obsidians? Was the obsidian so prized that deliberate and systematic exchange networks brought it into areas of demand? Was the "use life" of the obsidian microlithic tools simply shorter, such that more frequent "discard events" just *look* to us like a more mobile or more "networked" obsidian supply line?

Unfortunately, the information we need to answer the questions above is still lacking. Differences between the Lukenya Hill 1 and 2 assemblages may reflect different regimes of surface water availability. Less arid conditions and more abundant resource patches during Lukenya Hill 1 times may have allowed more sedentary groups to spend longer periods at Lukenya Hill, exploiting large and small game and plant foods, as do the !Kung and Hadza (Mabulla 2002). They would have had less contact with chert and obsidian sources, preferring to use local quartz, which was adequate for scraper technologies. The Lukenya Hill 2 microlithic sites, on the other hand, may have been part of settlement patterns similar to those of !Xõ and G/wi, who live in the driest part of the Kalahari where concentrated food and water is lacking. Group sizes are small, home ranges large, and mobility frequent. Such groups occupying Lukenya Hill had fairly frequent contact with scattered patches of chert and obsidian, including those from Central Rift sources. Because their occupational stays were short, they did not build up large quantities of local quartz. It is possible that high-ranking foods like migratory animals played an important role in their diets, and composite hunting weapons may have made the quest of these animals more efficient (Ambrose and Lorenz 1990). Unfortunately, the above scenario is one of many one could construct.

Lukenya Hill faunal remains from Middle and Later Stone Age contexts at Lukenya Hill suggests the animal foods consumed, but leave us with no evidence of other foods utilized or total proportion of these foods in the diet. Based on these faunal remains, Lukenya hunter-gatherers seemed to have concentrated on high-ranking, medium to large, migratory game (Marean 1990). Animal bone from the GvJm46 site was predominantly from one species, an extinct alcelaphine. Its position at the bottom of a steep cliff suggests that the locality was a kill site (Marean 1990:466). The teeth discovered there indicate a catastrophic mortality profile; that is, a herd structure of different ages and sexes is preserved in the faunal remains. Such a pattern is consistent with a drive site or other mass kill. Marean suggests that the kill site was used regularly at the end of the dry season. The Lukenya Hill people could have conducted drives when the animals were plentiful but killed animals though ambush or tracking at other times (Marean 1997). During Lukenya Hill 1 times, the seasonal use of tactical hunting techniques like driving may have been coupled with more diverse foraging in the near vicinity of the hill at other times of the year (Marean 1997). Unfortunately, the faunal remains leave no clues about the subsistence factors involved in the Lukenya Hill 1/Lukenya Hill 2 pattern. Although no plant remains were found at GvJm62, a phonolite, bored stone fragment and three dimpled anvils from GvJm62 attest to plant food procurement and processing activities during the Lukenya Hill 1 occupation (Barut 1997).

Just as in the Howieson's Poort case, however, one must keep in mind that functional and activity differences as well as the technological styles of different tool types probably account for much of the variation across Lukenya Hill 1 and Lukenya Hill 2. Naturally, typological differences ultimately reflect function in large part: Microliths are more efficient for cutting or using as projectile inserts and using scrapers for scraping tasks (Siegel 1985). In southern Africa, the scraper-dominated Later Stone Age assemblages are suited to domestic processing tasks, and microliths to hunting (Brooks 1984; Jacobson 1984). However, it is

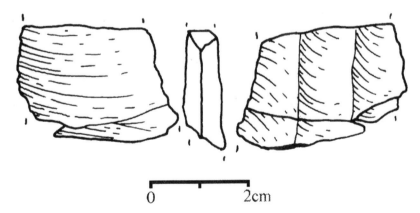

0   2cm

Figure 6.23.   Blade segment made on Central Rift Valley obsidian, GvJm62.

questionable if any one sort of microlithic tool was ever limited to a single function (Clark, Phillips, and Staley 1976; Clark 1977; Clark 1976:452; Moss 1983).

In summary, there are abundant signs of cultural-historical, activity, and land-use patterns in the Later Stone Age sequence at Lukenya Hill. Though one might argue the greater mobility of Lukenya Hill 2 groups is part of a wider pattern of more evolutionary significance, related to the adoption of advanced, efficient Later Stone Age technology (Ambrose and Lorenz 1990; Marean 1997), not all sequences demonstrate a link between blade technologies and greater mobility. Around Lake Eyasi, Middle and Later Stone Age people used local quartz, ignoring, or lacking contact, with chert sources 50-km to the north (Mabulla 1996).

Summing Up

Both the Howieson's Poort from Nelson Bay Cave and the Later Stone Age sequence at Lukenya Hill may tell us much about human behavioral capacities of the first biologically modern humans. The Howieson's Poort is a way of making stone tools that has long been considered out of place among the Middle Stone Age industries of South Africa. The Howieson's Poort from Nelson Bay Cave is an important segment of the South African Middle Stone Age. It is an industry that has long been considered anomalous among the Middle Stone Age industries of southern Africa that it precedes and follows. It has long been of interest for two distinct characteristics: Lithic assemblages set apart by large numbers of backed pieces struck from blade cores, and the selection of finer raw material types to make these backed pieces. These tool types are more usually associated with the Later Stone Age, becoming common after 40,000 years ago in Africa. The Howieson's Poort–backed pieces seem too small to be held in the hand. Consequently, it is thought that they were part of composite tools and formed parts of knives, spears, arrows, and the like.

Finding these tools in a Middle Stone Age context is interesting, because they are so much more at home in the Later Stone Age, especially after 40,000 years ago, particularly in southern and eastern Africa. An undoubted advantage of composite tools is that a greater diversity of different kinds of implements can be constructed. Certainly the Nelson Bay Cave sequence shows a diversity of different backed pieces, both in size, shape, and weight. What were these tools used for?

While microliths were often used as hafted hunting projectiles (Clark, J. D. 1977; Clark, Phillips, and Staley 1976; examples in Klein 1989:374; Phillipson 1976:218), they could also have been hafted knives, embedded in shredding boards, or used for a variety of purposes (Clark 1976:452; Phillipson and Phillipson 1970). Deacon has suggested that Robberg bladelets were hafted in stabbing spears similar to known Australian specimens (Mitchell 1988:211). Use-wear studies dispute a single function for microlithic tools and show that other lithic artifacts are also efficient projectiles. Hafted Later Stone Age microliths in South Africa were used primarily for cutting, sawing, or woodworking rather than as projectiles (Binneman 1997; Wadley and Binneman 1995). Odell and Cowan (1986) experimented with using unretouched flakes as projectiles and found they were adequate to the task. That the Nelson Bay Cave Levels 1 and 7 tools on the one hand and the Levels 5 and 6 tools on the other could have had very different functions is easily supportable.

Although microliths and scrapers were probably both multifunctional, their functions were probably different. Microliths and scrapers differ considerably in edge angle. Most microliths have very small edge angles, while scraper edge angles are generally between 35° and 80° (Merrick 1975; Siegel 1985). Siegel (1985) found through experiment that edge angle could reliably distinguish tools used for longitudinal motion, such as cutting, sawing, whittling, and carving, from tools used for transverse motions, including scraping, planing, and adzing. The former have edge angles between 26° and 35°, and the latter have edge angles greater than 35° (Siegel 1985:93). Thus while not all microliths were necessarily projectiles, it is likely that most composite tools made with hafted microliths were probably used for cutting as well. Scrapers can be associated with a variety of tasks, including scraping, but are generally less efficient at cutting tasks.

In fact, microlith- and scraper-based Later Stone Age sites have been found in other areas of Africa. In the Later Stone Age of the Dobe area of Botswana and the Namib Desert, Brooks (1984:48) and Jacobson (1984:76) have found both scraper-dominated and microlith-dominated sites. They suggest that the microlith-dominated sites are hunting-related, while the scraper-dominated sites were areas such as residential bases where food processing and manufacturing took place. In southwestern Cape, Parkington (1980) notes that open sites nearer the sea have higher proportions of backed microliths than sites in the mountains, where adzes are more common. Parkington interprets the open sites as summer occupations where microlith maintenance and manufacture took place.

In other words, even the Later Stone Age itself has many functional components that lack microliths. From this perspective again, the Howieson's Poort appears less and less anomalous. The hunter-gatherers who used Lukenya Hill as a seasonal station in their cycle of transhumance demonstrate the flexibility of their lifeway and the ingenuity of archaeology to draw information from the cold remains of ancient behaviors. The different cultural episodes at Lukenya Hill seem to indicate the sort of changes necessary to accommodate climatic alterations, the rise and fall of transregional interaction spheres, and changing strategies of stone tool transport.

The enigma of Howieson's Poort Industry may be that we consider it one. McBrearty and Brooks (2000) have challenged the argument that the evolution of modern behavior was an abrupt one associated with the transition from the Middle to Later Stone Age. Rather than seeing the Howieson's Poort as an irregularity, they have focused on other aspects of the Middle Stone Age in general to demonstrate that its makers were essentially modern in their behavior. The Middle Stone Age at Blombos shows some of the earliest bone points; harpoons from the Katanda site, if they can be accepted at Middle Stone Age, also attest to the evidence of cultural elaboration occurring at Middle Stone Age sites.

Backed blades, as part of complex, multicomponent tools, are a somewhat rare but important part of this accumulation of new technologies. That the Howieson's Poort Industry, as a special form of Middle Stone Age technology, may possess several variants demonstrates that complex tools were undergoing shifts in technological design within the 10,000-year-long span of the Howieson's Poort itself. In terms of stone preference and artifact size, there is significant variation within the Nelson Bay Cave sequence. Similar patterns of change in raw material and typology are found at the nearby sequence at Klasies River. This leads us to wonder how much variance exists within the entity we term the Howieson's Poort Industry. Could close examination of different Howieson's Poort sites across southern Africa allow one to distinguish functional or even stylistic or "ethnic" differences, sufficient to allow us to discern the annual cycles of the makers, or interaction spheres critical to them? Off hand, we may not have sufficient information to pursue this inquiry, but it seems more fruitful than the present categorizations of early occurrences of backing into what may be no more than a convenient *portmanteau* terminology.

Howieson's Poort forms an important part of the evidence for "modern" Middle Stone Age behavior. However, the key in accepting the "modernity" of Middle Stone Age behavior lies in making reliable estimations of behavior from ancient remains—the old "middle range" theory" problem that plagues most archaeological interpretations of any significance. In other words, how do we reliably infer past behavior from material remains?

Several compelling arguments still contradict the view that Middle Stone Age people were becoming behaviorally modern, while, at the same time, Middle Paleolithic Neanderthals were still practicing a "premodern culture" in Europe. Chief among them is the fact that many patterns noted in the Middle Stone Age archaeological record, and supposedly supportive of a modernity of the Middle Stone Age behavior hypothesis, can also be found in the Middle Paleolithic or earlier, and are also sporadic in their distribution. These include hafted and blade tools, tool transport, and signs of an aesthetic sense (see Hayden 1993; Kuhn and Bar-Yosef 1999). It may very well be that both Neanderthals and Middle Stone Age humans had similar *capacities*, in terms of their *abilities* to produce "modern" behavior, and that indicators of modernity are present in both the European and the African cultural assemblages (Soffer 1989). For this reason, it becomes important to investigate the assemblages that contain these "indicators" much more carefully.

The finding of variable technological styles within the Howieson's Poort from Nelson Bay Cave becomes extremely important. The differences between the upper and lower levels at Nelson Bay Cave show the suite of changes in all the *stages* of a technology that we associate with shifting technological styles. It seems unlikely that a single behavioral change, such as tool design, tool function, change in raw material selection, or increased mobility, could underlie the set of changes the sequence shows. Microliths from upper levels are clearly larger and thicker and of different shape than those from lower levels. Although one could argue that these differences are merely epiphenomenal to raw material selection, I believe this is unlikely. Typological variation between the middle levels and those on top and below is too great. Thin blades *could* have been made on quartzite and were made on quartzite some of the time. Furthermore, some backed pieces are made on local raw materials in both the lower and upper levels. I believe that microlith shapes changed to fit the requirements of different technological styles, which involved changes in raw material selection, tool manufacture, and tool function. It seems unlikely to me that the Howieson's Poort is exclusively about raw material or tool function, and much more likely that it is about a technological style, ways of skinning a cat, if you will, that appeared and then changed. Any style, by definition, will eventually drift and change.

What are the implications of this argument for whether Middle Stone Age people were behaviorally modern and whether they were more modern than the Neanderthals? First of all, it demonstrates that a lot of phenomena used to argue for Middle Stone Age modernity are, when writ large, much more complex than they seem. The Howieson's Poort is not about making hafted tools from exotic or rare raw materials, but seems to be about making hafted tools, per se, and selecting rare but widely distributed raw materials, but not necessarily at the same time. Clearly these two behavioral choices are decoupled when one examines the Howieson's Poort more carefully. Second, the shift in microlith size, shape, and raw material through the sequence certainly fits the expectations of time-restrictive patterning (Byers 1994)— indicative of a dynamic system of learning, innovating, and transmitting technology. In modern humans, these dynamic systems are represented in webs of symbols. When one considers as well that the South African Middle Stone Age sequence includes other restricted industries like the Stillbay (which is characterized by bifacial points and which underlies the Howieson's Poort at Blombos Cave; Henshilwood et al. 2001), the argument for relatively fine-grained time-restrictive patterning is strengthened.

We examined yet another instance of the modernity issue from East Africa and observed how a gradual shift to microlithic tool use is associated with land-use pattern changes. Differences in raw material availability and economy at the Lukenya sites show that bands inhabiting Lukenya Hill 2 sites moved more widely in the areas around the hill, had more contact with rarer chert and obsidian sources, and stayed at Lukenya Hill for shorter periods than those inhabiting Lukenya Hill 1 sites. The Lukenya Hill 1 sites, by contrast, were marked by longer occupations by groups that moved over smaller distances and had fewer contacts with rare raw material sources. They carried some obsidian as long use life, segmented blades and large tools, but quartz artifacts adequately served their needs. During longer occupations of Lukenya Hill 1 knappers used prodigious amounts of local quartz in an expedient way.

One might argue that the shift from Lukenya Hill 1 to Lukenya Hill 2 was driven simply by the invention of microlithic and composite tools that necessitated better chert and obsidian, leading them to select these raw materials with little change in their land-use patterns. Quartz, chert, and local obsidians are all found in essentially the same environments, although chert and obsidian bombs are rarer and more localized. Looking across the African Later Stone Age, however, one finds that even when chert is available, it was not necessarily preferred or required to make microliths over more ubiquitous and imputedly less desirable or flakeable quartz and quartzite. At Bimbe wa Mpalabwe, in Zambia, for example, there was a slight preference for chert over quartz for the making of microliths (19.7 percent of microliths being chert; 18.4 percent of microliths quartz), and chert was overwhelmingly preferred over the common quartz for scrapers (58 percent of scrapers being chert; 31 percent of scrapers quartz [Miller 1969:240]). Furthermore many sources of quartz quite amenable to conchoidal fracture were used to make microliths throughout Central Africa (Mercader and Brooks 2001). At Lukenya Hill, the appearance of microliths predates the extensive use of chert and obsidian (Barut 1994). The changes in raw material economy, especially core treatment, between Lukenya Hill 1 and Lukenya Hill 2 suggest that these two assemblages represent changes in land use. The different bands in the sequence may have had somewhat different annual journeys, covering larger foraging territories at one time than another; their interactions with other bands, through which obsidian moved, may also have been more frequent; and they chose to transport different *kinds* of obsidian, shifting to core transport in Lukenya Hill 2 as a means of more efficiently provisioning sites like Lukenya Hill with sufficient materials.

Is there evidence of the emergence of style at Lukenya Hill? Symbol-based social relationships for sharing information, resources, and risk are essential features of hunter-gatherer societies. Such systems may be embodied in the exchange of articles of adornment, the presence of art objects, and the elaboration of mortuary ritual. Unfortunately, we lack conclusive evidence of all these significant markers. However, we do know that Later Stone Age communities did have some of the first objects of bodily adornments, in the form of ostrich eggshell beads. Many archaeologists have related these beads to *hxaro*-like exchange networks (Robbins 1999; Wadley 1993). In East Africa, ostrich eggshell beads are widely distributed. They are found in the Sakutiek Industry from Enkapune ya Muto (Ambrose 1998) and at sites in northern Tanzania: in a Middle to Later Stone Age transition in the Middle to Upper Bed V at

Mumba Cave (Mehlman 1989:311), the scraper-based Later Stone Age Naseran Industry (Mehlman 1989:319), at Kisese II, and at the Later Stone Age Naisiusiu site at Olduvai Gorge (Mehlman 1989:386). However, ostrich eggshell beads are absent from other Pleistocene East African sites, including Lukenya Hill.

Among Kalahari hunter-gatherers, reciprocal exchange relationships have a similarly patchy distribution. They are practiced in areas of shareable, large resource patches, such as those inhabited by !Kung and Nharo groups. The !Xo, on the other hand, inhabit the driest part of the Kalahari where there are no large resource patches. They do not practice exchange relationships, since reciprocity is not a useful strategy where resources are generally scarce (Heinz 1979; Cashdan 1983). Most likely, similar contexts of relatively abundant and self-renewing resources were required for Pleistocene exchange relationships to be adaptive. At Lukenya Hill, Pleistocene assemblages do not contain ostrich eggshell beads. The region was drier than now and resource patches limited (Marean and Gifford-Gonzalez 1991).

In contrast, high-altitude and lakeshore sites like Enkapune ya Muto, Mumba, and Nasera Rockshelters, as well as Kisese II, could have supported rich food patches. The Kisese II faunal sequence shows that closed-habitat species make up around 20 percent of minimum nutrient intake throughout the sequence, even across the Pleistocene/Holocene boundary (Marean, Ehrhart, and Mudida 1990). Kisese is situated in a hilltop ecotone between open grassland and the woodlands of the hill itself, where more browsers thrived than in the more open surroundings of Lukenya Hill. Similarly, Upper Pleistocene faunal remains from Nasera Rockshelter include species typical of semiarid grassland and woodland as well as water-loving reduncines and duikers. This suggested vegetated areas nearby. Mumba inhabitants exploited tilapia, catfish, and achatinid snails (Mehlman 1989:362), and its shores also attracted a wide variety of other fauna. These were all areas with dependable food supplies, presenting ample opportunity to engage in socially useful exchange relationships.

One must keep in mind, however, that the majority of hunter-gatherer systems of land-use sharing are not associated with trade objects; the San practice seems to be unique in this case for historical reasons. Nevertheless, beadwork is a significant marker of behavior similar to that of modern hunter-gatherers for several reasons: first, it required knowledge of piercing and grinding technologies; second, it clearly attests to the presence of arbitrary, symbolic representational systems; third, on a social level, it is part of a culture where such representational systems were not just possible but desirable and useful as well (White, R. 1989, 1992). As is the case with technology, we cannot assume the desirability or superiority of new inventions, but need to appreciate their relationship to their cultural context. Personal adornment is clearly one of the most important ways in which people create both personal and social identity or style (Wiessner 1986). Social identity is the symbolic basis for permission-granting behaviors. Most often, objects of personal adornment are expensive, rare, imported, or labor-intensive. By the Holocene at least, ostrich eggshell beads are found in areas outside of ostrich habitats (Mitchell 1996). In many cultures objects of adornment serve to mark positions of authority, prestige, or other social differences. This marking is inherently symbolic; for example, among the Swazi, lion and elephant are important and powerful animals; clothing and body decoration using lion skin and ivory symbolize the social power of the wearer (Kuper 1973; in White 1992). Even among egalitarian hunter-gatherers, *hxaro* exchange involves a certain amount of competition for friends and mating partners, and success in weaving these social networks is sought after and recognized (Wiessner 1982a).

In the end, we can conclude that the Howieson's Poort and other Stone Age cultures beginning around 70,000 years ago were the first hunter-gatherers to do at least some things in the way that modern hunter-gatherers do. The people utilizing Howieson's Poort were adept at creating and experimenting with new technologies, in much the same way that the inhabitants of Lukenya Hill altered their land-use and tool raw material acquisition practices to compensate for environmental fluctuation. To that extent, they were full-fledged "modern" hunter-gatherers. It is to be expected that time/space diversity in the archaeological record of these early cultural moderns would take several tens of thousands of years to develop over the course of the Later Stone Age. Local adaptations, the elaboration of traditions of technological style, and increases in population were all a part of this developing diversity. One of the outcomes of this diversity was that, soon, the savannas of the subcontinent from Kenya to the Cape would be filled with new cultures, herdsmen driving their cattle from place to place and farmers opening clearings to raise their crops. The hunter-gatherers of tropical Africa had a new challenge, adapting to new ecosystems and interaction with new settlers and new ways of life.

7

Preludes to the Neolithic

Toward the end of the Middle Stone Age, hunter-gathering bands had assembled a fully modern cultural repertoire that included two major features: dynamically evolving technologies and systems of permission granting. Over the course of the Later Stone Age, these features would become more common and more diversified. Later Stone Age people explored the potentials of modern technology and interaction, responding to changing environments in a way previous peoples did not. Over the last 20,000 years in South Africa, for example, a succession of Later Stone Age industries—Robberg, Oakhurst, and Wilton—are associated closely with three distinct climate regimes.

The Robberg Industry of the latest Pleistocene (22,000 to 12,000 years ago) includes small bladelets from pyramid-shaped cores, polished bone points, and bone and shell beads. Robberg people hunted the large grazers of their grassland environment, including buffalo, hartebeest, and zebra (Figure 7.1). During the subsequent Oakhurst (or on the Cape, Albany) period, hunter-gatherers hunted both large animals and small browsing fauna of their changing environment, which was beginning to include more forest around the Pleistocene/Holocene transition. Their technology was dramatically different from those of Robberg people (Figure 7.2). They made use of local foods and materials, eating fish and making large quartzite scrapers. Finally during the Wilton Industry from 8,000 to 4,000 years ago, the environment was warm, dry, and, on the Cape, forested. Wilton people hunted small forest antelope such as bushbuck and steenbok. They used silicious materials to make small backed bladelets and small scrapers (Figure 7.3).

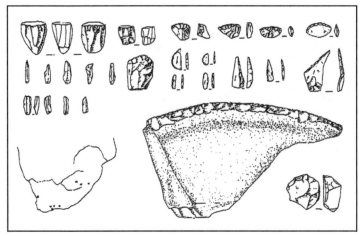

Figure 7.1. Distribution and characteristic artifacts of the Robberg. (From *Human Beginnings in South Africa* by H. J. Deacon and Janette Deacon [Claremont: New Africa Books]. Copyright © New Africa Books. Reprinted with permission.)

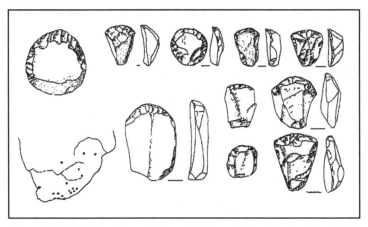

Figure 7.2. Distribution and characteristic artifacts of the Oakhusrt (Albany) Industry. (From *Human Beginnings in South Africa* by H. J. Deacon and Janette Deacon [Claremont: New Africa Books]. Copyright © New Africa Books. Reprinted with permission.)

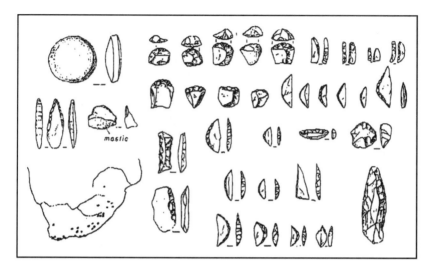

Figure 7.3. Distribution and characteristic artifacts of the Wilton Industry. (From *Human Beginnings in South Africa* by H. J. Deacon and Janette Deacon [Claremont: New Africa Books]. Copyright © New Africa Books. Reprinted with permission.)

Certainly it is true that earlier Early Stone Age and Middle Stone Age peoples also availed themselves of the resources that were available in their environments. As those environments changed, their food choices no doubt did also. What is new are the dramatic changes in technology and interaction that Later Stone Age people developed. In part, the choices they adopted enabled them to keep step with environmental change. By contrast, glacial and interglacial cycles are unrecognizable in the technological inventories of Early Stone Age and Middle Stone Age people. As far as we can tell from the archaeological record, Early and Middle Stone Age technological systems remained more or less unchanged in the face of environmental flux.

Certainly, Robberg, Oakhurst, and Wilton people had dramatically different food procurement methods and strategies. Based on their raw material procurement systems, it has been argued that their permission-granting systems varied also (Mitchell 2000). These three successive suites of material culture represent changes in technological style. That Oakhurst people made large quartzite scrapers and Wilton people small chert ones shows a different social context, in which every sequence of the *chaîne opératoire* entailed different technological choices (Deacon and Deacon 1999:127).

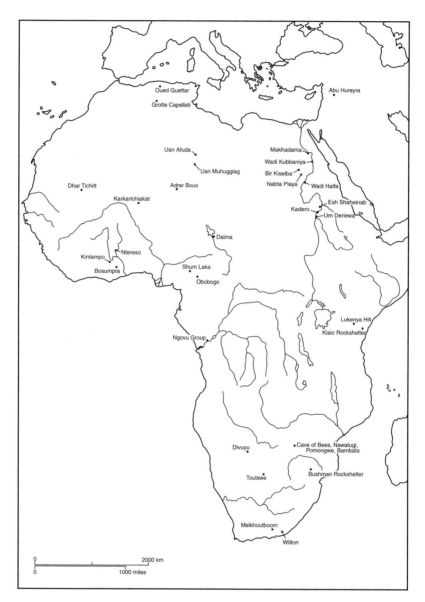

Figure 7.4.   Map of Africa showing sites mentioned in chapters 7 and 8.

The Holocene archaeology of Africa embodies the last episodes of hunter-gatherer activity. In a world increasingly dominated by larger populations of food producers, hunters continued to perfect the practice of advanced foraging. Marked by their characteristic microlithic blades, identical in form to the Howeison's Poort ones, but often smaller, Wilton bands in South Africa established home territories, leaving behind ample evidence of their various toolkits devised to sustain them within well-practiced annual circuits, utilizing the seasonal produce of local environments and wide-ranging interaction spheres to supply their material needs. When there were applicable surfaces, they were covered with elaborately decorated murals depicting their inner life. They represent an ideological universe still interpretable with reference to the belief systems and practices of the San (Robbins 1997; Lim 1997; Mitchell 1997).

Here, then, is the epitome of "modernity," hunter-gatherers ideally suited to the exploitation of their surroundings, effectively equipped technologically and socially. In addition to characteristic microlithic inserts and other worked stone, they made bone arrow points and link shafts and used wooden digging sticks and ostrich eggshell beads and containers. This tool inventory, as well as social and belief systems likened to that of historic San, lends credence to the idea of their place in the physical and cultural ancestry of some hunter-gathering peoples of more recent times (Deacon and Deacon 1999:129). We have seen, however, that the case is somewhat more complicated (Sealy and Pfeiffer 2000), that the hunter-gatherers of the ethnographic present often have long histories, involving their own trajectories of change as well as the presence of food producers in their territories.

Before understanding how African hunter-gatherer societies evolved and changed their lives and livelihoods to suit a "Neolithic" world, we must first review the processes initiating food production and domestication in Africa. The African "Neolithic" began as advanced foragers brought game animals, first cattle and later sheep and goats, under their control, developing pastoralism several thousand years before the first appearance of cereal agriculture. Africa, long a melting pot for breeds of unhumped cattle imported from Eurasia and the humped cattle of Asia, domesticated the indigenous aurochs (*Bos primigenius*) as early as 8,000 years ago, and established cattle pastoralism in the Sahara by at least 6,000 years ago (Clutton-Brock 1997:421). Nowhere broken to the yoke, the animals remained a food provider, less for their meat than for milk and blood. Cattle roving became part of long-established nomadic transhumant patterns, and initially shored up broad spectrum economies (Haaland 1992).

With an accomplished cultural repertoire, hunter-gatherers had adapted their increasingly diverse lifeways to many different environments, developing increasingly sophisticated collecting routines, affecting the yield of natural harvests in their vicinity. Often, this involved the exertion of greater amounts of human energy and labor into the food quest, requiring the maintenance of larger labor cohorts. This effort led in turn to the prospect of larger, more consistent harvests. Maintaining more people and keeping surpluses for future use affected social relations in some hunter-gathering communities. Their lifeway was evolving in new directions. They were learning to manage intensified and delayed production; and the development of intensified and delayed yields would be, in some but not all areas, a crucial first step toward a full-time reliance on domesticated plants and animals.

The evidence of intensification involves several long-term trends. The first of these is the gradual expansion of the diet over time: an increase in the numbers and kinds of foodstuffs used. Though it is difficult to believe that people neglected smaller game in the past, there was now a conscious effort to capture such prey, requiring new techniques and implements. In the case of plant foods, these were often of high nutritional value. The more a hunter-gatherer group depends on plant foods, the more it tends to focus on the most nourishing plant parts, such as nuts and seeds (Keeley 1995, 1999). On the down side, these foods required a new repertoire of preparatory procedures, such as grinding, roasting, or boiling. All these activities required a novel tool inventory, including baskets, rasps, hullers, pounders, or grinders. A need to boil water would soon yield a variety of containers out of pottery, in addition to food-preparation utensils. Unfortunately, evidence of early plant use is often limited to the circumstantial evidence of material culture—processing tools or sites, grinding tools, ground concavities in rocks, or bored stones used as digging weights, rather than actual plant remains (Young and Thompson 1999). A related sign of the transition to the new range of dietary choices was a general increase in human population densities.

Fishing first appeared in the Middle Stone Age and became widespread by the terminal Pleistocene in northern Africa, where it formed an important part of the diet in areas near water. In wetlands such as the Nile Valley in the late Pleistocene, fishing was combined with hunting and broad-spectrum plant collecting (Wetterstrom 1993). At Wadi Kubbaniya, large animals made up only 1 percent of the bone recovered. The small number of large animals may have been a function of harsh conditions during Last Glacial Maximum, a time when wetlands and meadows were supported on the floodplain, and little else in the vast desert.

Though not very important to the diet, hartebeest, auroch, and Dorcas gazelle were stalked and speared or captured with nets and traps.

The large numbers of fish bone at Wadi Kubbaniya point to the real heart of their subsistence. Over 90 percent of this was catfish, *Clarias sp.* During its annual spawn, at the beginning of the Nile floods, thick masses of *Clarias* migrate to the floodplain to lay eggs in shallow areas. A second fishing season began in the autumn, following the flood, as the catfish moved to deeper water, some were trapped in small pools on the plain. The large quantities of fish bone recovered suggest that once the fish were caught, they were dried or smoked for storage (Gautier and van Neer 1989:151–152). The catfish were only seasonally available, but could be stored for periods of up to five months, bridging the gap between fishing seasons. Waterfowl, like coots, geese, and ducks, migrated to the marshes in the winter months. These were easily captured with nets and traps.

The post-Pleistocene occupation of the Nile Valley repeats many of the themes seen at Wadi Kubbaniya, in particular the intensive collecting and storage of seasonally available resources found close at hand. At the terminal Pleistocene sites of Makhadma 2 and Makhadma 4, in the Nile Valley, further elaboration of this lifeway is evident. The two settlements demonstrate seasonal and activity specialization. Makhadma 2 contains only *Clarias*, caught during their swim upstream to spawn, while nearby Makhadma 4 has remains of Tilapia and other fish, probably pulled from recessional pools. Both places demonstrate signs of charcoal pits used for smoking fish, clear evidence of processing for storage (Vermeersch, Paulissen, and van Neer 1989). Throughout the Sahelian zone, early Holocene fisher/gatherers used dotted-wavy line pottery (Sutton 1977).

The Holocene Capsian Tradition *escargotières* in North Africa left behind large snail shell middens. Though the land snails seem to have been a large part of their diet, they also hunted and trapped small game animals like rabbits, as well as larger ones like gazelles, hartebeests, zebra, and wild cattle. Plant foods must have been gathered as well, for snails were only available for harvesting in the spring and autumn (Lubell and Sheppard 1997). At about the same time, 3,500 to 3, 000 years ago, in Congo, sites of the Ngovo group show *Canarium* and *Elaeis* remains together with evidence of forest hunting, including duiker, large rodents, forest pig, and the giant African snail (Eggert 1993).

Other evidence of an expanding food base comes from studies of small animal exploitation along the European shores of the Mediterranean (Stiner, Munro, and Surovell 2000), as well as other inquiries elsewhere in Europe and eastern Asia (Kuhn and Stiner 2001). These investigators examined the hunt of easy-to-catch, slow-moving animals, and other more difficult-to-catch, fast-moving animals. During the Middle Paleolithic, the small animals captured were, for the most part, reptiles, mollusks, prey that are easily acquired, and eggs. The capture of smaller, easy-to-kill animals was a strategy that even provided the australopithecines with sources of protein and fat (Lovejoy 1993). On the other hand, fast-moving prey were ignored during the Middle Stone Age, even though there is much evidence of hares in nearby wolf dens (Stiner 1993). Since contemporary Middle Stone Age settlements lack any evidence of hare consumption, we can only assume they lacked the technical ability to capture them.

During the Middle and early Later Stone Age, slow-moving, easy-to-catch limpets and turtles were important small prey along the Mediterranean Coast until their numbers declined, and limpet size decreased, due to the intensive effort of the collectors (Stiner, Munro, and Surovell 2000). During the Later Stone Age, however, hunters begin to add more difficult-to-catch prey to their bag. On the one hand, their technical systems were up to the innovative challenge; on the other, their increasing numbers probably made these new sources even more tempting. In tropical Africa, we find no sign that small swift animals like hares were a significant food source until the Holocene.

Another factor affecting human communities at this time, along with enhanced diets and food-getting diversity, was involvement in the production of new tools, storage facilities, and food-processing technologies (Casey 2000:132; Deacon 1984; Haaland 1992). Each of these had a direct effect. Novel implements sometimes required the use of new kinds of stone and stone-working techniques, like the granites pecked and ground into axes, pounders, or grindstones. Storage facilities were required that could protect against insect and rodent predation. Even more profoundly, storage is associated with very different attitudes toward ownership. In immediate-return systems, those who accumulate are obliged to redistribute at some point. Delayed return economies where resources are stored, on the other hand, are associated with ideas of private property and the presence of privileged individuals who manage and control the stores (Testart 1988:6). New foods and food-processing methods transferred the emphasis of food supply toward female-specific activities, enhancing women's roles. The old ways were changing, and in more ways than the fabrication of a new line of implements.

Energy and population increases came with concomitant penalties. Intensified production necessitated communities to exert a greater work effort in their subsistence practices than heretofore. Although intensification may be characterized by an overall increase in yields, it does not always produce an increased *net productivity*, since high yields are often attributable to increased labor and time put into production; a circular interplay of increased energy production allowing maintenance of the larger population needed to effectively work the system, and so forth (Moore 1981). Population increases before agriculture were substantial (Hassan 1981). Late Pleistocene hunter-gatherers created social and technological means to support greater cohorts. People began to outgrow the band and were becoming bound to stationary, renewable food sources.

Socially, however, these communities paid a price. The Wadi Kubbaniya people were able to achieve sharp increases in productivity. The Nile Valley's large populations were sharply conscripted during the widespread aridity of the Last Glacial Maximum. People here lived at high densities, and the diversity of stone tool industries implies sharp territorial boundaries, as one would expect for one of the few habitable areas in the Sahara at the time. As perhaps to be expected, the Wadi Kubbaniya period included stress, competition, and conflict—permanent cemeteries attest not only to claims to territory in general but also to evidence of warfare in the form of projectiles embedded in some 40 percent of the skeletons from the Wadi Halfa cemetery at 14,500 years ago (Wendorf and Schild 1980; Wendorf, Schild, and Close 1986). Here at least, population pressure and conflict were an important impetus to attempts to intensify food production.

Population increase is often implicated as a *prime mover* in long-term trends in human diet and the development of food production; others argue that it was a result, not a cause, of changes in diet. In any case, larger, more sedentary collecting cohorts and new dietary choices created an advantage for groups astute enough to realize the benefits of change. As populations grew, people sought food sources that regenerated quickly and rebounded rapidly from intensive human predation. The cognitive environment of the hunter-gatherer was permanently altered. Earlier hunters, as an efficient strategy, sought the largest game they could encounter but often foraged opportunistically around that goal (Hawkes, Hill, and O'Connell 1982). Now people sought out seeds, fish, and small animals that come in small highly nutritious packages. They may on occasion require almost as much energy to procure and prepare as they bring to the table. However, their advantages won out in the new context; as collectors moved from "traveling" to "processing," they sought the resources that were less peripatetic, reproduced quickly, and rebounded robustly to culling by human hunters.

People turned their attention to the procurement of the sort of resources whose acquisition was *capable* of being intensified, resources that allowed sustainable gleaning of increasing amounts of food and energy. The advantages of such a strategy are many. A diet focused on large game is physiologically dangerous. Aside from the hazards of the chase, animals are often in poor condition during African dry seasons, and humans run the risk of protein poisoning (Speth and Spielman 1983). Such a strategy could have had permanent consequences for the physiology and health of archaic people. Cachel (1997) suggests that the greater robusticity of Middle Stone Age hominids was a response to high-protein diets and the refinement of bone thickness during the transition to the Later Stone Age a beneficial result of improved diets, in particular their greater proportion of important dietary fats.

The arrival of the Holocene saw an increased use of plants and smaller animals. In Zimbabwe's Matopo Hills, at the Cave of Bees, Nswatugi, Pomongwe, and Bambata, excavation uncovered ample evidence of a rich array of plant and animal foods procured within the immediate vicinity (Walker 1995). The Pleistocene Middle Stone Age levels at Matopo sites have an abundance of bones from large migratory animals. There is a significantly broader array of food remains in Holocene Later Stone Age levels, where investigators identified 40 different animal species, or about 90 percent of the faunal remains, as belonging to smaller animals and reptiles like the mongoose, dassies, hares, tortoises, large lizards, small antelope, as well as eggs, fish and crabs, and insects, especially large quantities of a caterpillar (*Gonimbrasia belina*), the "mopane worm."

The capture of small animals suggests the use of snares and traps, assisted by nets from bark cordage similar to those preserved at Pomongwe (Walker 1995:221). About three-quarters of the plants and animals utilized can be found on the nearby inselbergs. Middle Stone Age occupants of these caves stalked large game on the open grasslands, "treading lightly on the landscape." The Later Stone Age inhabitants concentrated on hunting, as well as gathering marula nuts and insects, on the kopjes. A transition toward the capture of smaller animals and increased use of plant foods can be detected in South Africa as well, where *Watsonia* corms were found at Melkhoutboum (Deacon and Deacon 1999).

Hunter-gatherer lifeways at the end of the Pleistocene were a culmination of these processes of the broadening of dietary choices and technological diversification. In the Near East, hunter-gatherers began to intensively acquire and store grass seeds, like wheat barley, canary and meadow grasses, oats, and rye; gather wild legumes, fruits, and nuts; as well as hunting (Smith, B. 1998). Many of these intensification practices can be thought of as *preagricultural*, in that they are meant to enhance the yields of naturally occurring foods. Among their practices was the purposeful sowing and cultivation of economically useful plants. Hunter-gatherers may have practiced this precursor to full-fledged agriculture, still ongoing among herdsmen in northeast Africa (Keeley 1995).

Plant cultivation produces an ecosystem different from that roamed by traditional hunter-gatherers. It replaces the natural pulses that the nomadic bands responded to with ones orchestrated by human interference, involving the suppression or removal of natural mature vegetation and the tending or replanting of some favored areas to improve the availability of useful plants. A cultivated ecosystem is no longer responsive to naturally occurring pulses but to ones created by farmers. The alteration of environmental stasis is paid for by large subsidies of human energy to sustain an annual crop of rapidly growing, nutrient-consuming plants. The former steady-state having been disturbed, the cultivated ecosystem can only be effectively maintained by the constant vigilance of a sedentary farming population. As a result, the nomadic ways of the past are brought into question, as are cultural restraints on childbearing. Large populations spell the possibility of large harvests. Along with plant cultivation another key strategy introduced at this time was storage of food through drying, cooking, or other preparations, so that it can be consumed out of season or during famine times.

True agricultural systems resulted when *control of propagation* was added to the intensification strategies of cultivation and storage. When a species ability to reproduce is completely managed by human selection, the result is agriculture, the husbanding of plant and animal species fully dependent on humans to reproduce. Control of propagation, as opposed to monitoring wild produce, occurs when there is resolute selection of species in order to amplify particular traits and increase their utility to humans. Such traits include increased bulk, milk production, larger seed size or the clustering of seeds at the end of a stalk or stem, or strengthening the rachis holding seeds to the stem. This latter change prevents the plant from dispersing its seed naturally, thus conserving the seed for threshing and ensuring the plants dependence on humans.

This suite of complicated economic changes did not occur everywhere at the same rate. In some areas the degree of control of humans over plant species, or perhaps more properly the extent of symbiosis between food sources and human communities who tended them, varied greatly. Nevertheless, many experiments with the tending of former game animals or the raising of animal provender or foods for human consumption were under way. The more we learn about this period in the history of hunter-gatherers, the more we are inclined to reject the line demarking "hunter-gatherers" from "food producers." Certainly this process is no longer viewed as a "revolution" between disparate steady states, but a continuum of human and prey interactions in which forager resource management had an important and far-reaching role.

With the increasing recognition of the fuzzy line between hunting-gathering and food production when appraised from an ecological standpoint, several schemes come to mind attempting to arrange the protoagricultural practices of hunter-gatherers and foraging practices of farmers along a gradient. One recognized four food plant–yielding systems: wild–food plant procurement, wild–food plant production, wild–food plant cultivation, and domestication (Harris 1989; Figure 7.5).

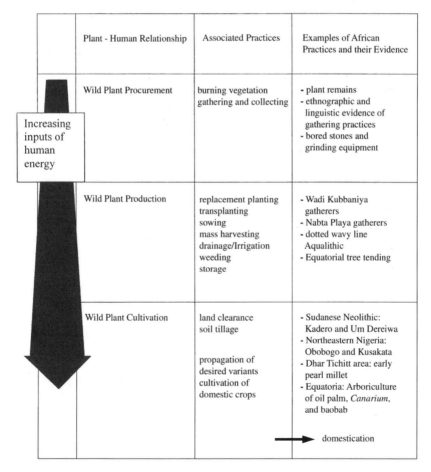

	Plant - Human Relationship	Associated Practices	Examples of African Practices and their Evidence
Increasing inputs of human energy	Wild Plant Procurement	burning vegetation gathering and collecting	- plant remains - ethnographic and linguistic evidence of gathering practices - bored stones and grinding equipment
	Wild Plant Production	replacement planting transplanting sowing mass harvesting drainage/Irrigation weeding storage	- Wadi Kubbaniya gatherers - Nabta Playa gatherers - dotted wavy line Aqualithic - Equatorial tree tending
	Wild Plant Cultivation	land clearance soil tillage propagation of desired variants cultivation of domestic crops	- Sudanese Neolithic: Kadero and Um Dereiwa - Northeastern Nigeria: Obobogo and Kusakata - Dhar Tichitt area: early pearl millet - Equatoria: Arboriculture of oil palm, *Canarium*, and baobab
			domestication

Figure 7.5. A continuum of human–plant relationships in Africa, based on Harris (1989).

Although this proposal does not include progressive interactions between humans and their food animals, one can construe a similar, although not necessarily coterminous, scheme of increasing interaction between humans and their food animals. This includes the development of sophisticated hunting techniques, removing noneconomical competitors or predators (Marean 1997). Another delayed-return strategy with reference to animals is pen-feeding in preparation for slaughter (di Lernia 1997, 2001). Intriguing evidence of husbanding of wild sheep comes from the Uan Afuda cave in southwestern Libya, where wild Barbary sheep were contained in a cave. The purpose of containment was presumably fattening for a planned slaughter, perhaps anticipating a period of food shortage (di Lernia 1997). The cave is evidence of experimentation with animal husbandry but this form of control never developed into full domestication (di Lernia 2001).

True herdspeople mind stock in the vicinity of their residence or move animals in the pastoralist pattern from one lush pasturage to another. In either case, a somewhat "symbiotic" relationship is developed. "Animals as food" was one of the imperatives of the traditional round, seeking the haunts of transient herds.

The Inception of
African Animal Husbandry

Pastoralism, a predominant lifeway in parts of tropical Africa from about 12° north latitude to 12° south latitude and much of arid East Africa, was an adroit solution to the natural circumstances of Africa, with its shifting rains and seasonally changing vegetation, ensuring access to lush grazing throughout the year. Pastoralism is an ingenious way, through the "middle-man" ruminant, to extract nourishing foods from otherwise inedible grasses and shrubs. Though it dictated a peripatetic existence as herds and families of herdsmen traveled from place to place, it only replaced a nomadic food quest with a more secure food supply. As "walking larders," cattle provided milk, blood, meat, hides, bone, and horn. They are by nature herd animals, and therefore convenient to keep in large numbers, as long as they can be provided with graze and water at least every other day. They fulfill the hunter's dictum—that the most efficient kill is of the largest animal in the environment. To adjust to this resource, however, those who adopted this way of life had to change socially and politically. Ideas of community and property common to hunter-gatherers no longer applied. The impulse to husband some breeds, putting them under the protection of the band, entailed not only the development of specialized technologies but new attitudes toward ownership. If food-sharing modes so prevalent among immediate-return hunters prevailed, then someone keeping cattle would have been persuaded to kill them and share the meat (Smith 1992). Following Testart (1988), it is likely that the keeping of cattle as a delayed-return investment was accompanied by concepts of private or kin group ownership, as it does today. In pastoral societies, cattle are not "public goods" nor are their products. They are private property and they pay a "delayed return," an investment in future value to owners or their descent groups. This is an attitude inherently at odds with the egalitarianism of "direct return economies," where the bounty of the hunt or collecting party is shared out equally in the here and now.

In its earliest form, stock-keeping was practiced within otherwise broad-spectrum collecting regimens. The transition to full-fledged pastoralism alters much of that, though some basic routines remain from their hunter-gatherer forebears. In broad-spectrum circumstances, the animals were herded primarily as a source of meat; in specialized pastoralism, they are kept for their blood and milk (Haaland 1992). In any case, early pastoralist societies buried their cows under tumuli at Nabta Playa (Wendorf and Schild 1998). Even at this early Holocene settlement in Egypt's Western Desert, cattle were revered.

As far as we can tell, the Nabta people combined pastoralism with fishing and plant-food collecting. It appears that early cattle were domesticated during a period of hostilities and social upheaval following brief but devastating "wild Nile" floods, which destroyed the floodplain's fisher-gatherer villages (Close 1996:46). A closer relationship with cattle may have been sought as a way of providing meat or milk "on the hoof" after the sources of a broader spectrum lifestyle became flooded. It is possible, based on the Nabta cattle burials, that animals were first kept for some religious purpose (Wendorf and Schild 1998). Being sacred sanctioned the husbanding relationship, easing the move to domestication (Smith 1992). The Nabta site establishes the long history of veneration of cattle in African societies (Herskovits 1926).

In any case, the early cattle herders of the Sahara pursued a generalized economy; they also hunted, fished, and collected wild grains. In this, they seem little changed from routine hunter-gatherers, except that they organized community around the necessity to tend stock. The exact context that led to their keeping cattle is unclear. The advantage of herding in conditions of environmental uncertainty is obvious. Initial attempts to control animals may have involved corralling them around large water sources during dry seasons or pen-feeding them in caves. Initially, the addition of pastoralism merely buttressed a broad-spectrum lifestyle.

The practice of specialized pastoralism begins about 6,000 years ago in the upper Nile Valley, where villages of sedentary fishers and gatherers were replaced about 5,300 years ago by small, ephemeral encampments of specialized mobile herdsmen conducting an annual circuit following the monsoon and maturing grasslands. Domesticated stock spread outward from the western Sahara over most of North Africa. At places like Adrar Bous, for example, they are found in horizons dated to 5,700 years ago. From the mid-Holocene onward, the end of the African Humid Period caused progressive drying of global climates and a drying trend in particular in North Africa. The once "wet Sahara" was returning to its desert state. As a response to this desertification, pastoralism continued its spread southward. Sometime between 4,000 and 3,500 years ago; Saharan people entered the Niger Basin, occupying cliff settlements at Dhar Tichitt in Mauritania, where, by 3,800 years ago, cattle pastoralism is associated with impressive dry stonework settlements. Typically, these people subsisted on their herds, while collecting seasonal wild plant foods from playa lakes and cultivating bulrush millet.

The spread of pastoralism into equatorial Africa may have been slowed by ecological factors, including diseases such as trypanomiasis, a parasite carried by the tsetse fly found in bushlands and woodlands (Gifford-Gonzalez 1998; Hanotte et al. 2002). Even today, tsetse infestation constrains cattle management in wooded areas, such as the *miombo* of the southeast. In many areas it is a shifting frontier: herds with an acquired, partial resistance to trypanomiasis can be introduced into some ecotones where grazing retarded the growth of woodland vegetation, limiting the tsetse threat (Giblin 1990).

Early pastoralists harvested and probably cultivated wild grains, but eventually used domesticates. The simplest method may have been the seeding of ground to be returned to later in the cycle. Wild cereals are fairly easy to sow broadcast and leave to grow and ripen. In forest zones, yams, as a root crop, are easily planted and left to mature on their own until the planter returns to the area. In Ethiopia, local crops like teff or ensete fulfilled the same function. Whether herdspeople desired sure pastures of grass to feed their animals, or whether transhumant collectors ensured a starchy staple, this cultivation was rudimentary, supplying a need at low cost and little effort—it is sometimes called "low-level" food production (Smith, B. 2001). Nevertheless, this activity formed a natural bridge between intensive collecting and full-fledged farming regimens.

Human–Food Plant Relationships in Africa

Collecting was an important preface to the domestication of food plants, in which, choosing within the spectrum of gathered foodstuffs, people would eventually concentrate on a select few. Once groups produced a "domesticate" by selective breeding, it was in most cases incorporated into a dietary inventory still rich with a great many wild foods (Smith, B. 2001). The proportion of wild to domesticated species in the diet varies widely. While Smith notes that the relative proportion of wild foods in the diet should decline over time, this is not necessarily true everywhere. In many parts of Africa, wild produce continued to be a significant part of the diet. In the tropical rain forest, for instance, farm products made up only 40 percent of the diet well into the nineteenth century (Vansina 1994–1995:17).

Wild Food Plant Procurement

Many African plant food species exist in a semidomesticated relationship with humans, including Abyssinian oats (*Avena abyssinica*), Guinea millet (*Brachiaria deflexa*), wild African rice (*Oryza glaberrima*), and safu plum (*Pachylobus edulis*) (Harlan 1989). These wild food plants are tended but not cultivated. Abyssinian oats grow as a weed in emmer and barley fields, and Ethiopian cultivators make no effort to get rid of it. As a result, *Avena abyssinica* evolved into two varieties, a nonshattering variety and semishattering one. The nonshattering form is reaped along with the emmer and barley. The semishattering ones are sometimes collected; though some is left in the fields to propagate for next season. Ethiopian farmers avoid putting all their eggs in one basket. If the plant most dependent on them fails, *Avena abyssinica*, a plant less dependent on humans, will be there to fall back on (Harlan 1992).

Over 60 species of wild grass seeds are commonly harvested in Africa (Jardin 1967). For example, *Paspalum scrobiculatum* grows along the roads and alongside rice, millet, and other domesticates in West Africa. Though it has not been domesticated in West Africa, domesticated varieties are found in India and Japan. There is also a long history of intimate relationships between people and selected trees and tubers in Africa. The baobab (*Adansonia sp.*), *Moringa sp.*, the karate or shea butter tree (*Butyrospermum*), and the oil palm *(Elaeis guineensis)* are a few examples. Karate, or the shea butter tree (*Butyrospermum*), grows in many parts of the Sahel in West Africa. Edible oil extracted from the fruit is important to the diet of savanna peoples. The tree enjoys a nearly sacred status. Though not cultivated, it is tended, resulting in a orchard-like savanna or nearly pure stands of *Butyrospermum* (Harlan, De Wet, and Stemler 1976:11). In the West African forests, cultivation of domestic yam and managed oil palm husbandry are often practiced together (Stahl 1993).

Many archaeologists have noted a relationship between old village sites and baobab, a wild tree whose wide distribution is a result of human propagation (Wickens 1982). In fact, wherever one comes across *Adansonia*, one is likely to find an abandoned village. This is not surprising, because the tree has many uses. The Swahili of East Africa have eighteen uses for this tree (Kusimba, C., personal communication 1996). Young baobabs rely on humans for survival; humans in turn depend on mature *Adansonia* for sustenance. The bark is used for fiber, while its leaves and roots are used as medicinal herbs. Its fruit is eaten and used as shampoo. While young, *Adansonia* are sometimes hollowed out, so that as they mature the opening deepens, becoming a cistern, trapping rainwater for use during the dry seasons.

The original habitat of the oil palm, *Elaeis guineensis*, is not the rain forest, but the margins of the wet forest zone. To thrive it needs the quantities of light provided by open village spaces and agricultural clearings. It remains a wild species but wed to areas of human habitation. Its occurrence in forest stretches devoid of human settlement is a sure sign that the area was once settled (Eggert 1993:324; Lavachery 2001). As in the case of the oil palm and the baobab, "dependence" is really mutual. The process of domestication was a process of co-evolution (Rindos 1984) Establishing a beneficial relationship between organisms, it increased the fitness of all involved. As food plants were altered, so was humanity's conception of their environment. As humans moved from "treading lightly on the landscape" in the Early and Middle Stone Age to intensively exploiting it, dramatically altering ecosystems, they too were transformed. At this time there is a significant decrease in the robusticity of the human skeleton and the size of the human dentition that seems tied to diet change and the increase in animal and plant sources of dietary fat (Cachel 1997). Significant reduction in sexual dimorphism is found along with the transition to food production (Lubell and Shepard 1997:326). Reduced sexual dimorphism is thought to mark a change from male hunting and the provisioning of females to female-based gathering. At this time, residential mobility decreased. These last two aspects suggest a swing toward collection of locally available foodstuffs and the increased importance of collectors, usually a female role.

Collectors of natural produce are dependent on natural pulses and seasonal succession of food plants. Farmers, to extend an analogy to the processes of domestication, effectively tame ecosystems, harnessing natural pulses to human needs. We have seen that hunter-gatherers shaped their surroundings, but theirs was a low-cost operation. The new breed of intensive collectors and their food-producing descendants gathered greater, more stable yields by absorbing much higher costs in technological innovation and social management.

Related Archaeological Evidence

Evidence of plant food remains from archaeological sites is notoriously sparse. Often archaeologists are dependent on extraordinary conditions to preserve indications of early plant exploitation, such as the waterlogged deposits of the Kalambo Basin or the parched conditions of some caves. Though evidence of plant use is rare from the early Paleolithic period, we can safely presume that they played an important role from the beginning. At Stralathan, a dry cave in South Africa's eastern Cape, remnants of grass bedding, similar to that identified by Clark at Kalambo, and a hearth with pieces of carbonized *Watsonia* corms and other plant remains were found in horizons dated to between 24,000 to 18,000 years ago, or just before onset of the Last Glacial Maximum. Some ash lenses at Klasies River may also indicate exploitation of this onion-like root (Deacon 1993). Middle Stone Age people ate Marula nuts at Bushman Rock Shelter. In the Later Stone Age, evidence of plant food use becomes much more common, which indicates increased human use of these sources as well as improved preservation. Many corms and oil-rich fruits were found stored in large pits with other plants at another South African dry cave, Melkhoutboum (Deacon 1976). In the tropical rain forests of Central Africa, long before any sign of cultivated crops or animal domestication, evidence of the consumption of palm (*Elaeis guineensis*) and canarium nuts (*Canarium schweinfurthii*) is very common on sites dating to the last 2,000 years.

More frequently in the African archaeological record, the only evidence we have of plant utilization is the equipment used to process seeds or nuts, usually grindstones or grinders, though other sorts of worked stone usually signify plant collecting as well. The first signs of plant processing implements appear around 40,000 years ago, when bored stones become common throughout southern, southeastern, and eastern Africa (Deacon, J. 1984). These stones are weights used to facilitate the action of digging sticks, used to dig up roots and smaller ground rodents, when more commonly utilized plant and animal foods were unavailable (Walker 1995). At early Holocene sites in the Matopo Hills, grindstones and bored digging stick weights are associated with quantities of Marula nut hulls (Walker 1995). The advantage of a strategy, incorporating collecting with the capture of smaller animals, is self-evident. These are small, easily gained food sources, capable of rapid replacement of losses due to human predation. Residential mobility was no longer advantageous, as plentiful, reliable food sources could be found close at hand and some of the risks attendant to the food quest reduced.

Wild Food Plant Production

Wild food plant production, if successful, brings a dramatic increase in the reliability and abundance of foodstuffs. Its practitioners replaced or sowed wild varieties, irrigating, weeding, reaping, harvesting, and storing the produce. The range of foodstuffs utilized is typically broad-spectrum, seeking to optimize local resources at low cost.

Related Archaeological Evidence

Wadi Kubbaniya lies along a tributary to the Nile, just north of Aswan. Today, the area is a floodplain 2-km wide, rimmed by sandstone cliffs where food plants are available. During the occupation of Wadi Kubbaniya 18,000 years ago, the Nile was smaller, still seasonal, but a slow-moving river. During its annual flood stage, the narrow valley was nearly completely under water. At other seasons, the countryside was an open plain of marshes and meadows, with shrubs and trees growing to the edge of the valley along the cliffs. Atop the neighboring cliffs, desert winds blew across light shrubs and bushes, forming a field of dunes. Most of the later Paleolithic sites were on the tops of these dunes, about 3-km from the mouth of the wadi. Only flooded in late summer, these elevated campsites offered an excellent overview of the swampy floodplain. The sites were small transitory camps, with bone and charcoal, stone tools, especially backed bladelets, heavy grinders, and shallow, heavy mortars.

Excellent preservation allows a very complete reconstruction of subsistence patterns at Wadi Kubbaniya. These include a large role for fish and tubers from wetland plants and a much smaller component of wild game. Plant foods at the Wadi Kubbaniya sites include a broad range of twenty-five types of seeds, fruits, and soft starchy vegetables, especially the tubers of wild nut-grass, *Cyperus rotundus,* a type of sedge. The tubers would have been available over longer periods, and the disturbed soil caused by digging out the roots stimulates further growth. Stands of nut-grass produce yields on a par with domestic barley fields (about 3-kg of edible parts per hectare). In fact, a few persons with digging sticks could have dug enough to meet several days' carbohydrate requirements in a matter of hours (Hillman 1989:180). Nutgrass would have been an important part of the diet, for it is abundant, productive, and reliable (Wetterstrom 1993:175). Other tubers, like club-rush (*Scirpus maritimus*), fruits, seeds, and plant parts, were found, but few of these have been identified.

Plant foods are nutritious, yet often indigestible. In order to be edible, many need extensive preparation, involving removing indigestible parts or chemically modifying toxic components. Some Wadi Kubbaniya tubers, like nut-grass and the club-rush, contain toxins that must be removed by grinding into flour detoxified by leaching before they can be eaten. This requires, in turn, boiling water and containers capable of holding water. Boiling water requires a whole new technology, one permitting stone boiling, by holding hot rocks in a potentially flammable container, or the fabrication of pots placed directly on a fire. The control of fire and its derivative, boiling water, opened many avenues into the exploitation of vegetable foods. The many grindstones found at Wadi Kubbaniya bear witness to the importance of seeds there.

The high calories of many plant foods would be expected to increase body fat, to the advantage of women and nursing mothers. Some increase in population may be a function of better nutrition and fewer failed pregnancies. Baby feces found at Wadi Kubbaniya suggest an advantage of the shift in these new diets was an ability to develop soft weaning foods for infants (Hillman 1989).

The occupation of the Wadi Kubbaniya area was as a station in an annual round, focused on fishing and hunting in the summer during the floods and tuber gathering after floodwaters receded. During the winter, the harvest of mature tubers was supplemented with nuts and seeds, along with edible parts of cattail and papyrus. At the same time, the inhabitants filled out their menu with the flesh of migratory ducks and geese hunted on the nearby marshes

By 8,000 years ago at the Nabta Playa, diets were enhanced by a broad spectrum of seed grains such as sorghum (Wasylikowa et al. 1997). Husbanding of these included reaping and storage, as well as purposeful sowing, tending, and weeding around these ostensibly wild cereals (Haaland 1992, 1996, 1999). Such practices lasted for more than 6,000 years before morphological changes gave rise to the first domesticated sorghum.

The tropical rain forests are also rich in evidence of intensified foraging lifestyles. Between 3,700 and 3,300 years ago, foragers living in central Ghana not only consumed land snails, as evidenced by deposits containing discarded snail shell, but also fruits, oil palm, and *Canarium schweinfurthii*, indicated by endocarps and seed husks, as well as the meat of arboreal primates and large reptiles. The oil palm played a significant role in the maintenance of forest populations, who very early practiced their protection (Lavachery 2001; Stahl 1993). Much as they do today, people husbanded and planted the trees, ensuring sufficient access to them. Because of human planting strategies, the two oil palms are found in many parts of the rain forest and its ecotone, a zone that Holocene hunter-gatherers often preferred (Mercader and Brooks 2001).

Wild Plant Food Cultivation

Now we come to economies that involve the practices we have already described, as well as conscious cultivation, and the beginnings of human manipulation to enhance desirable characteristics. Many attitudes attributable to full-time farmers become apparent, though domesticated varieties do not make an appearance until later. Not only were desirable variants grown, but people also invested time and effort in land clearance, soil preparation, and the care and maintenance of growing crops. These strategies go beyond the husbanding of naturally or casually sown stands. It is thought that earlier bands broadcast seed to be harvested later, but without the developed technology or attitudes of full-fledged farmers. Some transient herders in northeast Africa still do this. It is one way to ensure supplies in the course of their annual movement of their herds from one pasture to another. It is the sort of effort that suits hunter-gatherer routines, being that it is low cost and low maintenance, and merely assures the production of wild crops, presumably meant for on-the-spot consumption. Domestication processes, by contrast, start when plants with valued traits are selected for, replanted away from their wild sisters, and eventually become dependent on human intervention for their reproduction.

Related Archaeological Evidence

It is often difficult to distinguish wild from domestic varieties, and other traits like field clearance and preparation may be difficult to determine as well. Often one has to depend on analyses of pollen spectra in order to sample out times when vegetation is abruptly altered or when cereals flourish and replace forest. The appearance of new kinds of tools useful for working the soil or processing or storing grain; the polish on the surface of tools; or grain impressions on clay vessels, may be our only clue to plant production. Grinding stones, seemingly a sure sign, are in fact a part of Later Stone Age inventories, used by hunter-gatherers to process nuts and the seeds of wild food plants.

Throughout the African Neolithic, wild varieties of sorghum, millet, and similar grains were used well into the historical period; even in the zones of the wild progenitors evidence of domestication comes late. Sorghum (*Sorghum bicolor*) was first domesticated in Egypt and the Sudan, where people found it efficient to harvest wild cereals from stands in seasonally flooded depressions. This strategy was yet another low-cost effort, with good return on investment in harvesting equipment and storage facilities. Sorghum, which thrives wherever it is taken, is perfect for African conditions, being nutritious, hardy, and drought-resistant.

At Kadero and Um Direiwa on the Sudanese Nile, sorghum collection intensified to new levels. More than 30,000 grinder fragments were found at the latter site, suggesting an intensive collection and processing of cereals. These collectors stripped grain from the stalks, rather than winnowing them. This does not require alteration of the plant's structure. This special harvesting method may be one reason why morphological changes are not apparent in the sorghum used here, in spite of the intensive use of the plants implied by the massive quantities of grinders. These changes appear much later, about 2,000 years ago. In the meantime, harvesting and storing of cereals, as well as the manufacture of pottery and intensified acquisition of fish by net fishing not only enhanced sedentism but also augmented population densities. Survey of a short distance of the east bank of the Nile discovered twenty-two ostensibly stable, year-round settlements similar to Um Direiwa and dating to around 8,000 years ago (Haaland 1996, 1999).

Sorghum appears in a domesticated context around 2,000 years ago at Meröe, in the Sudan. Although native to Africa, it was cultivated 4,000 years ago in Yemen and India. In Mauritania, the first domesticated pearl millet was grown around 3,200 to 3,000 years ago (Amblard and Pernes 1989; Holl 1985, 1998a, 1998b). While actual grains are not preserved, there are impressions of early millet on pottery of this period at Karkarichinkat Sud, Maki, and Dhar Tichitt.

Subsistence patterns at Dhar Tichitt, Mauritania, suggest that the inhabitants had the basic components of a mixed agricultural economy. Not only did they keep herds of cattle and flocks of sheep or goats, but they collected and cultivated wild seeds like millet and hunted and fished in the vicinity (Holl 1985). Domesticated forms of sorghum appear later, about 2,000 years ago. This economic pattern, although one still primarily founded upon the collection and hunting of wild species, seems somewhat more advanced than those discussed earlier. The presence of domestic stock concurrent with an absence of domesticate forms of grain even implies a priority of stock management and that grain was cultivated first as animal fodder, supplying the needs of the herds. If that was the case, collected plant food remained a main source of human nutrition, as seems the situation here.

In equatorial Africa, humans developed similar closer relationships with staple plant foods. The large village at Obobogo in Cameroon, occupied around 3,000 years ago, yielded oil palm and *Canarium* remains, grinding equipment, polished stone, and iron slag. The stratified site of Kursakata, in northeast Nigeria, contains nearly 5-m of stratified cultural deposit and evidence of more than forty taxa of well-preserved fruits and grains. Most numerous were the remains of the cereals *Paniceae, Pennisetum,* and *Oryza* (Neumann, Ballouche, and Klee 1996:442). With the exception of *Brachiaria deflexa,* small-grained *Paniceae* is not usually cultivated; its appearance is a sure sign of full-scale collecting. In fact, *Paniceae* is the predominant grain found in the horizon from 2,860 years ago. Indications of the domestication of *Pennisetum,* or millet, occur shortly thereafter, or about 2,800 years ago. Over the next millennium, the people of Kursakata developed a mixed economy based on cultivated *Pennisetum* and collected *Paniceae.* In the late period, as the cultivation of *Oryza glaberrima* took root, cultivation of *Pennisetum* declined, but the collected *Paniceae* continued to play an important role in the economy (Neumann, Ballouche, and Klee 1996:447; Klee and Zach 1999).

Rockshelter sites of the equatorial region have evidence of exploitation of *Canarium schweinfurthii* and *Elaeis guineensis,* along with roulette-decorated pottery, metal, and stone tools (Mercader et al. 2000). In a core from Bosumtwi in Ghana, pollen of oil palm increases dramatically around 3,500 to 3,000 years ago, suggestive of an intensified management (Stahl 1993:265). Lavachery (2001) suggests the management of oil palm and other trees developed into systematic "arboriculture" based on replanting and tending of these trees in desired areas.

From Domestication Onward

More than forty domesticated plants were cultivated in the three major African centers, the Savanna, Forest Margin, and Ethiopian zones (Bower 1995). Over the rest of the continent, however, domesticated plants and animals were introduced either through the diffusion of the domesticated varieties or the movement of people carrying them. This process was one of introduction and local adaptation. Because cultivation was often secondary to pastoralism, as at Dhar Tichitt, archaeological evidence of cultivated grains is often missing from the sites of the first food producers in many areas, especially East Africa (Young and Thompson 1999), and the economies of these early Neolithic people are poorly known. Nevertheless, in many (but not all) areas they were the first potters or metalworkers; furthermore, their movements involved the transplanting of major linguistic and ethnic communities (Vansina 1990, 1994–1995). Eventually, full-scale mixed agriculture spread, to become established from North Africa to the Cape of southern Africa by 1,400 years ago (Sealy and Yates 1994).

Many analysts think of African agricultural systems as being extensive rather than intensive ones (Sutton 1994–1995). From a comparative perspective this is true, but it obscures the nature of African agriculture. As we have just seen, hunter-gatherers are tied to restrictive sets of natural pulses that necessitate mobile residential patterns. The sequence of pulses shapes their nomadic routines. African cultivators, on the other hand, must deal with the ecological consequences of high-energy inputs and outputs. Cultivation depletes soil nutrients.

In order to compensate for nutritionally poor tropical soil, African farmers often use slash-and-burn cultivation, where nutrients stored in mature vegetation are reduced to ash and worked into the soil to nurture crops for a few years. This is a higher cost procedure than intensive collecting, requiring a large exercise of manpower to prepare gardens and further work to maintain them. In the end, slash-and-burn cultivation is sufficient to sustain relatively small, dispersed populations, tied together by descent group linkages. To this extent African agriculture is extensive. Segmentary groups spread themselves over terrain and local groups open large clearings, most of which are in fallow, in order to support village level populations. Consequently, population densities over much of tropical Africa are quite low, with little opportunity for an intensified agricultural production. At the other end of the scale, the advanced collectors we have been discussing still had opportunity to intensify their harvests, whether they are of food plants or game.

These larger, more permanently based populations, living at densities unheard of in the world of hunter-gatherers, spread through segmentary lineage and other expansive organizations, ensuring through social connectivity adequate access to necessities. Social organizations based on leaders and lineage groups arose to manage flows of material and information. At the same time, an enlarged, interconnected community became a significant pathway for the propagation of epidemic disease and stresses incurred during harsh climate regimens like drought and famine. One could no longer travel to find more favorable conditions. Massive clearing of tropical forests opened up not only garden plots but also wet places for *Schistosoma* and the *Plasmodium falciparum*-carrying *anopheles* mosquito to breed (Pennisi 2001). Bilharziasis sapped the energies of whole communities. Malaria became a tropical scourge, countered genetically by the mutation and adaptation of the sickle cell condition, itself a scourge. Intensification, and the food-producing regimens that grew out it, was a mixed blessing. On the one hand, it provided ample food for populations that grew in response to its bounty, and the systemic requisite to supply adequate manual labor. On the other, it altered human lifeways; while negating the one that humanity had spent many thousands of years to develop. Given the seeming inevitability of the process of intensification and eventual food production, and its attractiveness in areas where hunting and gathering were difficult propositions, it is a wonder that any human groups remained as hunters.

Summing Up

Because of its ability to break the productive bounds of a particular ecosystem, food production is often considered "the greatest invention of all time" (Redman 1999:92). We have seen that it is a mixed blessing, but it does allow humans to extract energy from a particular ecosystem by orders of magnitude previously unknown. As a result, its introduction was accompanied by dramatic increases in carrying capacity, the population an environment could support. For example, about 150 hunters and gatherers lived in the early Neolithic village of Abu Hureyra in Jordan, but the number of residents increased to nearly 5,000 agriculturists (Moore et al. 2001). It was also accompanied by a transition to a settled life and the possibility of accumulation of goods by individuals and families. The high yields of agricultural harvests opened the doors to economies based on stored supplies rather than immediate return and the development of value that could be passed on from one generation to another. Having settled in permanent villages with reasonable expectation of year-round food supplies, communities were based on private or kin-group property and social stratification.

In some places, agricultural complexity and diversity proceeded without initiating an accompanying social and political complexity, by creating smallholder systems where individual households remain relatively independent economic and political units (Geertz 1963). In other places, changes in social organization accompanying the initiation of food-producing regimens brought forth hierarchically organized political and productive units, giving rise to an administrative sector out of a compromise between a need to be flexible in the face of environmental uncertainty and the need to pursue long-term plans (Redman 1999). In other words, a bureaucracy arose to guide decision making. As a result, the majority came to be controlled by a few administrative specialists. For better or worse, in Africa, the administration of food production, landholding, and material transfers acted as crucial precursors to the rise of complex, ranked societies in many areas. The question remains: Why did the practice of foraging persist for so many thousands of years after so many groups had adopted food-producing strategies?

8

Twilight of the Hunter-Gatherers

As of this writing, the hunting and gathering way of life is pretty much gone, though hunters and gatherers remained active in Africa well into the twentieth century, usually confined to marginal areas not suited to agriculture, such as deserts or tropical rain forests (Murdock 1968; Kent 1997). The Ju/'hoansi continued to forage the Kalahari Desert; the Okiek and other *Wandorobo* ("those without cattle") the East African mountains; the Waata, Boni, and Dahalo the desolate *nyika* of the Kenyan coast; and central African Pygmy bands in the forests and woodland glades. The ecological pattern of hunter-gatherer settlement suggests to some that twentieth century hunter-gatherers were relict peoples, remnants from the Later Stone Age who retreated into or stayed in marginal habitats while others were developing and using food production. We have already seen that the origins of present-day foragers, as well as their activities, are complex and controversial. The *Land Filled with Flies* debate even insinuated that some current foragers were people driven to marginal existences by their more powerful neighbors (Wilmsen 1989). Be that as it may, the continued pursuit of hunter-gathering in Africa is a tale of the relationships between the remaining foraging societies and the food producers they live among. Their persistent cultural existence is one dependent upon an age-old ability to adapt to changing circumstances through flexibility and social networks.

Kisio Rockshelter

The way the life of hunter-gatherers changed as new people and behaviors colonized the hinterland of eastern Africa can be seen at

Kisio Rockshelter, a hunter-gatherer camp of the last 1,000 years in the Tsavo National Park of southeastern Kenya, excavated by C. Kusimba (Figures 6.14, 8.1). The rockshelter had been inhabited twice, once around 100 years ago, and again around 1,000 years ago. Both the Lukenya and Kisio sites are in an *Acacia-Commiphora* bushland typical of arid East Africa (White 1983). The Tsavo region, however, is much drier than the Athi Plains, receiving as little as 200-mm of rain per year compared to around 500-mm of rain per year in the Athi Plains. Significantly, it is also at a much lower altitude (200- to 600-m, compared to 1,600- to 1,800-m at Lukenya Hill) and very hot. Due to its poor soils and desert climate, it has an abundance of animals that need very little water and can tolerate poor-quality forage (Olindo, Douglas-Hamilton, and Hamilton 1988; Wijngaarden and van Engelen 1985). The present-day Tsavo fauna includes elephant, buffalo, Burchell's zebra, kudu, impala, warthog, and dik-dik; large carnivores, including lion, leopard, and spotted hyaena; primates such as baboon and vervet monkey; and many species of insectivores, birds, reptiles, and amphibians (Figure 8.2; C. Kusimba and S. Kusimba 2000).

Figure 8.1. Kisio Rockshelter during excavation.

Figure 8.2.   Tsavo "red elephants" at a waterhole.

Lithic Assemblages from Kisio Rockshelter

The lithic assemblage at Kisio consists of 10,098 artifacts. Ninety-seven percent of these artifacts are made of locally available vein quartz. Other raw materials in the assemblage include a fine-grained rhyolitic igneous rock, cryptocrystalline silica, and locally available obsidian (Table 8.1). Almost half the cores in the Kisio assemblage are bipolar and 88 percent of the cores have three or fewer flake scars. There is very little retouch or platform preparation on the flakes, and only 1.4 percent of the artifacts were shaped tools (Table 8.2). Furthermore, very little recycling was employed at Kisio and only 1 of the 144 tools was a composite tool. These characteristics are similar to those of the quartz artifacts from GvJm46 and GvJm62 at Lukenya Hill and demonstrate that the majority of quartz artifacts were procured from the immediate vicinity, flaked once or twice, then discarded. Unlike at Lukenya Hill, no component of the lithic assemblage shows a significant use of curated strategies, such as the transport of Rift Valley obsidian to the site, the use of conservational bipolar flaking or formal tool manufacture, or the manufacture of

Count of Number	
Raw material	Total
Quartz	3,055
Chert	32
Lava	19
Obsidian	18
Chalcedony	4
Indurate sandstone	3
Quartzite	1
Magnetite	1
Grand Total	3,147

Table 8.1.   Raw Materials in the Kisio Rockshelter Lithic Assemblages

Reduction Stage	%
Debitage	85.4
Flakes	8.2
Cores	3.3
Tools	1.4

Table 8.2.   Reduction Stages in the Kisio Rockshelter Lithic Assemblages

composite tools. At Kisio Rockshelter, the lack of shaped tools or retouch and the lack of transport of nonlocal cores indicates an almost exclusive use of on-the-spot, expedient technology as far as lithic artifacts are concerned.

Faunal Assemblages from Kisio Rockshelter

Kisio Rockshelter's faunal assemblage was found in levels with abundant lithic material, pottery, iron artifacts, and beads. Furthermore, none of the bones displayed bore porcupine or carnivore toothmarks. Humans were the main accumulator and modifier of the Kisio bones. At Lukenya Hill, Marean described faunal assemblages based almost exclusively on migratory grazers. At Kisio, by contrast, the faunal remains are dominated by small nonmigratory animals (Table 8.3). In terms of Minimum Number of Individuals, the most common animals found were red and yellow hornbills, dik-dik, and hyrax, and in terms of NISP small bovids dominate over large ones. In addition, over

17 kg of land snail remains were recovered from Kisio. There were no domestic animals found at Kisio. Most of the species present, including the bovids, zebra, warthog, birds, hyrax, terrapin, frogs, chameleons, snakes, elephant shrews, rats, and gerbils, could have been food resources for humans. Ideally, taphonomic studies should be done to confirm that Kisio's small faunal remains were eaten by humans (Henshilwood 1997; Sampson 1998, 2000). Many of these species, including hyrax, frog, and hornbills, are still commonly hunted. Indeed, other

Taxonomic Classification	Common Name	MNI	NISP
Class Aves			
Order Anseriformes			
Family Anatidae			
Anas hottentota	Hottentot teal	1	1
Order Columbiformes			
Family Columbidae			
Oena capensis	Namaqua dove	1	1
Order Coraciiformes			
Family Bucerotidae			
Tockus erythrorhynchus	Red-billed hornbill	8	62
Tockus flavirostris	Yellow-billed hornbill	4	18
Tockus sp. indet.	Hornbill	1	10
Order Galliformes			
Family Phasianidae			
Coturnix delegorguei	Harlequin quail	1	1
Class Mammalia			
Order Artiodactyla			
Family Bovidae			
Tribe Aepycerotini			
Aepyceros melampus	Impala	2	5
Tribe Alcelaphini			
sp. indet.		2	6
Tribe Bovini			
Syncerus caffer	Buffalo	1	1
Tribe Cephalophini			
cf. *Cephalophus harveyi*	Harvey's red duiker	1	2
Tribe Neotragini			
Madoqua kirkii	Kirk's dik-dik	3	36
Tribe Tragelaphini			
Tragelaphus imberbis	Lesser kudu	1	1
Taurotragus oryx	Eland	1	3
sp. indet.		1	1
Family Suidae			
Phacochoerus africanus	Warthog	1	3

Table 8.3. MNI/NISP of Fauna from Kisio Rockshelter

Taxonomic Classification	Common Name	MNI	NISP
Order Hyracoidea			
Family Procaviidae			
Heterohyrax brucei	Bush/yellow-spotted hyrax	2	7
Order Lagomorpha			
Family Leporidae			
Lepus capensis	Cape hare	1	5
Order Macroscelidae			
Family Mascroscelididae			
Elephantulus sp. (*rufescens?*)	Elephant shrew	1	1
Order Perissodactyla			
Family Equidae			
Equus burchelli	Burchell's zebra	1	2
Order Primates			
Family Hominidae			
Homo sapiens	Human	1	16
Order Rodentia			
Family Cricetidae			
Cricetomys gambianus	Giant rat	1	1
Family Gerbillinae			
Tatera sp. indet.	Naked-soled gerbil	1	8
Taterillus emini	Gerbil	1	1
Class Reptilia			
Family Testudinidae			
Pelosios broadlyi	Freshwater terrapin	1	3
Order Squamata			
Family Varanidae			
Varanus exanthematicus	Savannah monitor lizard	1	10
Family Agamidae			
cf. *Agama agama*	Agama	1	5
Family Boidae			
Eryx colubrinus	Sand boa	1	3
Family Chamaeleonidae			
Chamaeleo sp. indet.	Chameleon	1	2
Family Colubridae			
Rhamphiophis oxyrhynchus	Brown-beaked snake	1	6
Psammophis sp. indet.	Sand snake	1	2
Family Viperidae			
Bitis arientans	Puff adder	1	6
Order Salientia			
Suborder Diplasiocoela			
sp. indet.	Frog		344

*Note: MNI and NISP was not calculated for any taxonomic levels above tribe

Table 8.3. continued

historic hunter-gatherers of Africa are known to have focused on similar small animal resources (Sampson 1998; Henshilwood 1997; Mutundu 1999). Because no permanent water is nearby, the Kisio shelter was most likely occupied briefly and sporadically. During these periods, local faunal were procured with the aid of expedient local tools.

Other classes of artifacts at Kisio show even more dramatic changes in historic hunter-gatherer lifeways compared to those of the Paleolithic at Lukenya Hill. The Kisio group was unmistakably linked through trade with surrounding peoples. First, over 200 European glass beads were found at Kisio; these were one of the most common trade items in East Africa in the mid- to late Iron Age. Second, several metal artifacts were recovered, including an arrowhead made of sheet metal, first introduced to East Africa by the British in the early nineteenth century (Figure 8.3). Plain and incised decorated pottery was also found, although no evidence of pottery or metal production was found at Kisio. The metal tools, then, unlike the lithic artifacts, were almost certainly a curated technology. Thorbahn (1979), after excavating similar rockshelter sites with wild fauna and trade items, attributed them to hunting and gathering peoples who, as the ivory trade grew, began to specialize in elephant hunting and the provision of caravans and other Tsavo groups with ivory, in exchange for blankets, grains,

Figure 8.3. Arrowhead of sheet metal used by the hunters of Kisio Rockshelter.

and milk products. Certainly, the Kisio occupation was a brief seasonal one, given the lack of permanent water nearby. One cannot rule out, however, that Kisio's inhabitants may have pursued a variety of subsistence practices at other periods or perhaps seasonally, such as herding and farming on a sporadic and seasonal basis; they may have lived in longer-term settlements at other times of the year, perhaps providing labor to an agricultural settlement (Wadley 1996). Intriguingly, Thorbahn (1979) reports on rockshelter occupations with domestic faunal remains in the Tsavo region. More sites need to be excavated before an exclusive "hunter-gatherer" economy can be attributed to the inhabitants of Kisio; by the same token, more evidence of interaction is needed to demonstrate what kinds of social linkages may have brought beadwork and metals to the Kisio people.

The way Kisio's Waata used the landscape was also dramatically different. The inhabitants of Lukenya Hill exploited an essentially open landscape concentrating on large, mobile fauna. Waata foragers, referred to pejoratively by their neighbors as Walyankuru (those who eat pig), spoke the Cushitic dialect of their Galla overlords (Cerulli 1922; Stiles 1982). The Waata were adept in the use of bows and poisoned arrows for hunting elephants and provided ivory to caravans heading to trade ports on the Kenya coast (Hobley 1895, 1912, 1929; Holis 1909). The Waata had patron-client relationships with their Oromo pastoralist overlords. "If they shoot an elephant one tusk is given to the Galla (Oromo) Chief" (Hobley 1895:557; 1929). Waataita agriculturalists from the Taita hills forged blood brotherhoods with Waata hunters for access to their secret knowledge of elephant hunting and, in turn, the lucrative ivory trade (C. Kusimba and S. Kusimba, field notes 1998–2000; Merritt 1975). In Tsavo, as in many parts of Africa, hunter-gatherers, pastoralists, and agriculturalists coexisted, bound by symbiotic relationships of exchange and intermarriage but also experiencing episodic conflicts (Table 8.4, Kusimba and Kusimba 2000; see also Ambrose 1986; Cronk and Dickson 2000; Smith 1998). Intergroup conflict over wealth-building resources such as cattle occurred in spite of alliances through which goods, information, and ritual power were exchanged (Merritt 1975; C. Kusimba and S. Kusimba, field notes 1998–2000). These relationships persisted well into the twentieth century. When the Tsavo National Park was gazetted in 1947, numerous human groups inside the park, who lived at least partly by hunting and gathering, were resettled around its outskirts (Hobley 1895; Stiles 1979, 1980). Many of these groups claimed descent from Waata hunter-gatherers of historical accounts.

	Waata	Oromo	Wataita	Coastal Fishers/ Urbanites
Environment	scrub/thicket	arid grasslands	wetter hill slopes	coasts, cities
Mobility	high	seasonal	sedentism/low mobility	sedentism
Social Organization	egalitarian/ heterarchical	lineage/clan	lineage/clan	ranked/stratified hierarchical
Trade Products	skins, meat, ivory, rhino horns, honey, beeswax, labor, ritual knowledge, medicines	milk, butter, meat, hides and skins, incense, domestic animals	crops, pottery, iron, rock crystal, finished tools	dried and/or smoked fish, beads, pottery, imported ceramics, metals, jewelry, tools, textiles
Ethic	egalitarian/ heterarchical	status-seeking, expansionist	status-seeking	status-seeking
Relationship with Coast	diplomatic trade	diplomatic trade	trade controlled by coast	
Type of Trade	individually contracted or person-to-person, symbiotic exchange —utilitarian goods or personal adornment	controlled by lineage/ethnic group or elders— utilitarian goods and prestige goods	controlled by lineage/ethnic group or elders— utilitarian goods and prestige goods	controlled by socioeconomic elites— utilitarian goods prestige goods

Table 8.4. Exchange Relationships among Hunter-Gatherers and Others in the Tsavo Region, Based on Historical Accounts

Processes of Persistence

There seem to be three *processes of persistence* by which the descendants of Later Stone Age hunter-gatherers continued their traditional lifeways under altered circumstances and sharing their territories with more numerous food-producing neighbors. These processes are enhancing the *symbiosis* between the differing communities, establishing *parallel* and complementary economies, and adopting a *peripatetic* lifeway. The processes of persistence involved, first, changes in technology. Hunter-gatherers altered or adopted new hunting strategies or preferred prey, because they intended to trade the fruits of the forage with their neighbors. For example, the economics of trade with neighbor farmers have a lot to do with the types of hunting practices chosen by Central African hunter-gatherers. Where forager women spend a lot of time working for farmers, they rarely participate in hunts; as a consequence, men hunt alone using bows and arrows. In areas where forager women's labor for agriculturalists is not so important, they tend to hunt with men by driving animals into the mens' nets. This type of hunting produces a large surplus that can be traded to agriculturalists (Bailey and Aunger 1989). The Mukogodo of montane East Africa husbanded hives for honey, exchanged with pastoralists; the widespread Batwa groups scattered along the lakes of eastern Africa exchanged lacustrine products for those of the land (Schadeberg 1999).

Second, stability in foragers' social and economic dealings with farmers, herdsmen, merchants, and others was forged by novel means of interaction. Mechanisms of interaction were already an integral and necessary element for foraging populations living as highly mobile, flexible, egalitarian bands. The introduction of farmers and herdsmen precipitated a reorientation of existing alliances to include food-producing kin, fictive kin, friends, trading partners, patrons, and so forth. At the same time, the foragers intended to maintain a distinct cultural identity, retaining one lifeway out of sight of their food-producing allies or patrons, and another in imitation of the food producers' institutions, developing a closer symbiotic relationship that sometimes included coresidence, intermarriage, and intensive interchanges of labor and food. Decidedly marginalized, relict hunter-gatherers in Africa have nevertheless experienced a long and influential contact with others over much of Africa and they retain a cultural persona and cultural boundary as hunter-gatherers (Cronk and Dickson 2000). Myths and stories of the hunter-gatherers' invisibility and short stature, and ethnonyms such as *batwa* (meaning "dwarf," "comrade," or "bushman") or *mumbonelekwapi* ("from where did you see me?", or "invisible") are widespread in sub-Saharan Africa (Clark, J. D. 1950–1951; Schadeberg 1999; Vansina 1990).

Central African hunter-gatherers lived *symbiotically* with farming neighbors for centuries, figuratively, as two (albeit unequal) halves of a single society (Grinker 1994). Sometimes, erstwhile foraging communities developed economies that *paralleled* those of their trading partners, with activities complementing or contrasting those of their neighbors sufficiently to ingratiate the two groups to one another. Another way they survived was to become flexible generalists, adapting to the needs of one or more societies engaging in labor, trade, ritual power, and the like. This last way might be called that of the *peripatetic*, peoples who subsist primarily through offering goods and services to the more settled communities they live among, and offering these services opportunistically to whomever may need them at the time, but maintaining endogamy and low status vis-à-vis others (Bollig 1987; Rao 1987). On the East African coast, this included hunters who provided caravans of coastal merchants with ivory and skins destined for the lucrative Indian Ocean trade.

An Instance of Symbiosis

Strategies of symbiosis include co-residence, intermarriage, and intensive exchanges of labor and food with allied farmers. Such relationships apparently have existed for many centuries between Central Africa's hunter-gatherers and their farming neighbors.

The hunter-gatherers of the Central African rain forests include more than twelve ethnic groups of pygmies, including the Efe, Sua, and Asua, and BaMbuti "pygmies" of Congo and the Central African Republic. The pygmy peoples, though a remnant of Later Stone Age inhabitants of the forests, are not related to the Khoisan relict populations of southeast and southern Africa. None of these foraging groups live independently. All are allied to village-dwelling farmers, who today call themselves the Lese, Bira, Baali, Mbo, Mdaaka, Budu, Nande, and others. These groups entered the West African rain forests about 2,000 years ago and the eastern Ituri forest about 1,000 years ago, where they found ancestors of present-day pygmies having been well established in their foraging routines for millennia (Mercader et al. 2000; Mercader and Brooks 2001).

For example, the Efe affiliate themselves with particular villagers as "partners" (Bailey 1991). They spend late June to mid-September in the forest when edible fruits, nuts, and honey are available. They make frequent day trips to Lese villages to trade their honey and meat and to assist in harvesting peanuts. In late September, after honey from the beehives within a band's range has been collected and rivers overflow their bounds the Efe camp near the villages, where women work in the gardens and men hunt. During the January to March dry season, the Efe reenter the forest to hunt. From April to June, the cultivated food is running low, and wild foods are not yet ripe; it is a famine period for both groups. Interestingly the agriculturists suffer more since they cannot transfer their village affiliations or collect in the forests like the Pygmies. The result for the Efe is a stylized annual round, synchronized to the periodicity of artificial and natural pulses and bound by symbolic linkages that underscore the compatibility of the two groups and their differing subsistence activities (Grinker 1994).

Throughout the twentieth century, the growth of farming populations relegated the resident hunter-gatherers to a minority status in the rain forests. Nevertheless, because of their complementary economic, social, and symbolic behavior, farmers and hunters alike believe themselves to be two halves of the same society (Grinker 1994; Turnbull 1965). Only their differing primary food-getting behaviors distinguish them.

The economic effort of forager and farmer is purposefully as different as possible. Each group's activities complement the other's. The symbiosis of these groups is further emphasized in the structuring of their relations. It is neither a simple market arrangement nor one enforced by a patron on a client. Involvement in economic and social ties requires Efe foragers and Lese farmers to become partners engaged in mutual exchanges (Grinker 1994). In Central Africa, the hunter-gatherer groups are organized along patrilineal lines, with each patriline linked to a particular village where partnerships are commonly established. Intermarriage, however, is common. Marriages of forager women to patrilineal farmers threaten the survival of hunter-gatherer bands in general. The "marrying out" of women may have been an important cause of the extinction of the hunter-gatherer lifeway over much of Africa (Bailey 1988).

How long this relationship has existed remains an open question. The relatively late and probably sporadic introduction of farmers to the tropical forest suggests that hunter-gatherers became a minority there fairly recently (Mercader et al. 2000). Hunter-gatherer encampments were discovered at Makubasi, as well as other cave sites, in the granite massif of the Ituri forest, associated with stone tools, and, later, iron tools, as well as pottery (Mercader et al. 2000). Comparison of early hunter-gatherer pottery of 1,000 years ago with that of recent farmers indicates a stylistic continuity and similarities in firing methods. It is suggested that interaction between the two has taken place for at least a millennium and that they shared not only foods but also technology over that time merging the two communities into a successful long-term lifestyle.

An Instance of Parallelism

Hunter-gatherer groups sometimes develop technologies and social forms that mimic those of nearby food producers, allowing interaction with them as component segments, while at the same time maintaining distinct cultural personae. The Okiek and other *Wandorobo* in Kenya were restricted to ecological situations too marginal to allow the keeping of cattle, especially mountaintops. Here, they hunted small mammals and husbanded, collected, and traded honey to the Masai and Nandi, thereby establishing an economic relationship with their pastoralist neighbors (Chang 1982; Blackburn 1982). Typically, the Okiek speak Maa, the language of the Masai in commerce with them, but use their own language among themselves. To facilitate the exchange of their honey for products made by the Masai, the Okiek imitate pastoralist institutions, taking on the clan names, age sets, circumcision ritual, and patrilineal kinship of their trading partners. In adopting the age set and clan system of the Masai, the Okiek defined ties of fictive kinship underlying serious exchange relationships. Every male Okiek had at least one trade partnership with a Masai man of the same clan and age set (Blackburn 1982). The mimicry of Masai institutions even penetrated the idea of private property. The beehives were deemed lineage property passed down from generation to generation, in the same way that Masai inherit cattle. The concept of "private" property is usually outside the hunter-gatherer repertoire, while here it assists in maintaining a structural parallel to an institution of the dominant society while retaining a separate ethnic foraging identity. The relationship, though not as close as that exhibited by the pygmies and their farming allies, did allow the creation of parallel institutions as a way of integrating them into the segmentary system of the pastoralists.

An Instance of the Peripatetic Way

The pygmies were profoundly integrated into economic and social arrangements with their farmer allies, so much so that the disparate groups tacitly formed a single social community. The *Wandorobo*, on the other hand, though providing a similar range of services, affixed themselves to their allies through economic alliances, reinforced by tactically imitating significant social attributes of the farmers. In both cases, a distinct ethnic identity as hunter-gatherers was retained. The Waata, too, retain a specific ethnic identity distinct from the pastoralists and farmers who share their territory. Like other such marginalized groups, they have adopted some customs and language from those they interact with. Unlike either the pygmies or the *Wandorobo*, the Waata, though beholden to pastoralist overlords and required to pay bounties in the form of ivory for the right to hunt the elephant herds "commercially," are otherwise independent, managing flexible economies and attuned to meeting the needs of others, offering their services at one time to the farmers, at others to the pastoralists, and at others to merchant proprietors managing the transfer of hides and ivory to the Swahili coast. They provided these groups with a variety of goods and services, including ivory and other bush products, farm labor, and crafts. At the same time, they were almost always an untouchable caste, forbidden to intermarry into the higher status groups they served. In this way, achieving opportunistic benefit, working with contingencies, and meeting the needs of others through exchanges, they manage to live in the interstices between and among established societies. To the others, they are part of the landscape, rather than acknowledged partners. So unobtrusive are they that even anthropologists never bothered to determine what they called themselves. As a result they appear in the literature under a variety of names (Stiles 1981:848).

The characterization of peripatetic hunter-gatherers is made difficult by their low social status, shifting identities, and a consequent low anthropological "visibility" (Bollig 1987). They are a very poorly studied group. However, there seem to be at least three distinct cultural groups of East African coastal hunters. The Kenya Boni inhabit tsetse-infested forest unsuitable for agriculture in the hinterland of the East African coast and the Dahalo and the Waata who live in a sparsely populated desert somewhat further inland from the coast. All speak Cushitic dialects (Stiles 1981:848). They have a varied set of alliances with their neighbors, Eastern Cushitic-speaking pastoralists and Bantu agriculturists. In all cases, the hunters occupy a very low status: contact with them is believed to be polluting and communal residence or intermarriage forbidden. It was believed that hunters ate low-status food, such as pig, porcupine, and reptile, leading to one of their ethnonyms, the *waliankuru*. However, they made themselves useful to all these neighboring groups, supplying ivory to the coastal trade. In return for this source of wealth, the hunters received pastoral products and immunity from attack by the Masai (Hobley 1895, 1912, 1929). At the same time, involvement with dominating societies was very limiting to the hunters, who were forbidden from owning cattle or assimilating into the pastoral societies.

Hunters provided neighboring farmers with bush products, field labor, wild gum and rubber, and craft items (Stiles 1981:854–855). They used commerce to add to their worth, dealing in iron or wooden objects as the ivory trade waxed and waned. The Boni, skilled woodworkers, traded wooden objects, rope, water lily bulbs, and gourd containers for milk products, goats, or money. Some, like the forest Boni, farmed from time to time, although their harvests were only occasionally successful. A Waata seasonal round was defined for the most part by the host society; they work for them in good times, but withdraw to foraging when drought or disease strikes the cattle (Bollig 1987). The Boran of Ethiopia engaged in hunting, woodcutting, skin tanning, pottery production, ritual services, and grave digging, and assumed the role of executioner (Haberland 1963; Straube 1963). Today, the Waata guard the gardens of the Pokomo of the Tana River, make palm wine, and continue to hunt and gather southeast of the Taita Hills (Bollig 1987:207; C. Kusimba and S. Kusimba 1998–2000).

The cultural ambiguity of the relationship of peripatetics to the people they live among is exemplified by the attitude of the Gabbra to the Waata. The Waata are an indispensable part of Gabbra ritual, participating in almost all life-cycle ceremonies: birth, death, marriage, and generation transition rites, and performing circumcision and infibulations (Haberland 1963:150). At the same time, they are held in contempt for breaking food taboos, being irreligious, or destroying fertility, and pursuing a life "outside culture." The Waata are truly Africa's gypsies, dependent on the economic choices and whims of others, living a life their hosts find contemptible, yet enjoying their independence. At the same time, the economic and social pliancy of the Waata, doing a lot of things for a variety of people, fits them into the highly stratified societies, like the Oromo or the Swahili, as a kind of "untouchable" caste. As a result, they are still there today.

Summing Up

What caused hunter-gatherer groups to choose one or the other of these three strategies of persistence? For that matter how much is known about the interaction between foragers and their neighbors during the past century, much less the distant past? Anthropology has observed and recorded some of the ways that hunter-gatherers related to others. Some investigators have even attempted to reconstruct the meeting of these disparate cultures in eastern and southern Africa sometime in the fourth or fifth century (for example Miller 1969). Rock art in the Matopo Hills depicting herdsmen and their cattle, if we attribute it to hunter-gatherers, shows the hunters knew that their territories were filling with others. It is apparent, also, that sometimes these two communities may have had little in common and little contact; they remained estranged across frontiers in many areas (Thorp 1997). If this was the case, then the history of contact and the process of adopting relationships with food producers occurred, perhaps, in a climate of duress. We have indicated the effect on food procurement and the constraints placed on acquiring the large, mobile game hunters still sought in many areas.

In the ethnographic cases we examined, social relationships tend to work to the disadvantage of less numerous and politically weaker hunter-gatherers. The hunter-gatherer populations have tended to be reduced to clients of their more numerous, prosperous, and powerful neighbors, or marginalized to the least tempting pieces of real estate that food producers find inadequate for their operations and that serve the foragers poorly. It would seem that we answer the questions that open this chapter simply; hunter-gatherers, historically, have been opportunistic, striving to find low-cost solutions to environmental problems. In the case of symbiosis, parallelism, and a peripatetic course, they manage to survive as cultural entities, with their own ways and history. They may have adapted to new social environments, but they remain culturally distinct. We can still observe them as hunter-gatherers. As said earlier, revisionist debates attempted to determine whether the end product of millennia of contact with "foreign" colonists, Cushitic-speaking pastoralists, Bantu-speaking farmers, Swahili traders, and Europeans were still reliable models of prehistoric hunter-gatherer behaviors. That debate blends into this one, concerning the historical reconstruction of latter-day foraging peoples.

On the one hand, some argue that foragers existed as relict hunters on the fringes of food-producing societies ever since the inception of these food-getting strategies. Embedded in this idea is the contention that for the greater part of history adherents of these different economies had little cultural contact and less influence on one another. In which case, their relationships with food producers are relatively recent and have not strongly affected their cultures. Alternatively, others counter that hunting and gathering peoples have had a long and complex interrelationship with food producers for many millennia and that many features of their current lifeways are the product of that interaction (Headland and Reid 1989; Schrire 1980). Some even have argued that many groups now pursuing a hunter-gatherer existence were once, if only part-time, farmers or pastoralists, sometime in the past (Wilmsen 1989:94, 99).

In some cases, the ancestries of people who today practice hunter-gathering have been questioned. The pygmy populations of the Central African rain forests seem to be remnants of earlier Later Stone Age hunter-gatherers, who now live in intense symbiosis with neighboring farmers. However, it has been put forward that they could not have survived in the rain forest before attaining access to farmed foods. In other words, their arrival in the rain forest accompanied the influx of food producers; and any sustained occupation required continued reliance on the farmer's produce (Bailey et al. 1989). The symbiotic relationship enlarged the range of these foraging folk, widening opportunities for retaining a distinct cultural identity and for living, as they do, both as a part of a host culture and separate from it. Resolution of this contention started an inquiry into the quality of the plant and animal foods available in the forest (Bahuchet, McKay, and de Garine 1991; Colinvaux 1991). If, as many investigators contend, the rain forest is rich in plant and animal foods, then some time in the past, the Pygmy foragers chose a symbiotic lifeway rather than being forced into one. The history of hunter-gatherer occupancy of the rain forest appears to have a considerable time depth (Eggert 1993; Kipnis 1998; Mercader and Brooks 2001). Foragers were, apparently, well established there when they met the first farmers; apparently they saw the virtue of tapping into an alternative food source.

The forest dwellers adapted successfully to an invasion of their territory by others. In other cases, the history of today's foragers is more disputed. Some believe the Okiek established their relationship with the Maa-speaking Masai pastoralists after having been disenfranchised as farmers and pastoralists (Chang 1982:271). The majority of historians and ethnographers, however, seem to believe they are largely autochthonous. In an extreme situation, they found a reasonable way to survive while retaining their cultural persona, imitating assimilation of characteristic features of the dominant culture. In this way, they became acceptable to the others, persisting as a distinct group, with special functions in the alliance. This (as well as symbiosis) was also a strategy conducive to extinguishing cultural identity, as they assimilated more and more of the dominant culture.

Archaeology and history try to illuminate the different pathways taken in order to persist, detecting changes in technology and interaction necessary for some groups to stay viable, yet still associate with others. Some hunter-gatherer groups were pushed quietly into extinction. Parallel and symbiotic relationships often disguise "poison pills" drawing foragers into absorption and cultural extinction. Pygmy groups, often, lose personnel to intermarriage with their neighbors; generations are lost, effectively snuffing out some bands (Bailey 1988). The foragers' quandary is one of persisting, with a separate cultural identity, in the face of a dominant culture and an altered ecological situation. A one-time *Wandorobo*, the Mukogodo (or Yatta) in Central Kenya made the transition to pastoralism during the twentieth century. A brief review of their history demonstrates the hazards, as well as purported benefits, of parallelism as a way toward viable interaction. Until the 1930s, the Mukogodo inhabited caves in Kenya's central highlands, where they husbanded bees for trade with Maa-speaking neighbors, whose language they adopted. Hunting territories and beehives were owned by patrilines and beehives used as bridewealth. Early in the twentieth century, living in highland forest, they hunted mostly small animals such as hyrax and small antelope, kept beehives, and modeled their social organization on the lineages and clans of neighboring pastoralists (Mutundu 1999). They acquired domestic sheep and goats and eventually cattle as bridewealth, solidifying trade and creating even more desire for the marriages of their daughters into Masai patrilineal society. As a result, the Mukogodo gained wealth as the proprietors of cattle while losing title to their daughters' progeny. This state of affairs eventually led to the Mukogodo's transition to full-time food production (Cronk 1989) and to being absorbed into the pastoralist groups they cooperated with.

Other foragers, on the other hand, adopted a "gypsy-like" existence, assuring survival as a low caste but as a critical component of the more dominant societies they lived among. Gaining reputation through significant rituals, they created a unique, somewhat protected and arcane place in their host societies. As a result, some live on to the present day, though whether as Cushitic-speaking descendants of Later Stone Age groups or as a people persuaded into the forager lifeway by circumstances and powerful neighbors is yet to be determined.

Having said this, one must confess to being leery of pigeonholing any one group or another into any of these categories of persistence. The processes are evident, but so too are the very complex histories of some groups. The San, for example, seem to have followed a *parallel* course sometime in the past. Losing contact with the food producers they engaged, some were marginalized to the Kalahari, where they sometimes find recourse to a peripatetic existence, working for the more numerous and prosperous folk who surround them. During the reign of the Tswana in the eighteenth and nineteenth centuries, their relationship with cattle-keepers was as the Waata and Galla. Forced to give ivory and skins to their overlords, they clearly had a lowly social status (Wilmsen 1989). At the same time, we have the present-day example of them pursuing a somewhat customary hunter-gatherer existence in the desert wastes of the Kalahari. In many ways, the recent history of tropical Africa's hunter-gatherers is as obscure as their Pleistocene beginnings.

Though there is now a common understanding, supported by archaeology, that the hunter-gatherers of the Congo rain forest are remnants of preexistent forest populations, their close physical similarity to the others they interact with suggested that they were an offspring of that population, lately moved into forested areas under duress. We have seen the reasoning countering this plausible explanation. The debate over the history and cultural and physical identity of groups like the Congo hunter-gatherers highlights the paucity of reliable information, archaeological as well as historical, on hunter-gatherers since the introduction of food-producing regimes in subtropical Africa, and the origins of present-day groups of hunter-gatherers. It is obvious that a few are the remnants of Later Stone Age cultural groups and that others adopted this way of life as a strategy of persistence.

Unlike the Congo foragers, the Khoisan peoples of southern Africa are as a group physically distinct from neighboring food producers. They also exhibit continuity to Later Stone Age hunter-gatherers, a lineage that runs through the Wilton and related groups all the way back to the Middle Stone Age inhabitants of the south. Yet, even this genealogy is insecure when relating present-day foragers of the Kalahari, who apparently have been food producers from time to time in the past.

That there is a debate at all is itself a powerful testament to a woeful lack of information about hunter-gatherers and hunting and gathering as an alternative economic strategy at a time when many others invented or adopted food production as their chief means of sustenance. There is a tendency in history and archaeology to a kind of implicit progressivism, focusing on the most complex phenomenon available at any one time as the most important. This relegated hunter-gatherer studies to the margins of the discussion on the origins of food production, implying, as nineteenth-century thinkers had, that foragers were an interesting evolutionary step, but one surpassed by superior food-getting technologies. Even those with a specific interest in hunter-gatherer studies have deliberately sought out the history of the most pristine or isolated cases, while those living in symbiosis or as clients of food-producing societies have received far less attention. Only recently have debates over origins and history caused us to look at more recent foraging.

By far the most visible debate surrounding hunter-gatherer history is that of the Ju/'hoansi case, because as an empirical model they figure so prominently in current thinking about hunter-gatherers. If the features of their way of life are merely a product of recent interaction, then as a source of ethnographic analogy for archaeology these ethnographies can be questioned. By the same token, it can be argued that even if these Kalahari foragers do not retain an unblemished genealogy of "Paleolithic" behavior, the way they conduct themselves as hunter-gatherers may exemplify the manner and mode of earlier hunter cultural behavior. One may argue that they are attempting to solve ecological problems akin to those of Pleistocene hunters; therefore, their approach ought to reconstruct those of their predecessors. Having foregone the implication of a pristine descent we can still use the circumstances of modern groups to plausibly model the recent past.

Let us consider the case of Ju/'hoansi *hxaro*, a classic example of hunter-gatherers in a desert living as small, dispersed groups using far-reaching exchange networks to create a web of kinship and social obligation (Wiessner 1982a, 1986). The adaptive advantages of *hxaro* exchanges are well known, serving to explain how reciprocal relationships are fostered, maintained, and inherited through time, and how these reciprocal relationships provide a basis for visiting, marriage, and resource sharing, while distributing risk among far-flung band-level societies. It has been a productive source of ethnographic analogy in African archaeology (Mitchell 1996; Wadley 1993).

The *hxaro* exchanges create linkages that sometimes go far beyond a visiting, or pooled risk, circle of partners. These exchanges sometimes extend along *nama cheesi*, or paths for things, networks that can extend over several hundred kilometers and connect several hundred persons. Such a path is made up of many smaller segments of between five and eight people who know one another (Wiessner 1994). Most of the visiting, marriages, and so on enabled by *hxaro* take place within these smaller segments. So why are the *nama cheesi* so long? It is difficult to visualize the need for so complex a system under ordinary circumstances of life in the desert. However, *hxaro* systems may be a product of Iron Age interaction, developed to provide access to trade items after pastoralists and farmers began colonizing the Kalahari (Wiessner 1994). If this is the case, then Kalahari exchange networks have a recent origin, reflecting an adaptation to neighboring groups rather than a reflection of some ancient social behaviors. In any event, gift exchanges of the *hxaro* sort, marking the reciprocal relationships between foragers, occur very rarely. In fact, this sort of system exists only among the Ju/'hoansi and Nharo.

The geographical reach of individual *nama cheesi* interaction spheres grew as a function of their role as pathways, bringing valuable goods—metal, glass beads, tobacco, and pottery—into the Kalahari from major trade centers beyond the San areas (Wiessner 1994:118). Continued attention to maintaining these pathways was necessitated by the critical nature of participation in the cross-Kalahari trade, using its connectivity to ease access to critical material circulation, facilitating a transition to, and life in, the desert. Reciprocities are a fact of life in rural Africa today, where even a casual gift obligates a response. That extensive interaction spheres were required in the vast expanses of the Kalahari is self-evident. That local exchange arrangements, of the *hxaro* type, could date back to Middle Stone Age hunter-gatherers is not only self-evident but also supported by the archaeology of transported stone, shared technology, and the like. The *nama cheesi* networks extended a noncapital obligation of reciprocity over a broad area, essentially adapting an established mode of material transfers to changed conditions.

But the circumstances of post-Neolithic hunter-gatherers required, as we have seen, more than an ability to adapt specific cultural features to new circumstances; they also needed accommodation to new people and novel means of food-getting and social strategies. Archaeology and history have examined the Ju/'hoansi case in order to determine the present situation as either a result of their isolation from, or involvement with, others. In the first instance, we could explain behaviors of Kalahari hunters as a highly adapted version of traditional ones; in the second that they are the result of interaction with others. These positions are not only poles apart but also ones capable of synthesis; the complex origins of these people can be rationalized as sets of adaptive behavior reacting to a wide range of cultural influences, some inherited and others acquired. All our sources suggest that the Kalahari was witness to the impact of pastoralism, the development of stratified chiefdoms based on wealth, reckoned in heads of cattle and the growth of wide-ranging trading combines. The extent of the hunter-gatherers involvement with these herdsmen, chiefs, and traders is a subject of debate. Apparently, the San became subservient clients of herders and farmers sometime in the sixteenth century, when the Tswana colonized the region, exacting tribute from hunter-gatherers and preventing them from owning property (Vierich 1982:218). In a sense, these immigrant landlords dominated the San, making them into serfs (Schrire 1980; Wilmsen 1989). According to Wilmsen, though, the San had been earlier entrepreneurs, supplying ivory, gold, and game skins to seventh- to twelfth-century trading settlements at Divuyu, Nqoma, and Toutswe that were involved in networks that extended to Indian Ocean trading ports. These villages relied on the San to provide trade goods such as salt, ivory, game, ores, and skins, as well as labor, for which, in return, they received payment in grains, cows, metal, and pottery (Wilmsen 1989:70–72). During this period, the San were cattle owners, and, during the nineteenth century, they were involved in hunting elephant and ostrich for the ivory and feather trade. According to this reading of history, Kalahari hunter-gatherers became locked into foraging only recently, following their disenfranchisement at the hands of the Tswana and colonial settlers. This reconstruction of the past, supported by archaeology, implies that interaction between hunters and herders goes back 1,200 years (Wilmsen and Denbow 1990).

However, some have argued that some San, in fact, were isolated or essentially unchanged by the development of trade, complexity, and colonialism in southern Africa (Solway and Lee 1990; Lee and Guenther 1991). It has even been posited that some in the very dry sandveld of the western Kalahari had no significant contact with pastoralists until the nineteenth century (Smith and Lee 1997; Yellen and Brooks 1989). This contention, too, seems supported by archaeology. There is no apparent change in the character of the Kalahari Later Stone Age throughout this period, except for some small amounts of pottery. Hunter-gatherers are known to have possessed ceramics and iron, as products of trade, curation, or even their own handiwork (Musonda 1989; Mazel 1992; Mercader et al. 2001). To some archaeologists, the San had little or no involvement with Iron Age communities moving into their areas, after the fifth century A.D., or with the more complex societies and mercantile economies of the last thousand years that followed soon thereafter (Sadr 1997; Yellen and Brooks 1989). Apparently, the San, or at least some of those identified in the archaeology, lived as traditional hunter-gatherers, apart from others, free of foreign influence, but also in relative economic impoverishment throughout most of the second millennium.

On the face of it, we appear to have a quandary. One derived from the nature of the palimpsest left by the past, the emphasis we place on the material remains that make it up, or our reading of it. This is neither

the time nor the place to dissect, much less explain, archaeological in-
terpretative theory. The debate outlined here tends only to highlight
how elusive our grasp of the past can be when we try to pinpoint the
history of nonliterate peoples. Some San may have interacted with local
pastoralists or farmers; others may not have. Some may have participated in commercial undertakings that reached the Indian Ocean trade;
others may not have. Some may have made pottery, some may have
traded for it and iron tools; others may not have, and so forth. In attempting to conflate the past to fit a particular case, we may be short-
changing the very people we are attempting to comprehend. At the
same time, interpretive debates should, and need to be, resolved, since
archaeology may be our only source of information on the lifeways of
foragers, and the practice of foraging, following the coming of food production. However, it is the process of *resolution*, our understanding the
intricacies of the palimpsest we are reading, that creates our quandary.

Often it is difficult to identify the behaviors of hunter-gatherers
and the food producers, merchants, and others with whom they interacted. Nevertheless, apparently arcane debates over the proportion of
worked stone or wild animal bone to foreign-made objects or evidence
of domestic stock illuminate pathways toward understanding how
hunter-gatherers managed to persist in an increasingly strange world
run by others. How do we recognize evidence of significant, as opposed to circumstantial, interaction (Bollong and Sampson 1999)? A
hunter crossing an abandoned hamlet picking up a useful pottery
sherd is operating as an archaeologist, curating the fragment for some
future personal use. Discovery of the sherd among a hunter's toolkit
points toward a proximity to pottery makers, but not necessarily to real
interaction. Similarly, domestic stock hunted or poached could leave
the same sort of faunal evidence as food animals gotten through exchange. The examples of archaeological interpretation are endless and
reliant on context; farmers hunt and hunters make pottery. Earlier, we
discussed transported stone as evidence of interaction spheres; geology
was proof of origin and the distances traveled. One could rationalize
the means of transport. The ubiquity of *hxaro* and *nama cheesi* imply the
transport of things over long distances with no face-to-face interaction
between the producers and the end-users. Yet, found in ancient assemblages they may be evidence of extended contact, circumstantial contact, or no contact whatsoever. For example, ostrich eggshell beads
have been found in villages in the Victoria Falls region, a long way
from the nearest ostriches, or ostrich-hunters for that matter (Vogel,
personal communication). Obviously, the beads, or the shell, came
from sources south of the Zambezi and suggest far-ranging trade net-

works; what they do not indicate is meaningful interaction between two disparate groups. How the shell was obtained in the first place and became part of the exchange network of Early Iron Age farmers can only be speculated on. Herein lies the crux of our quandary. We wish to know the fate of the Later Stone Age hunter-gatherer, and the archaeology is often not as clear-cut as we would wish. This is not to disparage any of the effort expended on the San, or any other problem, but to suggest how very difficult it is to work backward from a living group in order to identify not only its predecessors but also the sometimes ephemeral interactions they may have had with others.

Differentiating a farming hamlet from a forager's camp is relatively straightforward. Their material remnants are demonstrably different. Often, though, it is difficult to distinguish between the encampments of hunters and pastoralists. It is even difficult to speculate about hunter and pastoralist interactions in many cases, particularly if there are only minimal signs of pottery or domestic cattle, which seems to be the case at the Kalahari sites (Yellen and Brooks 1989; Sadr 1997).

In the southwestern Cape, Khoikhoi herder and San hunter sites are differentiated on the basis of the relative proportions of wild to domestic food plant remains, the relative frequency of formal worked stone tools, pottery usage, and the size of ostrich eggshell beads (Smith, Sadr, Gribble, and Yates 1991). The case can be easily made that the patent demarcation of their settlements indicates separate ways of life, maintained over the past 1,400 years since domestic animals were first brought into the area. However, a technical case could be made that given the wide variation in bead size and relative proportion of domestic to wild fauna remains found at these sites, any sort of definite attribution to either herder or hunter settlement is difficult to make (Schrire 1992; Wadley 2001). The point to all this is that we have evidence of two contemporary but contrasting food-getting regimes in the area; however, we have nothing to associate them into a relationship that we could pinpoint as interactive or allied in ways similar to the ethnographic cases cited above. Apparently, the erstwhile Later Stone Age foraging populations of southern Africa went their separate ways; some as herdsmen, while others pursued their traditional foraging habits. One or the other, or some of both of these populations were ancestors of the San. This may have a relevance to the question of the purity of their credentials as models of Pleistocene behavior; but it also returns us to our basic assertion of hunter-gatherers as adaptive and opportunistic, as able to make their way in the world and able to maintain their distinctive way of life and cultural identity while living alongside others.

The earliest hominids in eastern Africa engaged in a variety of "social" and "scavenging" habits that were soon to be refined into the behaviors we attribute to a predecessor like *Homo ergaster*, behaviors that would lend order to their lifeway, imposing social responsibility on relationships of reciprocity and the care of the young and elderly. In time, the simple requirements imposed on nuclear family bands expanded to include the political orchestration of extra-community marriage, building new nuclear families, bridging space, and access to necessities through human chains linking kindreds, environments, and resources. These interaction spheres permitted exchanges of vital information and essential material circulation. New forms of humanity evolved, taking advantage of novel technologies to spread mankind into the varied environments of Africa.

Without looking back on the whole of human history, we can say that the hunter-gatherer way of life was an efficient organization, preserving valuable ecological knowledge and educating new generations, while mediating the basic, psychological needs of its members. In time, human technologies adapted to confront Earth's varied environmental mosaic, progressing from the most simple kinds of worked stone edge to more elaborate and efficient compound tools, using little stone, adding planning to the preparation and maintenance of critical implements. The advanced hunter knew the ways of his prey, and looked forward to its periodic appearances in the landscape in the same way that collectors gauged the seasons and their produce. Out of their routine familiarity with the natural world grew a new set of practices we recognize as food production. This process started with the husbanding of food animals, shifting them from one well-watered place to another for grazing, and came to include the cultivation of cereals. Cultivation originally increased the reliability and yield of food and led, in some cases, to domesticated plant foods and regulated food supplies as well as permanent settlements and centralizing political institutions. Yet, the hunter-gatherer persisted, not as a relict society but as an alternative lifeway. In this adaptive form, hunter-gatherers insinuated themselves into the sphere of the farmer and herdsman, drawing sustenance from a novel food source. Though their status may be marginalized, or socially dubious, they survived into the present day, their way of life as opportunistic today as it was a million years ago, when we began our journey from the open plains of East Africa.

Appendix: Stone Artifacts in the Howieson's Poort Levels at Nelson Bay Cave

Howieson's Poort assemblage Level 1: Mostly backed pieces on quartzite

Level One	quartzite	quartz	silcrete	chert	Total
scraper	38	2	3	4	47
backed	70	4	2	1	77
burin	1	0	0	0	1
notch	7	0	1	0	8
tool fragments	10	1	1	2	14
Total	126	7	7	7	147

Howieson's Poort assemblage Level 2: Mostly scrapers, some backed pieces on quartzite

Level Two	quartzite	silcrete	chert	Total
scraper	33	0	0	33
backed	10	1	1	12
burin	3	0	0	3
borer	2	0	0	2
blade	1	0	0	1
tool fragments	0	1	0	1
notch	0	0	2	2
Total	49	2	3	54

Howieson's Poort assemblage Level 3: Mostly scrapers, some backed pieces on quartzite

Level Three	quartzite	quartz	silcrete	chert	Total
scraper	5	2	1	0	8
backed	1	2	1	0	4
burin	0	0	0	0	0
bec	0	0	1	0	1
misc. mod	0	0	1	0	1
tool fragments	10	0	0	3	13
Total	16	4	4	3	27

Howieson's Poort assemblage Level 4: Mostly scrapers, some backed pieces on quartzite

Level Four	quartzite	quartz	silcrete	chert	Total
scraper	4	0	0	1	5
backed	2	0	1	1	4
ret blade	2	0	0	0	2
notch		0	1	0	1
tool fragments	1	0	2	2	5
Total	9	0	4	4	17

Howieson's Poort assemblage Level 5: Mostly backed pieces on nonquartzite raw materials

Level Five	quartzite	quartz	silcrete	chert	Total
scraper	1	1	2	3	7
backed	0	1	10	2	13
casual trim	0	2	0	0	2
tool fragments	0	0	0	0	0
Total	1	4	12	5	22

Howieson's Poort assemblage Level 6: Mostly backed pieces on nonquartzite raw materials

Level Six	quartzite	quartz	silcrete	chert	Total
scraper	1	0	2	0	3
backed	5	4	3	7	19
tool fragments	1	0	3	0	4
Total	7	4	8	7	26

Howieson's Poort assemblage Level 7: Mostly scrapers, some backed pieces on quartzite

Level Seven	quartzite	quartz	silcrete	chert	Total
scraper	30	1	1	0	32
backed	23	1	3	5	32
burin	2	0	0	0	2
Total	55	2	4	5	66

Howieson's Poort assemblage Level 8: Mostly scrapers, two pieces on quartzite

Level Eight	quartzite	Total nonquartzite	Total
scraper	20	2	22
backed	1	0	1
burin	2	0	2
Total	23	2	25

Howieson's Poort assemblage Level 9: Mostly scrapers

Level Nine	quartzite	Total
scraper	9	9
Total	9	9

Howieson's Poort assemblage Level 10

Level Ten	quartzite	Total
scraper	5	5
backed	1	1
Total	6	6

References

Adams, J. M., and H. Faure. 1997. QEN Review and Atlas of Palaeovegetation: Preliminary Land Ecosystem Maps of the World since the Last Glacial Maximum. Oak Ridge National Laboratory, Tenn., USA. www.esd.ornl.gov/projects/qen/adams1.html.

Alvard, M. S. 1993. Testing the Ecologically Noble Savage Hypothesis: Interspecific Prey Choice by Piro Hunters of Amazonian Peru. *Human Ecology* 21:355–387.

Amblard, S., and J. Pernes. 1989. The Identification of Cultivated Pearl Millet (*Pennisetum*) amongst Plant Impressions on Pottery from Oued Chebbi (Dhar Oualata, Mauritania). *African Archaeological Review* 7:117–126.

Ambrose, S. H. 1986. Hunter-Gatherer Adaptations to Non-Marginal Environments: An Ecological and Archaeological Assessment of the Dorobo Model. *Sprache und Geschichte in Afrika* 7:11–42.

———. 1998. Chronology of the Later Stone Age and Food Production in East Africa. *Journal of Archaeological Science* 25:377–392.

———. 2001. Paleolithic Technology and Human Evolution. *Science* 291:1748–1753.

Ambrose, S. H., and K. Lorenz. 1990. Social and Ecological Models for the Middle Stone Age of South Africa. In *The Emergence of Modern Humans: An Archaeological Perspective*. P. Mellars, ed. Pp. 3–33. Edinburgh: Edinburgh University Press.

Andrevsky, W. 1994. Raw Material Availability and the Organization of Technology. *American Antiquity* 59:21–34.

Asfaw, B., T. White, O. Lovejoy, B. Latimer, S. Simpson, and G. Suwa. 1999. *Australopithecus garhi*: A New Species of Early Hominid from Ethiopia. *Science* 284:629–635.

Aucour, A.-M., C. Hillaire-Marcel, and R. Bonnefille. 1994. Late Quaternary Biomass Changes from ^{13}C Measurements in a Highland Peatbog from Equatorial Africa (Burundi). *Quaternary Research* 41:225–233.

———. 1995. Physical Environment and Site Choice in South Africa. *Journal of Archaeological Science*:343–353.

Avital, E., and E. Jablonka. 2000. *Animal Traditions: Behavioral Inheritance in Evolution*. Cambridge: Cambridge University Press.

Bahuchet, S. 1990a. The Aka Pygmies: Hunting and Gathering in the Lobaye Forest. In *Food and Nutrition in the African Rain Forest*. C. M. Hladik, S. Bahuchet, and I. De Garine, eds. Pp. 19–23. Paris: UNESCO.

———. 1990b. Food Sharing among the Pygmies of Central Africa. *African Study Monographs* 11(1):27–53.

Bahuchet, S., D. McKay, and I. de Garine. 1991. Wild Yams Revisited: Is Independence from Agriculture Possible for Rain Forest Hunter-Gatherers? *Human Ecology* 19(2):213–243.

Bailey, B., and R. Aunger. 1989. Net Hunters versus Archers: Variation in Women's Subsistence Strategies in the Ituri Forest. *Human Ecology* 17:273–297.

Bailey, R. C. 1988. The Significance of Hypergyny for Understanding the Subsistence Behavior of Contemporary Hunters and Gatherers. In *Diet and Subsistence: Current Archaeological Perspectives*. B. V. Kennedy and G. M. LeMoine, eds. Pp. 57–65. Calgary: University of Calgary Press.

———. 1991. The Behavioral Ecology of Efe Pygmy Men in the Ituri Forest, Zaire. Anthropological Papers of the Museum of Anthropology, University of Michigan, no. 87.

Bailey, R. C., et al. 1989. Hunting and Gathering in Tropical Rain Forest: Is It Possible? *American Anthropologist* 91:59–82.

Bailey, R., and T. Headland. 1991. The Tropical Rainforest: Is It a Productive Environment for Human Foragers? *Human Ecology* 19:261.

Balikci, A. 1968. The Netsilik Eskimos: Adaptive Processes. In *Man the Hunter*. R. B. Lee and I. De Vore, eds. Pp. 78–82. Chicago: Aldine.

Balter, M. 2002. From a Modern Human's Brow—or Doodling? *Science* 295:247–249.

Bar-Yosef, O., and M. E. Kislev. 1989. Early Farming Communities in the Jordan Valley. In *Foraging and Farming: The Evolution of Plant Exploitation*. D. Harris and G. Hillman, eds. Pp. 632–642. London: Unwin Hyman.

Bar-Yosef, O., and B. Vandermeersch. 1993. Modern Humans in the Levant. *Scientific American* 4:94–100.

Barham, L. 1987. The Bipolar Technique in Southern Africa: A Replication Experiment. *South African Archaeological Bulletin* 42:45–50.

———. 2002. Systematic Pigment Use in the Middle Pleistocene of South-Central Africa. *Current Anthropology* 43:181–190.

Barnard, A. 1992. *Hunters and Herders of Southern Africa: A Comparative Ethnography of the Khoisan Peoples*. Cambridge: Cambridge University Press.

———. 1999. Images of Hunters and Gatherers in European Social Thought. In *The Cambridge Encyclopedia of Hunters and Gatherers*. R. Lee and R. Daly, eds. Pp. 375–383. Cambridge: Cambridge University Press.

Barth, F. 1969. Introduction. In *Ethnic Groups and Boundaries: The Social Organization of Culture Difference*. F. Barth, ed. Pp. 9–38. Prospect Heights, Ill.: Waveland Press.

Barton, R., A. Currant, Y Fernandez-Jalvo, J. C. Finlayson, P. Goldberg, R. Macphail, P. B. Pettit, and C. B. Stringer. 1999. Gilbraltor Neanderthals and Results of Recent Excavations in Gorham's, Vanguard, and Ibex Caves. *Antiquity* 73:13–23.

Barut, S. 1994. Middle and Later Stone Age Lithic Technology and Land Use in East African Savannas. *African Archaeological Review* 12:44–70.

———. 1996. Later Stone Age Obsidian Source Use at Lukenya Hill, Kenya. In *Aspects of African Archaeology*. G. Pwiti and R. Soper, eds. Pp. 303–313. Harare: University of Zimbabwe Publications.

———. 1997. Lithic Raw Material Use at Lukenya Hill, Kenya. Ph.D. diss., University of Illinois. University Microfilms, Ann Arbor.

Basgall, M. 1987. Resource Intensification among Hunter-Gatherers: Acorn Economies in Prehistoric California. In *Research in Economic Anthropology*, Volume 9. Pp. 21–52. Greenwich, Conn.: JAI Press.

Bednarik, R. G. 1994. Art Origins. *Anthropos* 89:169–180.

Bickerton, D. 1992. *Language and Species*. Chicago: University of Chicago Press.

Binford, L. R. 1962. Archaeology as Anthropology. *American Antiquity* 28:217–225.

———. 1972. Model Building, Paradigms, and the Current State of Paleolithic Research. In *An Archaeological Perspective*. S. and R. L. Binford, eds. Pp. 244–294. New York: Seminar Press.

———. 1977. Forty-Seven Trips. In *Stone Tools as Cultural Markers*. R. V. S. Wright, ed. Pp. 24–36. Canberra: Australian Institute of Aboriginal Studies.

———. 1979. Organization and Formation Processes: Looking at Curated Technologies. *Journal of Anthropological Research* 35:255–273.

———. 1980. Willow Smoke and Dogs Tails: Hunter-Gatherer Settlement Systems and Archaeological Site Formation. *American Antiquity* 45:4–20.

———. 1984. Bones of Contention: A Reply to G. Isaac. *American Antiquity* 49:164–167.

———. 1987. Searching for Camps and Missing the Evidence? Another Look at the Lower Paleolithic. In *The Pleistocene Old World: Regional Perspectives*. O. Soffer, ed. Pp. 17–31. New York: Plenum Press.

Binford, L. R., and J. O'Connell. 1984. An Alyawara Day: The Stone Quarry. *Journal of Anthropological Research* 40:406–432.

Binneman, J. 1997. Usewear Traces on Robbery Bladelets from Rose Cottage Cave. *South African Journal of Science* 93:479–482.

Bird, R. 1999. Cooperation and Conflict: The Behavioral Ecology of the Sexual Division of Labor. *Evolutionary Anthropology* 8:65–75.

Bird-David, N. 1992. Beyond "The Hunting and Gathering Mode of Subsistence": Culture-Sensitive Observations on the Nayaka and Other Modern Hunter-Gatherers. *Man* 27:19–44.

———. 1998. Beyond the Original Affluent Society: A Culturalist Reformulation. In *Limited Wants, Unlimited Means: A Reader in Hunter-Gatherer Economics and the Environment.* J. Gowdy, ed. Pp. 115–137. Washington, D.C.: Island Press.

Blackburn, R. 1982. In the Land of Milk and Honey: Okiek Adaptations to their Forests and Neighbors. In *Politics and History in Band Societies.* E. Leacock and R. B. Lee, eds. Pp. 283–305. New York: Cambridge University Press.

Bleed, P. 1986. The Optimal Design of Hunting Weapons. *American Antiquity* 51:737–747.

Blumenschine, R. 1988. An Experimental Model of the Timing of Hominid and Carnivore Influence on Archaeological Bone Assemblages. *Journal of Archaeological Science* 15:483–502.

———. 1995. Percussion Marks, Tooth Marks, and Experimental Determinations of the Timing of Hominid and Carnivore Access to Long Bones at FLK Zinjanthropus, Olduvai Gorge, Tanzania. *Journal of Human Evolution* 29:21–51.

Blumenschine, R., J. A. Cavallo, and S. D. Capaldo. 1994. Competition for Carcasses and Early Hominid Behavioral Ecology: A Case Study and Conceptual Framework. *Journal of Human Evolution* 27:197–213.

Boëda, E. 1988. Le concept laminaire: Rupture et filiation avec le concept Levallois. In *L'Homme de Neanderthal: La Mutation.* Volume 8. J. K. Kozlowski, ed. Pp. 41–59. Liège: Eraul 35, University of Liège.

———. 1991. Approche de la variabilité des systèmes de production lithique des industries dupaleolithice inférieur et moyen: Chronologique d'une variabilité attendée. *Techniques et Cultures* 17–18:37–79.

———. 1993. Le débitage discoide et le débitage levallois recurrent centripète. *Bulletin de la Société Préhistorique Française* 90:392–404.

Boëda, E., J.-M. Geneste, and L. Meignen. 1990. Identification de chaînes opératoires lithiques du paléolithique ancien et moyen. *Paleo* 2:43–79.

Bollig, M. 1987. Ethnic Relations and Spatial Mobility in Africa: A Review of the Peripatetic Niche. In *The Other Nomads: Peripatetic Minorities in Cross-Cultural Perspective.* A. Rao, ed. Pp. 179–228. Kölner Ethnologische Mitteilungen Volume 8. Cologne: Bohlau Verlag.

Bollong, C. A., and C. G. Sampson. 1999. Later Stone Age Herder-Hunter Interactions Reflected in Ceramic Distributions in the Upper Seacow River Valley. *South African Journal of Science* 95(4):171–180.

Bollong, C. A., C. G. Sampson, and A. Smith. 1997. Khoikhoi and Bushman Pottery in the Cape Colony: Ethnohistory and Later Stone Age Ceramics of the South African Interior. *Journal of Anthropological Archaeology* 16:269–299.

Bonnefille, R., and G. Riollet. 1988. The Kashiru Sequence (Burundi): Paleoclimate Implications for the Last 40,000 Years B.P. in Tropical Africa. *Quaternary Research* 30:19–35.

Bonnefille, R., J. Roeland, and J. Gruot. 1990. Temperature and Rainfall Estimates for the Past 40,000 Years in Equatorial Africa. *Nature* 346:347–349.

Bousman, C. B. 1993. Hunter-Gatherer Adaptations, Economic Risk and Tool Design. *Lithic Technology* 18:59–86.

Bower, J. 1995. Early Food Production in Africa. *Evolutionary Anthropology* 4:130–139.

Brain, C. K., and P. Shipman. 1993. The Swartkrans Bone Tools. *Transvaal Museum Monograph* 8:195–215.

Brantingham, P. J., J. Olsen, J. Rech, and A. Krivoshapkin. 2000. Raw Material Quality and Prepared Core Technologies in Northeast Asia. *Journal of Archaeological Science* 27:255–271.

Brauer, G. 1992. Africa's Place in the Evolution of *Homo sapiens*. In *Continuity or Replacement: Controversies in* Homo sapiens *Evolution*. G. Brauer and F. Smith, eds. Pp. 83–98. Rotterdam: A. A. Balkema.

Braun, D. 1986. Midwestern Hopewellian Exchange and Supralocal Interaction. In *Peer Polity Interaction and Socio-political Change*. C. Renfrew and J. Cherry, eds. Pp. 117–126. Cambridge: Cambridge University Press.

Brook, G., D. Burney, and J. Cowart. 1990. Desert paleoenvironmental data from cave speleothems with examples from the Chihuauan, Somali-Chalbi, and Kalahari Deserts. *Paleography, Paleoclimatology, Paleoecology* 76:311-329.

Brook, G. A., K. A. Haberyan, and S. De Filippis. 1991. Evidence of a Shallow Lake at Tsodilo Hills, Botswana 17,500 to 15,000 B.P.: Further Confirmation of a Widespread Late Pleistocene Humid Period in the Kalahari Desert. *Paleoecology of Africa* 22:165–175.

Brooks, A. S. 1984. San Land Use Patterns, Past and Present: Implications for Southern African Prehistory. In *Frontiers: Southern African Archaeology Today*. M. Hall, G. Avery, D. M. Avery, M. L. Wilson, and A. J. B. Humphreys, eds. Pp. 40–52. BAR International Series 207. Oxford: British Archaeological Reports.

———. 1996. Behavior and Human Evolution. In *Contemporary Issues in Human Evolution*. W. E. Meikle, F. C. Howell, and N. G. Jablonski, eds. Pp. 135–166. San Francisco: California Academy of Sciences.

Brooks, A. S., D. M. Helgren, J. M. Cramer, A. Franklin, W. Hornyak, J. M. Keating, R. G. Klein, W. J. Rink, H. P. Schwarcz, J. N. L. Smith, K. Stewart, N. E. Todd, J. Verniers, and J. E. Yellen. 1995. Dating and Context of Three Middle Stone Age Sites with Bone Points in the Upper Semliki Valley, Zaire. *Science* 268:548–553.

Brooks, A. S., and P. Robertshaw. 1990. The Glacial Maximum in Tropical Africa: 22,000–12,000 B.P. In *The World at 18,000 B.P. Volume 2: Low Latitudes*. C. Gamble and O. Soffer, eds. Pp. 120–169. London: Unwin Hyman.

Brown, J. L. 1964. The Evolution of Diversity in Avian Territorial Systems. *Wilson Bulletin* 76:160–169.

Bunn, H., and E. Kroll. 1986. Systematic Butchery by Plio/Pleistocene Hominids at Olduvai Gorge, Tanzania. *Current Anthropology* 27:431–452.

Burch, E. S. 1998. The Future of Hunter-Gatherer Research. In *Limited Wants, Unlimited Means: A Reader in Hunter-Gatherer Economics and the Environment.* J. Gowdy, ed. Pp. 201–217. Washington, D.C.: Island Press.

Butzer, K. W. 1982. Geomorphology and Sediment Stratigraphy. In *The Middle Stone Age at Klasies River Mouth, South Africa.* R. Singer and J. Wymer, eds. Pp. 33–43. Chicago: University of Chicago Press.

Byers, A. M. 1994. Symboling and the Middle-Upper Palaeolithic Transition: A Theoretical and Methodological Critique. *Current Anthropology* 35:369–399.

Cachel, S. 1997. Dietary Shifts and the European Upper Palaeolithic Transition. *Current Anthropology* 38:579–603.

Cachel, S., and J. W. K. Harris. 1996. The Paleobiology of *Homo Erectus*: Implications for Understanding the Adaptive Zone of This Species. In *Aspects of African Archaeology.* G. Pwiti and R. Soper, eds. Pp. 3–11. Harare: University of Zimbabwe Publications.

Carr, P. J., ed. 1994. *The Organization of North American Prehistoric Chipped Stone Tool Technologies.* Archaeological Series 7. Ann Arbor, Mich.: International Monographs in Prehistory.

Casey, J. 2000. *The Kintampo Complex the Late Holocene on the Gambaga Escarpment, Northern Ghana.* Cambridge Monographs in African Archaeology 51. Oxford: Archaeopress.

Cashdan, E. 1983. Territoriality among Human Foragers: Ecological Models and an Application to Four Bushmen Groups. *Current Anthropology* 24:47–66.

———. 1985. Coping with Risk: Reciprocity among the Basarwa of Northern Botswana. *Man* 20:454–474.

Cerulli, E. 1922. *Folk-Literature of the Galla of Southern Abyssinia.* Harvard African Studies 3.

Chang, C. 1982. Nomads without Cattle: East African Foragers in Historical Perspective. In *Politics and History in Band Societies.* E. Leacock and R. Lee, eds. Pp. 269–282. Cambridge: Cambridge University Press.

Clark, D. L. 1976. Mesolithic Europe: The Economic Basis. In *Problems in Economic and Social Archaeology.* G. De G. Sieveking, I. H. Longworth, and K. E. Wilson, eds. Pp. 449–481. London: Duckworth.

Clark, J. D. 1950–1951. A Note on the Pre-Bantu Inhabitants of Northern Rhodesia and Nyasaland. *South African Journal of Science* 47:80–85.

———. 1958. Some Stone Age Woodworking Tools in Southern Africa. *South African Archaeological Bulletin* 13:144–152.

———. 1969. *Kalambo Falls Prehistoric Site.* Cambridge: Cambridge University Press.

———. 1970. *The Prehistory of Africa.* London: Thames and Hudson.

———. 1974. *Kalambo Falls Prehistoric Site II: The Later Prehistoric Cultures.* Cambridge: Cambridge University Press.

——. 1975. Africa in Prehistory: Peripheral or Paramount? *Man* 10:175–198.

——. 1977. Interpretations of Prehistoric Technology from Ancient Egyptian and Other Sources, Part II. *Paléorient* 3:127–150.

——. 1980a. Early Human Occupation of African Savanna Environments. In *Human Ecology in Savanna Environments*. D. R. Harris, ed. Pp. 41–71. London: Academic Press.

——. 1980b. Raw Material and African Lithic Technology. *Man and Environment* 4:44–55.

——. 1984. Old Stone Tools and Recent Knappers: Late Pleistocene Stone Technology and Current Flaking Techniques in the Zaire Basin. *Zimbabwea* 1:8–22.

——. 1988. The Middle Stone Age of Eastern Africa and the Beginnings of Regional Identity. *Journal of World Prehistory* 2:235–305.

——. 1989. The Origin and Spread of Modern Humans: A Broad Perspective on the African Evidence. In *The Human Revolution: Behavioral and Biological Perspectives on the Origin of Modern Humans*. P. Mellars and C. Stringer, eds. Pp. 565–588. Princeton, N.J.: Princeton University Press.

——. 1994. The Acheulean Industrial Complex in Africa and Elsewhere. In *Integrative Paths to the Past*. R. S. Coruccini and R. L. Ciochon, eds. Pp. 597–637. Englewood Cliffs, N.J.: Prentice Hall.

Clark, J., and K. Brown. 2001. The Twin Rivers Kopje, Zambia: Stratigraphy, Fauna, and Artefact Assemblages from the 1954 and 1956 Excavations. *Journal of Archaeological Science* 28:305–330.

Clark, J. D., J. L. Phillips, and P. S. Staley. 1976. Interpretations of Prehistoric Technology from Ancient Egyptian and Other Sources, Part I. *Paléorient* 2:323–388.

Clastres, P. 1972. The Guayaki. In *Hunters and Gatherers Today*. M. B. Bicchieri, ed. Pp. 138–174. New York: Holt, Reinhart, and Winston.

Clist, B. 1999. Traces de très anciennes occupations humaines de la forêt tropicale au Gabon. In *Challenging Elusiveness: Central African Hunter-Gatherers in a Multidisciplinary Perspective*. K. Biesbrouck, S. Elders, and G. Rossel, eds. Pp. 61–74. Leiden, Netherlands: Universiteit Leiden Research School CNWS.

Close, A. 1992. Holocene Occupation of the Eastern Sahara. In *New Light on the Northeast African Past*. F. Klees and R. Kuper, eds. Pp. 155–183. Cologne: Heinrich-Barth-Institut.

——. 1996. Plus Ça Change: The Pleistocene-Holocene Transition in Northeast Africa. In *Humans at the End of the Ice Age: The Archaeology of the Pleistocene-Holocene Transition*. L. Straus, B. Eriksen, J. Erlandson, and D. Yesner, eds. Pp. 43–60. New York: Plenum.

Close, A. E., and C. G. Sampson. 1999. Tanged Arrowheads from Later Stone Age Sites in the Seacow River Valley (South Africa). *South African Archaeological Bulletin* 54(170):81–89.

Clottes, J. 1996. Thematic Changes in Upper Paleolithic Art: A View from the Grotte Chauvet. *Antiquity* 70:276–288.

Clutton-Brock, J. 1997. The Expansion of Domestic Animals in Africa. In *Encyclopedia of Precolonial Africa*. J. O. Vogel, ed. Pp. 418–424. Walnut Creek, Calif.: AltaMira Press.

Coetzee, J. A. 1967. Pollen Analytical Studies in Eastern and Southern Africa. *Paleoecology of Africa* 3:1–146.

Coetzee, J. A., and E. M. Van Zinderen Bakker. 1989. Paleoclimatology of East Africa during the Last Glacial Maximum: A Review of Changing Theories. In *Quaternary and Environmental Research on East African Mountains*. W. C. Mahaney, ed. Pp. 189–198. Rotterdam: A. A. Balkema.

Colinvaux, P. 1991. The Rain-Forest Ecosystem as a Resource for Hunting and Gathering. *American Anthropologist* 93:153–162.

Cooke, C. K. 1984. The Industries of the Upper Pleistocene in Zimbabwe. *Zimbabwea* 1:23–27.

Cornellisen, E. 1997. Central African Transitional Cultures. In *Encyclopedia of Precolonial Africa*. J. Vogel, ed. Pp. 312–332. Walnut Creek, Calif.: AltaMira Press.

Cosgrove, D. 1985. Prospect, Perspective, and the Evolution of the Landscape Idea. *Transactions of the Institute of British Geographers* 10:45–62.

Cotterell, B., and J. Kamminga. 1987. The Formation of Flakes. *American Antiquity* 52:675–708.

Cronk, L. 1989. From Hunters to Herders: Subsistence Change as a Reproductive Strategy among the Mukogodo. *Current Anthropology* 30:224–234.

Cronk, L., and B. Dickson. 2000. Public and Hidden Transcripts in the East African Highlands: A Comment on Smith (1998). *Journal of Anthropological Archaeology* 20:113–121.

Cruz-Uribe, K. 1983. The Mammalian Fauna from Redcliff Cave, Zimbabwe. *South African Archaeological Bulletin* 38:7–16.

d'Errico, F., J. Zilhão, M. Julien, C. Baffier, and J. Pelegrin. 1998. Neanderthal Acculturation in Western Europe? *Current Anthropology* 39:S2–S44.

Damas, D. 1972. The Copper Eskimo. In *Hunters and Gatherers Today*. M. B. Bicchieri, ed. Pp. 3–50. New York: Holt, Reinhart, and Winston.

Dart, R. 1957. The Osteodontokeratic Culture of *Australopithecus prometheus*. *Memoir of the Transvaal Museum* 10.

Davies, N. B. 1978. Ecological Questions about Territorial Behavior. In *Behavioral Ecology: An Evolutionary Approach*. J. R. Krebs and N. B. Davies, eds. Pp. 317–350. Sunderland: Sinauer.

Deacon, H. 1976. *Where Hunters Gathered: A Study of Holocene Stone Age People in the Eastern Cape*. Claremont: South African Archaeological Survey.

———. 1989. Late Pleistocene Paleoecology and Archaeology in the Southern Cape, South Africa. In *The Human Revolution: Behavioral and Biological Perspectives on the Origins of Modern Humans*. P. Mellars and C. Stringer, eds. Pp. 547–564. Edinburgh: Edinburgh University Press.

———. 1993. Planting an Idea: An Archaeology of Stone Age Gatherers in South Africa. *South African Archaeological Bulletin* 48:86–93.

———. 1999. Personal Communication.

Deacon, H., and J. Deacon. 1999. *Human Beginnings in South Africa: Uncovering the Secrets of the Stone Age*. Walnut Creek, Calif.: AltaMira Press.

Deacon, H. J., A. S. Talma, and J. C. Vogel. 1988. Biological and Cultural Development of Pleistocene People in an Old World Southern Continent. In *Early Man in the Southern Hemisphere*. J. R. Prescott, ed. Pp. S23–S31. Adelaide: Department of Physics and Mathematical Physics, University of Adelaide.

Deacon, H., and S. Wurz. 1996. Klasies River Main Site, Cave 2: A Howieson's Poort Occurrence. In *Aspects of African Archaeology*. G. Pwiti and R. Soper, eds. Pp. 213–218. Harare: University of Zimbabwe Publications.

Deacon, J. 1978. Changing Patterns in the Late Pleistocene: Early Holocene Prehistory of Southern Africa as Seen from the Nelson Bay Cave Stone Artifact Sequence. *Quaternary Research* 10:81–111.

———. 1984. Later Stone Age People and Their Descendants in Southern Africa. In *Southern African Prehistory and Paleoenvironments*. R. G. Klein, ed. Pp. 221–328. Rotterdam: A. A. Balkema.

———. 1990. Weaving the Fabric of Stone Age Research in Southern Africa. In *A History of African Archaeology*. P. Robertshaw, ed. Pp. 39–58. London: James Curry.

Deacon, J., and N. Lancaster. 1988. *Late Quaternary Paleoenvironments of Southern Africa*. Oxford: Oxford Science Publications.

Deacon, T. 1997. *The Symbolic Species: The Co-Evolution of Language and the Brain*. New York: Norton.

de Heinzelin, J., J. C. Clark, T. White, W. Hart, P. Renne, G. WoldeGabriel, Y. Beyene, and E. Vrba. 1999. Environment and Behavior of 2.5 Million-Year Old Bouri Hominids. *Science* 284:625–629.

deLaguna, F. 1990. Tlingit. In *The Handbook of North American Indians, Volume 7: The Northwest Coast*. W. Suttles, ed. Pp. 203–228. Washington, D.C.: Smithsonian Institution Press.

deMenocal, P. B. 1995. Plio-Pleistocene African Climate. *Science* 270:53–59.

———. 2001. Cultural Responses to Climate Change during the Late Holocene. *Science* 292:667–673.

deMenocal, P. B., J. Ortiz, T. Guilderson, J. Adkins, M. Sarnthein, L. Baker, and M. Yarusinski. 2000. Abrupt Onset and Termination of the African Humid Period: Rapid Climate Response to Gradual Insolation Forcing. *Quaternary Science Reviews* 19:347–361.

Dibble, H. 1987. The Interpretation of Mousterian Scraper Morphology. *American Antiquity* 52:109–117.

———. 1992. Local Raw Material Exploitation and Its Effects on Lower and Middle Paleolithic Assemblage Variability. In *Raw Material Economies among Prehistoric Hunter-Gatherers*. A. Montet-White and S. Holen, eds. Pp. 33–47. Lawrence: University of Kansas Publications in Anthropology 19.

di Lernia, S. 1997. Cultural Control over Wild Animals during the Early Holocene: The Case of Barbary Sheep in Central Sahara. In *Before Food Production in North Africa*. Savino di Lernia and Giorgio Manzi, eds. Pp. 113–126. Forli: ABACO.

———. 2001. Dismantling Dung: Delayed Use of Food Resources among Early Holocene Foragers of the Libyan Sahara. *Journal of Anthropological Archaeology* 20:408–411.

di Lernia, Savino, and G. Manzi. 1997. *Before Food Production in North Africa*. Forli: ABACO.

Dowson, T. 1996 Re-production and Consumption: The Use of Rock Art Imagery in Southern Africa Today. In *Miscast: Negotiating the Presence of the Bushmen*.

Dwyer, P., and M. Minnegal. 1985. Andaman Islanders, Pygmies, and an Extension of Horn's Model. *Human Ecology* 13:111–120.

Dyson-Hudson, N., and E. Smith. 1978. Human Territoriality: An Ecological Assessment. *American Anthropologist* 80:21–41.

Ebert, J. I. 1992. *Distributional Archaeology*. Albuquerque: University of New Mexico Press.

Edgerton, R. 1992. *Sick Societies: Challenging the Myth of Primitive Harmony*. New York: Free Press.

Eggert, M. 1993. Central Africa and the Archaeology of the Equatorial Rainforest: Reflections on Some Major Topics. In *The Archaeology of Africa: Food, Metals and Towns*. T. Shaw, P. Sinclair, B. Andah, and A. Okpoko, eds. Pp. 289–329. London/New York: Routledge.

Elenga, H., D. Schwartz, and A. Vincens. 1994. Pollen Evidence of Late Quaternary Vegetation and Inferred Climate Change in Congo. *Palaeogeography, Palaeoclimatology, Palaeoecology* 109:345–356.

Elenga, H., A. Vincens, and D. Schwartz. 1991. Presence d'elements forestiers Montagnards sur les Plateaux Batéké (Congo) au pléistocène supérieur: Nouvelles Données Palynologiques. *Paleoecology of Africa* 22:239–252.

Ericson, J. E., and T. K. Earle. 1982. *Contexts for Prehistoric Exchange*. New York: Academic Press.

Errington, F., and D. Gewertz. 1993. Anthropology at Its Best: The 1993 Annual Meeting. *Anthropology Newsletter* 34:1, 26.

Féblot-Augustins, J. 1993. Mobility Strategies in the Late Middle Paleolithic of Central Europe and Western Europe: Elements of Stability and Variability. *Journal of Anthropological Archaeology* 12:211–265.

Feit, H. A. 1994. The Enduring Pursuit: Land, Time, and Social Relationships in Anthropological Models of Hunter-Gatherers and in Subarctic Hunters' Images. In *Key Issues in Hunter-Gatherer Research*. E. S. Burch and L. J. Ellanna, eds. Pp. 421–439. Oxford: Berg.

Fiedler, L., and J. Preuss. 1985. Stone Tools from the Inner Zaire Basin (Region de l'Equator, Zaire). *African Archaeological Review* 3:179–187.

Flanagan, J. 1989. Hierarchy in Simple "Egalitarian" Societies. *Annual Review of Anthropology* 18:245–266.

Foley, R. 1999. Hunting Down the Hunter-Gatherers. *Evolutionary Anthropology* 8:115–117.

Fox, R. G. 1969. Professional Primitives: Hunters and Gatherers in Nuclear Southeast Asia. *Man in India* 36:93–98.

Freeman, L. 1994. Torralba and Ambrona: A Review of Discoveries. In *Integrative Paths to the Past*. R. Corruccini and R. Ciochon, eds. Pp. 597–637. Englewood Cliffs, N.J.: Prentice Hall.

Frost, G. T. 1980. Tool Behavior and the Origins of Laterality. *Journal of Human Evolution* 9:447–459.

Gamble, C. 1999. *The Paleolithic Societies of Europe*. Cambridge: Cambridge University Press.

Gang, G. Young. 2001. The Middle and Later Stone Ages in the Mukogodo Hills of Central Kenya. BAR Series S964. *Cambridge Monographs in African Archaeology* 52.

Gasse, F., and F. A. Street. 1978. Late Quaternary Lake-Level Fluctuations in Environments of the Northern Rift Valley and Afar Regions (Ethiopia and Djibouti). *Palaeogeography, Palaeoclimatology, Palaeoecology* 24:279–325.

Gautier, A., and W. van Neer. 1989. Animal Remains from the Late Paleolithic Sequence at Wadi Kubbaniya. In *The Prehistory of North Africa, Volume 2: Paleoeconomy, Environment and Stratigraphy*. A. Close, ed. Pp. 119–158. Dallas: Southern Methodist University Press.

Geertz, C. 1963. *Agricultural Involution*. Berkeley: University of California Press.

Geneste, J.-M. 1988. Systèmes d'approvisionnement en matières premières au paléolithique moyen et au paléolithique supérieur en aquitaine. In *L'Homme de Neanderthal: La Mutation*, Volume 8. J. K. Kozlowski, ed. Pp. 61–70. Liège: Eraul 35, University of Liège.

———. 1989. Economie des ressources lithiques dans le mousterien du sudouest de la France. In *L'Homme de Neanderthal: La Subsistance*, Volume 6. Marylène Patou and Leslie G. Freeman, eds. Pp. 75–97. Liège: Eraul 33 University of Liège.

Giblin, J. 1990. Trypanosomiasis Control in African History: An Evaded Issue. *Journal of African History* 31:59–80.

Gibson, T. 1988. Meat Sharing as a Political Ritual: Forms of Transaction versus Modes of Subsistence. In *Hunters and Gatherers, Volume 2: Property, Power and Ideology*. T. Ingold, D. Riches, and J. Woodburn, eds. Pp. 165–179. New York: St. Martin's.

Gifford-Gonzalez, D. 1998. Early Pastoralists in East Africa: Ecological and Social Dimensions. *Journal of Anthropological Archaeology* 17(2):166–200.

Goodwin, A. J. H., and van Riet Lowe, C. 1929. The Stone Age Cultures of South Africa. *Annals of the South African Museum* 27.

Goodyear, A. 1989. A Hypothesis for the Use of Cryptocrystalline Raw Materials among Paleoindian Groups of North America. In *Eastern Paleoindan*

Lithic Resource Use. C. Ellis and J. Lothrop, eds. Pp. 1–10. Boulder, Colo.: Westview Press.

Gould, R., and S. Saggers. 1985. Lithic Procurement in Central Australia: A Closer Look at Binford's Idea of Embeddedness in Archaeology. *American Antiquity* 50:117–135.

Gowdy, J. 1999. Hunter-Gatherers and the Mythology of the Market. In *The Cambridge Encyclopedia of Hunters and Gatherers.* R. Lee and R. Daly, eds. Pp. 391–398. Cambridge: Cambridge University Press.

Gramly, R. M. 1976. Upper Pleistocene Archaeological Occurrences at Site GvJm22, Lukenya Hill, Kenya. *Man* 11:319–344.

Gramly, R. M., and G. P. Rightmire 1973. Fragmentary Cranium and Dated Later Stone Age Assemblage from Lukenya Hill, Kenya. *Man* 8:571–579.

Griffin, P. B. 1984. Forager Resource and Land Use in the Humid Tropics: The Agta of Northeastern Luzon, The Phillipines. In *Past and Present in Hunter-Gatherer Societies.* C. Schrire, ed. Pp. 95–121. New York: Academic Press.

Grinker, R. 1994. *Houses in the Rainforest: Ethnicity and Inequality among Farmers and Foragers in Central Africa.* Berkeley: University of California Press.

Grun, R., N. J. Shackleton, and H. J. Deacon. 1990. Electron-Spin Resonance Dating of Tooth Enamel from Klasies River Mouth Cave. *Current Anthropology* 31:427–432.

Gubser, N. J. 1965. *The Nunamiut Eskimos, Hunters of Caribou.* New Haven: Yale University Press.

Guilmet, G. M. 1977. The Evolution of Tool-Using and Tool-Making Behavior. *Man* 12:33–47.

Flanagan. 1989. Hierarchy in Simple "Egalitarian" Societies. *Annual Review of Anthropology* 18:245–266.

Haaland, R. 1992. Fish, Pots, and Grain: Early and Mid-Holocene Adaptations in the Central Sudan. *The African Archaeological Review* 10:43–64.

———. 1996. A Socio-Economic Perspective on the Transition from Gathering, Cultivation to Domestication, a Case Study of Sorghum in the Middle Nile Region. In *Aspects of African Archaeology.* G. Pwiti and R. Soper, eds. Pp. 391–401. Harare: University of Zimbabwe Publications.

———. 1999. The Puzzle of the Late Emergence of Domesticated Sorghum in the Nile Valley. In *The Prehistory of Food: Appetites for Change.* C. Godsen and J. Hather, eds. Pp. 397–418. London: Routledge.

Haberland, E. 1963. Zum Problem der Jäger und besonderen Kasten in nordost- und ost Afrika. *Paideuma* 9:136–155.

Haberyan, K. A., and R. E. Hecky. 1987. The Late Pleistocene and Holocene Stratigraphy and Palaeoliminology of Lakes Kivu and Tanganyika. *Palaeogeography, Palaeoclimatology, Palaeoecology* 61:169–197.

Hamilton, A. C. 1982. *Environmental History of East Africa: A Study of the Quaternary.* New York: Academic Press.

———. 1987. Vegetation and Climate of Mt. Elgon during the Late Pleistocene and Holocene. *Paleoecology of Africa* 18:283–304.

———. 2000. History of Forests and Climate. In *The Conservation Atlas of Tropical Forests: Africa*. J. A. Sayer, C. Harcourt, and N. Collins, eds. Pp. 17–25. New York: Simon and Shuster.

Hanotte, O., D. Bradley, J. Ochieng, Y. Verjee, E. Hill, and E. Rege. 2002. African Pastoralism: Genetic Imprints of Origins and Migrations. *Science* 296:336–339.

Harlan, J. 1989. Wild-Grass Seed Harvesting in the Sahara and Sub-Sahara of Africa. In *Foraging and Farming: The Evolution of Plant Exploitation*. D. Harris and G. C. Hillman, eds. Pp. 79–98. London: Unwin Hyman.

———. 1992. Indigenous African Agriculture. In *Agricultural Origins in World Perspective*. P. J. Watson and C. W. Cowan, eds. Pp. 59–69. Washington, D.C.: Smithsonian Institution Publications in Anthropology.

Harlan, J. R., DeWet, J., and A. Stemler. 1976. *Origins of African Plant Domestication*. Mouton: The Hague.

Harris, D. R. 1989. An Evolutionary Continuum of People-Plant Interaction. In *Foraging and Farming: The Evolution of Plant Exploitation*. D. Harris and G. C. Hillman, eds. Pp. 11–24. London: Unwin Hyman.

Hassan, F. 1981. *Demographic Archaeology*. New York: Academic Press.

Hastenrath, S., and J. E. Kutzbach. 1983. Paleoclimatic Estimates from Water and Energy Budgets of East African Lakes. *Quaternary Research* 19:141–153.

Hawkes, K. 1993a. Why Hunter-Gatherers Work: An Ancient Version of the Problem of Public Goods. *Current Anthropology* 34:341–361.

———. 1993b. On Why Male Foragers Hunt and Share Food: Reply to Hill and Kaplan. *Current Anthropology* 34:706–710.

———. 2000. Big Game Hunting and the Evolution of Egalitarian Societies. In *Hierarchies in Action: Cui Bono?* M. Diehl, ed. Pp. 59–83. Southern Illinois University: Center for Archaeological Investigations, Occasional Paper 27.

———. 2001. Is Meat the Hunter's Property? Big Game, Ownership, and Explanations of Hunting and Sharing. In *Meat-Eating and Human Evolution*. C. Stanford and H. Bunn, eds. Pp. 219–236. Oxford: Oxford University Press.

Hawkes, K., and J. O'Connell. 1981. Affluent Hunters? Some Comments in the Light of the Alyawara Case. *American Anthropologist* 83:622–626.

Hawkes, K., H. Hill, and J. F. O'Connell. 1982. Why Hunters Gather: Optimal Foraging and the Ache of Eastern Paraguay. *American Ethnologist* 9:379–398.

———. 1989. Hardworking Hadza Grandmothers. In *Comparative Socioecology of Mammals and Man*. V. Standen and R. Foley, eds. Pp. 341–366. London: Blackwell.

———. 1991. Hunting Income Patterns among the Hadza: Big Game, Common Goods, Foraging Goals, and the Evolution of the Human Diet. *Philosophical Transactions of the Royal Society B* 334:243–251.

———. 1992. Hunting Income Patterns among the Hadza: Big Game, Common Goods, Foraging Goals and the Evolution of the Human Diet. In *Foraging Strategies of Monkeys, Apes, and Humans*. A. Whiten and E. M. Widdowson, eds. Pp. 83–91. Oxford: Oxford Science Publications.

———. 1995. Hadza Children's Foraging: Juvenile Dependency, Social Arrangements, and Mobility among Hunter-Gatherers. *Current Anthropology* 36:688–700.

———. 1997. Hadza Women's Time Allocation, Offspring Production, and the Evolution of Long Postmenopausal Life Spans. *Current Anthropology* 38:551–577.

Hawkes, K., J. F. O'Connell, and N. G. Blurton-Jones. 2001a. Hadza Meat Sharing. *Evolution and Human Behavior* 22:113–142.

———. 2001b. Hunting and Nuclear Families: Some Lessons from the Hadza about Men's Work. *Current Anthropology* 42:681–710.

Hawkes, K., J. F. O'Connell, and L. Rogers. 1997. The Behavioral Ecology of Modern Hunter-Gatherers and Human Evolution. *Trends in Ecology and Evolution* 12:29–32.

Hayden, B. 1990. Nimrods, Piscators, Pluckers, and Planters: The Emergence of Food Production. *Journal of Anthropological Archaeology* 9:31–69.

———. 1993. The Cultured Capacities of Neanderthals: A Review and Re-evaluation. *Journal of Human Evolution* 24:113–146.

Haynes, G. 2002. The Catastrophic Extinction of North American Mammoths and Mastodonts. *World Archaeology* 33:391–416.

Headland, T. 1997. Revionism in Ecological Anthropology. *Current Anthropology* 38:605–630.

Headland, T., and L. Reid. 1989. Hunter-Gatherers and Their Neighbors from Prehistory to Present. *Current Anthropology* 30(1):43–66.

Heinz, H. J. 1979. The Nexus Complex among the !Xõ Bushmen of Botswana. *Anthropos* 74:465–480.

Henshilwood, C. 1997. Identifying the Collector: Evidence for Human Processing of the Cape Dune Mole—*Bathyergus suillus*, from Blombos Cave, Southern Cape, South Africa. *Journal of Archaeological Science* 24:659–662.

Henshilwood, C., and J. Sealy. 1997. Bone Artifacts from the Middle Stone Age at Blombos Cave, Southern Cape, South Africa. *Current Anthropology* 38(5):890–895.

Henshilwood, C. S., J. Sealy, R. Yates, K. Cruz-Uribe, P. Goldberg, F. E. Grine, R. G. Klein, C. Poggenpoel, K. van Niekerk, and I. Watts. 2001. Blombos Cave, Southern Cape, South Africa: Preliminary Report on the 1992–1999 Excavations of the Middle Stone Age Levels. *Journal of Archaeological Science* 28:421–448.

Herskovitz, M. 1926. The Cattle Complex in East Africa. *American Anthropologist* 28:230–272, 361–368, 494–528.

Hewes, G. W. 1973. An Explicit Formulation of the Relation between Toll-Using and Early Human Language Emergence. *Visible Language* 7:101–127.

Hill, K., and H. Kaplan. 1993. On Why Male Foragers Hunt and Share Food. *Current Anthropology* 34:701–706.

Hillman, G. C. 1989. Late Paleolithic Plant Foods, from Wadi Kubbaniya in Upper Egypt: Dietary Diversity Infant Weaning, and Seasonality in a Riverine Environment. In *Foraging and Farming: The Evolution of Plant*

Exploitation. D. Harris and G. C. Hillman, eds. Pp. 207–234. London: Unwin Hyman.

Hitchcock, R. K., and J. I. Ebert. 1989. Modeling Kalahari Hunter-Gatherer Subsistence and Settlement Systems: Implications for Development Policy and Land Use Planning. *Anthropos:*447–462.

Hladik, C. M., and A. Hladik. 1990. Food Resources of the Rain Forest. In *Food and Nutrition in the African Rain Forest.* C. M. Hladik, S. Bahuchet, and I. De Garine, eds. Pp. 14–18. Paris: UNESCO.

Hobbes, T. 1973 [1651]. *Leviathan.* London: J. M. Dent and Sons.

Hobley, C. W. 1895. Upon a Visit to Tsavo and the Taita Highland. *Geographical Journal* 5:545–561.

——. 1912. The Wa-lungulu or Araingulu of the Taru Desert. *Man* 12:18–21.

——. 1929. *Kenya from Chartered Company to Crown Colony.* London: Frank Cass.

Holis, A. C. 1909. A Note of the Graves of Wanyika. *Man* 9:145.

Holl, A. F. C. 1985. Subsistence Patterns of the Dhar Tichitt Neolithic, Mauritania. *The African Archaeological Review* 3:151–162.

——. 1998a. Livestock Husbandry, Pastoralisms, and Territoriality: The West African Record. *Journal of Anthropological Archaeology* 17(2):143–165.

——. 1998b. The Dawn of African Pastoralisms: An Introductory Note. *Journal of Anthropological Archaeology* 17:81–96.

——. 2000. Metals and Prehistoric African Society. In *Ancient African Metallurgy.* J. Vogel, ed. Pp. 1–82. Walnut Creek, Calif.: AltaMira Press.

Holloway, R. 1968. Culture: A Human Domain. *Current Anthropology* 10:395–412.

Holy, L. 1986. *Strategies and Norms in a Changing Matrilineal Society.* Cambridge: Cambridge University Press.

Howell, F., G. Cole, and M. Kleindienst. 1962. Isimila, an Acheulean Occupation Site in the Iringa Highlands. In *Actes du Quatrième Congrès Panafricain de Préhistoire.* G. Mortelmans and J. Nenquin, eds. Pp. 43–80. Tervuren, Bellgium: Musée Regional de L'Afrique Centrale.

Huntingford, G. W. B. 1931. Free Hunters, Serf Tribes, and Submerged Classes in East Africa. *Man* (O. S.) 31:22–228.

Iliffe, J. 1996. *Africans: A History of the Continent.* Cambridge: Cambridge University Press.

Ingbar, E. E. 1994. Lithic Material Selection and Technological Organization. In *The Organization of North American Prehistoric Chipped Stone Tool Techniques.* P. J. Carr, ed. Pp. 45–56. Archaeological Series 7. Ann Arbor, Mich.: International Monographs in Prehistory.

Inizan, M., H. Roche, and J. Tixier. 1992. *Technology of Knapped Stone.* Meudon: Cercle de Recherche et d'Etudes Préhistoriques and Centre National de la Recherche Scientifique.

Inskeep, R. R. 1987. *Nelson Bay Cave, Cape Province, South Africa: The Holocene Levels.* Bar International Series 357 (I).

Isaac, G. L. 1978a. Food Sharing and Human Evolution: Archaeological Evidence from the Plio-Pleistocene of East Africa. *Journal of Anthropological Research* 34:311–325.

————. 1978b. The Food Sharing Behavior of Protohuman Hominids. *Scientific American* 238:90–108.

————. 1984. The Archaeology of Human Origins: Studies of the Lower Pleistocene in East Africa, 1971–1981. *Advances in World Archaeology* 3:1–87.

————. 1986. Foundation Stones: Early Artefacts as Indicators of Activities and Abilities. In *Stone Age Prehistory: Studies in Honor of Charles McBurney*. G. N. Bailey and P. Callow, eds. Pp. 221–241. Cambridge: Cambridge University Press.

Ivey, P. K. 2000. Cooperative Reproduction in Ituri Forest Hunter-Gatherers: Who Cares for Efe Infants? *Current Anthropology* 41:856–866.

Jacobson, L. 1984. Hunting versus Gathering in an Arid Ecosystem: The Evidence from the Namib Desert. In *Frontiers: Southern African Archaeology Today*. M. Hall, G. Avery, D. M. Avery, M. L. Wilson, and A. J. B. Humphreys, eds. Pp. 75–79. BAR International Series 207. Oxford: British Archaeological Reports.

Jardin, C. 1967. *List of Foods Used in Africa*. Rome: Food and Agriculture Organization.

Jaubert, J., M. Lorblanchet, H. Laville, R. Slott-Moller, A. Turq, and J. Brugal. 1990. *Les Chausseurs d'Aurochs de la Borde*. Paris: Documents d'Archaeologie Française 27.

Jenike, M. 2001. Nutritional Ecology: Diet, Physical Activity and Body Size. In *Hunter-Gatherers, an Interdisciplinary Perspective*. C. Panter-Brick, R. Layton, and P. Rowley-Conwy, eds. Pp. 205–238. Cambridge: Cambridge University Press.

Johnson, T. C., C. A. Scholz, M. R. Talbot, K. Kelts, R. D. Ricketts, G. Ngobi, K. Beuning, I. Ssemmanda, and J. W. McGill. 1996. Late Pleistocene Dessication of Lake Victoria and Rapid Evolution of Cichlid Fishes. *Science* 273:1091–1093.

Jolly, D., I. C. Prentice, and R. Bonnefille. 1998. Biome Reconstruction from Pollen and Plant Macrofossil Data for Africa and the Arabian Peninsula at 0 and 6000 years ago. *Journal of Biogeography* 25:1007–1027.

Karlin, C., S. Ploux, P. Bodu, and N. Pigeot. 1993. Some Socio-Economic Aspects of the Knapping Process among Groups of Hunter-Gatherers in the Paris Basin Area. In *The Use of Tools by Human and Non-Human Primates*. A. Berthelet and J. Chavaillon, eds. Pp. 318–340. Oxford: Clarendon.

Keeley, L. 1995. Protoagricultural Practices among Hunters and Gatherers. In *Last Hunters, First Farmers*. T. D. Price and A. Gerbrauer, eds. Pp. 95–126. Santa Fe, N.M.: SAR Press.

————. 1999. Use of Plant Foods among Hunter-Gatherers: A Cross-Cultural Survey. In *Prehistory of Agriculture: New Experimental and Ethnographic Approaches*. P. C. Anderson, ed. Pp. 6–14. Los Angeles: Institute of Archaeology, University of California.

Keeley, L., and N. Toth. 1981. Microwear Polishes on Early Stone Tools from Koobi Fora, Kenya. *Nature* 293:464–465.

Keller, C. M. 1966. The Development of Edge Damage Patterns on Stone Tools. *Man* 1:501–511.

Kelly, R. 1983. Hunter-Gatherer Mobility Strategies. *Journal of Anthropological Research* 39:277–306.

———. 1988. The Three Sides of a Biface. *American Antiquity* 53:717–734.

———. 1992. Mobility/Sedentism: Concepts, Archaeological Measures, and Effects. *Annual Review of Anthropology* 21:43–66.

———. 1995. *The Foraging Spectrum: Diversity in Hunter-Gatherer Lifeways.* Washington, D.C.: Smithsonian Institution Press.

Kelly, R., and L. Todd. 1988. Coming into the Country: Early Paleoindian Hunting and Mobility. *American Antiquity* 53:231–244.

Kent, S. 1992. The Current Forager Controversy: Real versus Ideal Views of Hunter-Gatherers. *Man* 27:45–70.

———. 1997. *Cultural Diversity among Twentieth Century Foragers: An African Perspective.* Cambridge: Cambridge University Press.

Kibunjia, M. 1994. Pliocene Archaeological Occurrences in the Lake Turkana Basin. *Journal of Human Evolution* 27:159–171.

Kipnis, R. 1998. Early Hunter-Gatherers in the Americas: Perspectives from Central Brazil. *Antiquity* 72:581–592.

Klee, M., and B. Zach. 1999. The Exploitation of Wild and Domesticated Food Plants at Settlement Mounds in Northeast Nigeria (1800 Cal BC to Today). In *The Exploitation of Plant Resources in Ancient Africa.* M. Van der Veen, ed. Pp. 81–88. New York: Kluwer Academic/Plenum.

Klein, R. G. 1972. The Late Quaternary Mammalian Fauna of Nelson Bay Cave (Cape Province, South Africa): Its Implications for Megafaunal Extinctions and Environmental and Cultural Change. *Quaternary Research* 2:135–142.

———. 1978. Preliminary Analysis of the Mammalian Fauna from the Redcliff Stone Age Cave Site, Rhodesia. Occasional Papers of the National Museums of Rhodesia, Series A, *Human Sciences* 4:74–80.

———. 1980. Environmental and Ecological Implications of Large Mammals from Upper Pleistocene and Holocene Sites in Southern Africa. *Annals of the South African Museum* 81:223–283.

———. 1984. Later Stone Age Faunal Samples from Heuningneskrans Shelter (Transvaal) and Leopard's Cave (Zambia). *South African Archaeological Bulletin* 39:109–116.

———. 1989. Biological and Behavioral Perspectives on Modern Human Origins in Southern Africa. In *The Human Revolution: Behavioral and Biological Perspectives on the Origin of Modern Humans.* P. Mellars and C. Stringer, eds. Pp. 529–546. Princeton, N.J.: Princeton University Press.

———. 1992. The Archaeology of Modern Human Origins. *Evolutionary Anthropology* 1:5–20.

———. 1999. *The Human Career.* Chicago: University of Chicago Press.

Klein, R. G., and K. Cruz-Uribe. 1996. Exploitation of Large Bovids and Seals at Middle and Later Stone Age Sites in South Africa. *Journal of Human Evolution* 31:315–334.

———. 2000. Middle and Later Stone Age Large Mammal and Tortoise Remains from Die Kelders Cave 1, Western Cape Province, South Africa. *Journal of Human Evolution* 38(1):169–195.

Knecht, H. 1992. The Role of Innovation in Changing Upper Paleolithic Organic Projectile Technologies. *Techniques et Culture* 17.

Knutsson, K. 1969. Dichotomization and Integration. In *Ethnic Groups and Boundaries: The Social Organization of Culture Difference*. Pp. 86–100. Prospect Heights, Ill.: Waveland Press.

Kratz, C. A. 1981. Are the Okiek Really Maasai? Or Kipsigis? Or Kikuyu? *Cahiers d'Études Africaines* 79:355–368.

Kuhn, S., and O. Bar-Yosef. 1999. The Big Deal about Blades: Laminar Technologies and Human Evolution. *American Anthropologist* 101.

Kuhn, S., and M. Stiner. 2001. The Antiquity of Hunter-Gatherers. In *Hunter-Gatherers, An Interdisciplinary Perspective*. C. Panter-Brick, R. Layton, and P. Rowley-Conwy, eds. Pp. 99–142. Cambridge: Cambridge University Press.

Kuhn, S. L. 1992. On Planning and Curated Technologies in the Middle Paleolithic. *Journal of Anthropological Research* 48:185–214.

———. 1994. A Formal Approach to the Design and Assembly of Mobile Toolkits. *American Antiquity* 59:426–442.

———. 1995. *Mousterian Lithic Technology: An Ecological Perspective*. Princeton, N.J.: Princeton University Press.

Kuper, A. 1973. Costume and Cosmology: The Animal Symbolism of the Ncwala. *Man* 8:613–630.

———. 1982. *Wives for Cattle: Bridewealth and Marriage in Southern Africa*. London: Routledge and Paul.

Kusimba, C. M. 1999. *The Rise and Fall of Swahili States*. Walnut Creek, Calif.: AltaMira Press.

Kusimba, C. M., D. Killick, and D. Creswell. 1994. Indigenous and Imported Metals in Swahili Sites on the Kenyan Coast. *MASCA Research Papers in Science and Archaeology* 11:63–78.

Kusimba, C. M., and S. Kusimba. 1998–2000. Field Notes, Tsavo Archaeological Research Project.

Kusimba, C., and S. Kusimba. 2000. Hinterlands and Cities: Investigations of Economy and Trade in the Tsavo Region, Kenya. *Nyame Akuma*, no. 54.

Kusimba, S. 1999. Hunter-Gatherer Land Use Patterns in Later Stone Age East Africa. *Journal of Anthropological Archaeology* 18:165–200.

———. 2001. The Pleistocene Later Stone Age in East Africa: Excavations and Lithic Assemblages from Lukenya Hill. *African Archaeological Review* 18:77–123.

Kusimba, S., and F. Smith. 2001. Acheulean. In *The Encyclopedia of Prehistory.* P. Peregrine and M. Ember, eds. Pp. 1–22. New York: Kluwer Academic/ Plenum Publishers.

Lahr, M. M., and R. Foley. 1994. Multiple Dispersals and Modern Human Origins. *Evolutionary Anthropology* 3:48–60.

Lam, Y. M., O. M. Pearson, and C. M. Smith. 1996. Chin Morphology and Sexual Dimorphism in the Fossil Hominid Mandible Sample from Klasies River Mouth. *American Journal of Physical Anthropology* 100:545–557.

Lamb, H. F., F. Gasse, A. Benkaddour, N. El Hamouti, S. van der Kaars, W. T. Perkins, N. J. Pearce, C. N. Roberts. 1995. Relation between Century-Scale Holocene Arid Intervals in Tropical and Temperate Zones. *Nature* 373:134–137.

Lavachery, P. 2001. The Holocene Archaeological Sequence of Shum Laka Rock Shelter (Grassfields, Western Cameroon). *African Archaeological Review* 18(4):213–247.

Leakey, L. S. B. 1965. *Olduvai Gorge, 1951–1960. Volume I: A Preliminary Report on the Geology and Fauna.* Cambridge: Cambridge University Press.

Leakey, L. S. B., and M. D. Leakey. 1964. Recent Discoveries of Fossil Hominids in Tanganyika: At Olduvai and Near Lake Natron. *Nature* (London) 202:4927, 5–7.

Leakey, M. D. 1971. *Olduvai Gorge. Volume III.* Cambridge: Cambridge University Press.

Lee, R. B. 1968. What Hunters Do for a Living: How to Make Out on Scarce Resources. In *Man the Hunter.* R. B. Lee and I. DeVore, eds. Pp. 30–48. Chicago: Aldine.

———. 1976. Introduction. In *Kalahari Hunter-Gatherers: Studies of !Kung San and Their Neighbors.* R. Lee and I. DeVore, eds. Pp. 3–24. Cambridge, Mass.: Harvard University Press.

———. 1979. *The !Kung San: Men, Women, and Work in a Foraging Society.* Cambridge: Cambridge University Press.

———. 1984. *The Dobe !Kung.* New York: Holt, Rinehart and Winston.

Lee, R. B., and R. Daly. 1999. Introduction. In *The Cambridge Encyclopedia of Hunters and Gatherers.* R. Lee and R. Daly, eds. Pp. 1–19. Cambridge: Cambridge University Press.

Lee, R. B., and I. De Vore, eds. 1968a. *Man the Hunter.* Chicago: Aldine.

———. 1968b. Problems in the Study of Hunter-Gatherers. In *Man the Hunter.* R. B. Lee and I. De Vore, eds. Pp. 3–12. Chicago: Aldine.

Lee, R., and M. Guenther. 1991. Oxen or Onions? The Search for Trade (and Truth) in the Kalahari. *Current Anthropology* 32(5):592–601.

Lemonnier, P. 1992. *Elements for an Anthropology of Technology.* Anthropological Papers of the Museum of Anthropology, University of Michigan, no. 87.

Lim, I. L. 1997. Eastern African Rock Art. In *Encyclopedia of Precolonial Africa.* J. O. Vogel, ed. Pp. 362–67. Walnut Creek, Calif.: AltaMira Press.

Livingstone, D. A. 1971. A 22,000-Year Pollen Record from the Plateau of Zambia. *Limnology and Oceanography* 6:349–356.

Lovejoy, O. 1993. Modeling Human Origins: Are We Sexy Because We're Smart, or Smart Because We're Sexy? In *The Origin and Evolution of Humans and Humanness*. D. T. Rasmussen, ed. Pp. 1–28. Boston: Jones and Bartlett.

Lubell, D., and P. J. Sheppard. 1997. Northern African Advanced Foragers. In *The Encyclopedia of Precolonial Africa*. J. O. Vogel, ed. Pp. 325–329. Walnut Creek, Calif.: AltaMira.

Mabulla, A. Z. P. 1996. Middle and Later Stone Age Lithic Technology at Lake Eyasi, Tanzania. Ph.D. diss., University of Florida. University Microfilms, Ann Arbor.

Mabulla, A. Z. 2002. Archaeological Implications of Hadzabe Forager Land Use in the Eyasi Basin, Tanzania. Unpublished MS.

MacDonald, D. H., and B. S. Hewlett. 1999. Reproductive Interest and Forager Mobility. *Current Anthropology* 40:501–523.

MacDonald, K., and W. Van Neer. 1994. Specialized Fishing Peoples in the Later Holocene of the Mema Region, Mali. In *Fish Exploitation in the Past: Proceedings of the 7th Meeting of the ICAZ Fish Remains Working Group*. W. Van Neer, ed. Pp. 243–252. Tervuren, Belgium: Musée Royal de L'Afrique Centrale.

MacEachern, S. 1994. Symbolic Reservoirs' and Intergroup Relations' West African Examples. *African Archaeological Review* 12:205–224.

Maley, J. 1987. Fragmentation de la forêt dense humide Africaine et extension des biotopes montagnards au quaternaire récent: Nouvelles données polliniques et chronologiques. Implications paléoclimatiques et biogéographiques. *Paleoecology of Africa* 18:307–334.

Mandryk, C. S. 1993. Hunter-Gatherer Social Costs and the Nonviability of Submarginal Environments. *Journal of Anthropological Research* 49:39–71.

Manega, P. 1993. Geochronology, Geochemistry, and Isotopic Study of the Plio-Pleistocene Hominid Sites and the Ngorongoro Volcanic Highland in Northern Tanzania. Ph.D. diss., Department of Geology, University of Colorado—Boulder.

Marean, C. W. 1990. Late Quaternary Paleoenvironments and the Faunal Exploitation in East Africa. Ph.D. diss., University of California—Berkeley. Ann Arbor: University Microfilms.

——. 1992a. Implications of Late Quaternary Mammalian Fauna from Lukenya Hill (South-Central Kenya) for Paleoenvironmental Change and Faunal Extinctions. *Quaternary Research* 37:239–255.

——. 1997. Hunter-Gatherer Foraging Strategies in Tropical Grasslands: Model Building and Testing in the East African Middle and Later Stone Age. *Journal of Anthropological Archaeology* 16:189–225.

Marean, C., and Z. Assefa. 1999. Zooarcheological Evidence for the Faunal Exploitation Behavior of Neandertals and Early Modern Humans. *Evolutionary Anthropology* 8:22–23.

Marean, C. W., C. L. Ehrhart, and N. Mudida. 1990. Late Quaternary Mammalian Fauna in Eastern Africa: Its Relevance for Environmental Change and Faunal Extinctions. Paper presented at the Sixth International Conference of the International Council for Archaeology, Washington D.C., May 1990.

Marean, C., and D. Gifford-Gonzalez. 1991. Late Quaternary Extinct Ungulates of East Africa and Paleoenvironmental Implications. *Nature* 350:418–420.

Marks, A. 1988. The Curation of Stone Tools during the Upper Pleistocene: A View from the Central Negev, Israel. In *Upper Pleistocene Prehistory of Western Eurasia*. H. Dibble and A. Montet-White, eds. Pp. 275–285. Philadelphia: University of Philadelphia Museum.

Marshall, F. and E. Hildebrand. 2002. Cattle before Crops: The Beginnings of Food Production in Africa. *Journal of World Prehistory* 16:99–143.

Marshall, L. 1976. *The !Kung of Nyae Nyae*. Cambridge, Mass: Harvard University Press.

Masao, F. T. 1982. On Possible Use of Unshaped Flakes: An Ethnohistorical Approach from Central Tanzania. *Ethnos* 47:262–270.

Mauss, M. 1924 (1990). *The Gift*. Trans. W. D. Halls. New York: Norton.

Mazel, A. D. 1992. Early Pottery from the Eastern Part of Southern Africa. *South African Archaeological Bulletin* 47:3–7.

McBrearty, S. 1986. The Archaeology of the Muguruk Site, Western Kenya. Ph.D. diss., University of Illinois—Urbana. Ann Arbor: University Microfilms.

———. 1991. Recent Archaeological Research in Western Kenya and Its Implications for the Status of Sangoan Industry. In *Cultural Beginnings: Approaches to Understanding Hominid Lifeways in the African Savanna*. J. D. Clark, ed. Pp. 159–176. Bonn: Monographien 19, Forschunginstitut für Vor- und Frühgeschichte, Römisch-Germanisches Zentralmuseum.

McBrearty, S., and A. S. Brooks. 2000. The Revolution That Wasn't: A New Interpretation of the Origin of Modern Human Behavior. *Journal of Human Evolution* 39(5):453–563.

McHenry, H., and K. Coffing. 2000. Australopithecus to Homo: Transformations in Body and Mind. *Annual Review of Anthropology* 29:125–146.

Mehlman, M. J. 1989. Later Quaternary Archaeological Sequences in Northern Tanzania. Ph.D. diss., University of Illinois. Ann Arbor: University Microfilms.

Mercader, J. 2002. Forest People: The Role of African Rainforests in Human Evolution and Dispersal. *Evolutionary Anthropology* 11:117–124.

Mercader, J., and A. Brooks. 2001. Across the Forest and Savannas: Later Stone Age Assemblages from Ituri and Semliki, Democratic Republic of Congo. *Journal of Anthropological Research* 57:197–217.

Mercader, J., M. Garcia-Heras, and I. Gonzales-Alvarez. 2000. Ceramic Tradition in the African Rainforest: Characterization Analysis of Acient and Modern Pottery from Ituri, D. R. Congo. *Journal of Archaeological Science* 27:163–182.

Merrick, H. V. 1975. Change in Later Pleistocene Lithic Industries in Eastern Africa. Ph.D. diss., University of California—Berkeley. Ann Arbor: University Microfilms.

Merrick, H. V., and F. H. Brown. 1984. Obsidian Sources and Patterns of Source Utilization in Kenya and Northern Tanzania: Some Initial Findings. *African Archaeological Review* 2:129–152.

Merrick, H., F. Brown, and M. Connelly. 1990. Sources of Obsidian at Ngamuriak and Other South-Western Kenyan Sites. In *Early Pastoralists of South-Western Kenya* P. Robertshaw, ed. Pp. 173–181. Nairobi: British Institute in Eastern Africa Memoir 11.

Merritt, H. 1975. A History of the Taita. Ph.D. diss. Ann Arbor: University Microfilms.

Metcalfe, D., and K. R. Barlow. 1992. A Model for Exploring the Optimal Trade-Off between Field Processing and Transport. *American Anthropologist* 94:340–356.

Miller, G. H., P. B. Beaumont, H. J. Deacon, A. S. Brooks, P. E. Hare, and A. J. T. Jull. 1999. Earliest Modern Humans in Southern Africa Dated by Isoleucine Epimerization in Ostrich Eggshell. *Quaternary Science Reviews* 18:1537–1548.

Miller, G. H., P. Beaumont, and A. B. Johnson. 1992. Pleistocene Geochronology and Paleothermometry from Protein Diagenesis in Ostrich Eggshells: Implications for the Evolution of Modern Humans. *Philosophical Transactions of the Royal Society, London B* 337:149–158.

Miller, S. F. 1969. Contacts between the Later Stone Age and the Early Iron Age in South Central Africa. *Azania* 4:81–90.

———. 1979. Lukenya Hill, GvJm46, Excavation Report. *Nyame Akuma* 14:31–34.

Milo, R. 1998. Evidence for Hominid Predation at Klasies River Mouth, South Africa, and Its Implications for the Behavior of Early Modern Humans. *Journal of Archaeological Science* 25:99–133.

Minichillo, Tom. 1999. A Hard Rock Is Good to Find: Foraging Strategies and Lithic Resource Modeling. Paper presented at the 64th Annual Meeting of the Society for American Archaeology, Chicago.

Mitchell, P. 1988. Human Adaptation in Southern Africa during the Late Glacial Maximum. In *Prehistoric Cultures and Environments in the Late Quaternary of Africa*. J. Bower and D. Lubell, eds. Pp. 163–214. BAR International Series 405. Oxford: British Archaeological Reports.

———. 1992. Last Glacial Maximum Hunter-Gatherers in Southern Africa as an Example of a High-Technology Foraging System. Paper presented at the Twelfth Biennial Conference of the Society of Africanist Archaeologists, Los Angeles, March 1992.

———. 1996. Prehistoric Exchange and Interaction in Southeastern Southern Africa: Marine Shells and Ostrich Eggshell. *African Archaeological Review* 13:35–76.

————. 1997. Southern African Advanced Foragers. In *Encyclopedia of Pre-colonial Africa*. J. O. Vogel, ed. Pp. 341–46. Walnut Creek, Calif.: AltaMira Press.

————. 2000. The Organization of Later Stone Age Lithic Technology in the Caledon Valley, Southern Africa. *African Archaeological Review* 17:141–176.

Monahan, C. 1996. New Zooarchaeological Data from Bed II, Olduvai Gorge, Tanzania: Implications for Hominid Behavior in the Early Pleistocene. *Journal of Human Evolution* 31:93–128.

Moore, A. M., G. C. Hillman, and A. J. Legge. 2001. *Village on the Euphrates: The Excavation of Abu Hureyra*. Oxford: Oxford University Press.

Moore, J. 1981. The Effects of Information Networks in Hunter-Gatherer Societies. In *Hunter-Gatherer Foraging Strategies: Ethnographic and Archaeological Analyses*. B. Winterhalder and E. Smith, eds. Pp. 194–217. Chicago: University of Chicago Press.

Morgan, L. 1964 [1877]. *Ancient Society*. New York: Kerr.

Moss, E. H. 1983. *The Functional Analysis of Flint Implements: Pincevent and Pont D'Ambon, Two Case Studies from the French Paleolithic*. BAR International Series 177. Oxford: British Archaeological Reports.

Movius, H., N. C. David, H. M. Bricker, and B. R. Clay. 1968. The Analysis of Certain Major Classes of Upper Paleolithic Tools. *Bulletin of the American School of Prehistoric Research* 26:1–17.

Murdock, G. P. 1968. The Current Status of the World's Hunting and Gathering Peoples. In *Man the Hunter*. R. B. Lee and I. De Vore, eds. Pp. 13–20. Chicago: University of Chicago Press.

Musonda, F. 1989. The Significance of Pottery in Zambian Later Stone Age Contexts. *The African Archaeological Review* 5:147–58.

Mutundu, K. 1999. Ethnohistoric Archaeology of the Mukogodo in North-Central Kenya: Hunter-Gatherer Subsistence and the Transition to Pastoralism in Secondary Settings. *Cambridge Monographs in African Archaeology 47*. Oxford: Archaeopress.

Myers, F. 1986. *Pintupi Country, Pintupi Self*. Washington, D.C.: Smithsonian Institution Press.

Nash, S. 1996. Is Curation a Useful Heuristic? In *Stone Tools: Theoretical Insights into Human Prehistory*. G. H. Odell, ed. Pp. 81–99. New York: Plenum.

Nelson, C. M., and J. K. Mengich. 1984. Early Development of Pastoral Adaptation in the Central Highlands of Kenya. In *Origins and Early Development of Food-Producing Cultures in Northeast Africa*. L. Krzyzaniak, ed. Pp. 481–487. Poznan: Polish Academy of Sciences.

Nelson, M. C. 1992. The Study of Technological Organization. In *Advances in Archaeological Method and Theory, Volume 3*. M. B. Schiffer, ed. Pp. 57–100. Tucson: University of Arizona Press.

Nettle, D., and R. Dunbar. 1997. Social Markers and the Evolution of Reciprocal Exchange. *Current Anthropology* 38:93–99.

Neumann, K., A. Ballouche, and M. Klee. 1996. The Emergence of Plant Food Production in the West African Sahel: New Evidence from Northeast Nigeria and Northern Burkina Faso. In *Aspects of African Archaeology*. G. Pwiti and R. Soper, eds. Pp. 303–313. Harare: University of Zimbabwe Publications.

O'Connell, J. F., and K. Hawkes. 1981. Alyawara Plant Use and Optimal Foraging Theory. In *Hunter-Gatherer Foraging Strategies: Ethnographic and Archaeological Analyses*. B. Winterhalder and E. A. Smith, eds. Pp. 99–126. Chicago: University of Chicago Press.

———. 1988. Hadza Hunting, Butchering, and Bone Transport and Their Archaeological Implications. *Journal of Anthropological Research* 44:113–161.

O'Connell, J. K., K. Hawkes, and N. G. Blurton Jones. 1999. Grandmothering and the Evolution of *Homo erectus*. *Journal of Human Evolution* 26:461–485.

Odell, G. H. 1981. The Morphological Express at Function Junction: Searching for Meaning in Lithic Tool Types. *Journal of Anthropological Research* 37:319–342.

———. 1994. A North American Perspective on Recent Archaeological Stone Tool Research. *Palimpsesto: Revista de Arqueologia* 3:109–122.

Odell, G. H., B. D. Hayden, J. K. Johnson, M. Kay, T. A. Morrow, S. E. Nash, M. S. Nassaney, J. W. Rick, M. F. Rondeau, S. A. Rosen, M. J. Shott, and P. T. Thacker. 1996. Some Comments on a Continuing Debate. In *Stone Tools: Theoretical Insights into Human Prehistory*. G. H. Odell, ed. Pp. 377–392. New York: Plenum Press.

Olindo, P. M., I. Douglas-Hamilton, and P. Hamilton. 1988. The 1988 Tsavo Elephant Count. Unpublished Report to the Kenya Wildlife Service. Nairobi.

Panter-Brick, C., R. Layton, and P. Rowley-Conwy. 2001. Lines of Inquiry. In *Hunter-Gatherers, an Interdisciplinary Perspective*. C. Panter-Brick, R. Layton, and P. Rowley-Conwy, eds. Pp. 1–11. Cambridge: Cambridge University Press.

Parkington, J. E. 1980. Time and Place: Some Observations on Spatial and Temporal Patterning in the Later Stone Age Sequence in Southern Africa. *South African Archaeological Bulletin* 35:73–83.

———. 1986. Stone Tool Assemblages, Raw Material Distributions, and Prehistoric Subsistence Activities: The Late Stone Age of South Africa. In *Stone Age Prehistory: Studies in Memory of Charles McBurney*. G. N. Bailey and P. Callow, eds. pp. 181–194. Cambridge: Cambridge University Press.

———. 1990. A Critique of the Consensus View on the Age of Howeison's Poort Assemblages in South Africa. In *The Emergence of Modern Humans: An Archaeological Perspective*. P. Mellars, ed. Pp. 34–55. Edinburgh: Edinburgh University Press.

Parry, W. J., and R. L. Kelly. 1987. Expedient Core Technology and Sedentism. In *The Organization of Core Technology*. J. K. Johnson and C. A. Morrow, eds. Pp. 285–304. Boulder, Colo.: Westview Press.

Pearson, O. 2000. Postcranial Remains and the Origin of Modern Humans. *Evolutionary Anthropology* 9:229–247.

Pelegrin, J. 1990. Prehistoric Lithic Technology: Some Aspects of Research. *Archaeological Reviews from Cambridge* 9:116–125.

———. 1993. A Framework for Analyzing Prehistoric Stone Tool Manufacture and a Tentative Application to Some Early Stone Industries. In *The Use of Tools by Human and Non-Human Primates*. A. Berthelet and J. Chavaillon, eds. Pp. 302–317. Oxford: Clarendon Press.

Pelegrin, J., C. Karlin, and P. Bodu. 1988. Chaînes opératoires: Un outil pour le préhistorien. In *Technologie Préhistorique*. J. Tixier, ed. Pp. 37–53. Notes et Monographies Techniques du CRA 25. Paris: Centre National de Recherches Scientifiques.

Pennisi, E. 2001. Malaria's Beginnings: On the Heels of Hoes? *Science* 293: 416–417.

Perlès, C. 1993. Ecological Determinism, Group Strategies, and Individual Decisions in the Conception of Prehistoric Stone Assemblages. In *The Use of Tools by Human and Non-Human Primates*. A. Berthelet and J. Chavaillon, eds. Pp. 267–280. Oxford: Clarendon.

Peters, J. 1989. Late Pleistocene Hunter-Gatherers at Ishango (Eastern Zaire): The Faunal Evidence. *Revue de Paléobiologie* 8(1).

Peterson, J. 1978. Hunter-Gatherer/Farmer Exchange. *American Anthropologist* 80:335–351.

Phillipson, D. W. 1993. *African Archaeology*. Cambridge: Cambridge University Press.

Phillipson, L., and D. W. Phillipson. 1970. Patterns of Edge Damage on the Late Stone Age Industry from Chiwemupula, Zambia. *Zambia Museums Journal* 1:40–75.

Pikirayi, I. 2001. *The Zimbabwe Culture*. Walnut Creek, Calif.: AltaMira Press.

Plummer, T., and L. Bishop. 1994. Hominid Paleoecology at Olduvai Gorge, Tanzania as Indicated by Antelope Remains. *Journal of Human Evolution* 27:47–75.

Pobiner, B. 1999. The Use of Stone Tools to Determine Handedness in Hominids. *Current Anthropology* 40:90–92.

Potts, R. 1996. *Humanity's Descent: The Consequences of Ecological Instability*. New York: Morrow.

Rambo, A. T. 1985. *Primitive Polluters: Semang Impact on the Malaysian Tropical Rainforest Ecosystem*. Ann Arbor, Mich.: Museum of Anthropology, University of Michigan.

Rao, A. 1987. The Concept of Peripatetics: An Introduction. In *The Other Nomads: Peripatetic Minorities in Cross-Cultural Perspective*. A. Rao, ed. Pp. 1–32. Cologne: Bohlau Verlag.

Redman, C. 1999. *Human Impact on Ancient Environments*. Tucson: University of Arizona Press.

Relethford, J. H. 1995. Genetics and Modern Human Origins. *Evolutionary Anthropology* 4:53–63.

———. 1998. Genetics of Modern Human Origins and Diversity. *Annual Reviews in Anthropology* 27:1–23.

Renfrew, C., and J. Cherry (eds.). 1986. *Peer Polity Interaction and Socio-political Change*. Cambridge: Cambridge University Press.

Richardson, J. L., and R. A. Dussinger. 1986. Paleolimnology of Mid-Elevation Lakes in the Kenya Rift Valley. *Hydrobiologia* 143:167–174.

Richardson, J. L., and A. E. Richardson. 1972. The History of an East African Rift Lake and Its Climatic Implications. *Ecological Monographs* 42:499–534.

Rightmire, G., and H. Deacon. 1991. Comparative Studies of Late Pleistocene Human Remains from Klasies River Mouth, South Africa. *Journal of Human Evolution* 20:131–156.

Rindos, D. 1984. *The Origins of Agriculture: An Evolutionary Perspective*. New York: Academic Press.

Robbins, L. H. 1997. Eastern African Advanced Foragers. In *Encyclopedia of Precolonial Africa*. J. O. Vogel, ed. Pp. 330–40. Walnut Creek, Calif.: AltaMira Press.

———. 1999. Direct Dating of Worked Ostrich Eggshell in the Kalahari. *Nyame Akuma* no. 52:11–16.

Robbins, L. H., M. L. Murphy, G. A. Brook, A. H. Iverster, A. C. Campbell, R. G. Klein, R. G. Milo, K. M. Stewart, W. S. Downey, and N. H. Stevens. 2000. Archaeology, Paleoenvironment, and Chronology of the Tsodilo Hills White Paintings Rock Shelter, Northwest Kalahari Desert, Botswana. *Journal of Archaeological Science* 27(11):1085–1113.

Robbins, L. H., M. L. Murphy, A. C. Campbell, G. A. Brook, D. M. Reid, K. A. Haberyan, and W. S. Downey. 1998. Test Excavations and Reconnaissance: Paleoenvironmental Work at Toteng, Botswana. *South African Archaeological Bulletin* 53(168):125–132.

Robbins, L. H., M. L. Murphy, N. J. Stevens, G. A. Brook, A. H. Iverster, K. A. Haberyan, R. G. Klein, R. Milo, K. M. Stewart, D. G. Mattiesen, and A. J. Winkler. 1996. Paleoenvironment and Archaeology of Drotskys Cave— Western Kalahari Desert, Botswana. *Journal of Archaeological Science* 23(1):7–22.

Robbins, L., M. Murphy, K. Stewart, A. Campbell, and G. Brook. 1994. Barbed Bone Points, Paleoenvironment, and the Antiquity of Fish Exploitation in the Kalahari Desert, Botswana. *Journal of Field Archaeology* 21:257–264.

Roberts, N., M. Taieb, P. Barker, B. Danati, M. Icole, and D. Williamson. 1993. Timing of the Younger Dryas Event in East Africa from Lake-Level Changes. *Nature* 366:146–164.

Robertshaw, P. 1990. The Development of Archaeology in East Africa. In *A History of African Archaeology*. P. Robertshaw, ed. Pp. 78–94. London: James Currey.

Roche, H., A. Delagnes, J.-P. Brugal, C. Feibel, M. Kibunjia, V. Mourre, and P.-J. Texier. 1999. Early Hominid Stone Tool Production and Technical Skill 2.34 Myr Age in West Turkana, Kenya. *Nature* 399:57–60.

Roebroeks, W., J. Kolen, and E. Rensink. 1988. Planning Depth, Anticipation, and the Organization of Middle Paleolithic Technology: The Archaic

Natives Meet Eve's Descendants. *Helinium, Revue Consacré à l'Archéologie des Pays-Bas, de la Belgique et du Grand-Duché du Luxembourg* 28:17–34.

Rogers, M., J. W. K. Harris, and C. Feibel. 1994. Changing Patterns of Land Use by Plio-Pleistocene Hominids in the Lake Turkana Basin. *Journal of Human Evolution* 27:139–158.

Roscoe, P. 2002. The Hunters and Gatherers of New Guinea. *Current Anthropology* 43:153–162.

Rousseau, J.-J. 1973 [1750–62]. *The Social Contract and Discourses*. London: Dent.

Sackett, J. R. 1982. Approaches to Style in Lithic Archaeology. *Journal of Anthropological Archaeology* 1:59–112.

———. 2000. Human Antiquity and the Old Stone Age: The Nineteenth Century Background to Paleoanthropology. *Evolutionary Anthropology* 9:37–49.

Sadr, K. 1997. Kalahari Archaeology and the Bushman Debate. *Current Anthropology* 38:104–112.

———. 1998. The First Herders at the Cape of Good Hope. *African Archaeological Review* 15:101–132.

Sahlins, M. D. 1972. *Stone Age Economics*. Chicago: Aldine.

———. 1998 [1972]. The Original Affluent Society. In *Limited Wants, Unlimited Means: A Reader on Hunter-Gatherer Economics and the Environment*. J. Gowdy, ed. Pp. 5–41. Washington, D.C.: Island Press.

Sampson, C. G. 1988. *Stylistic Boundaries among Mobile Hunter-Foragers*. Washington, D.C.: Smithsonian Institution Press.

———. 1998. Tortoise Remains from a Later Stone Age Rock Shelter in the Upper Karoo, South Africa. *Journal of Archaeological Science* 25:985–1000.

———. 2000. Taphonomy of Tortoises Deposited by Birds and Bushmen. *Journal of Archaeological Science* 27(9):779–788.

———. 2001. Personal Communication.

Schadeberg, T. 1999. Batwa: The Bantu Name for the Invisible People. In *Challenging Elusiveness: Central African Hunter-Gatherers in a Multidisciplinary Perspective*. K. Biesbrouck, S. Elders, and G. Rossel, eds. Pp. 21–40. The Netherlands: Universiteit Leiden Research School CNWS.

Schrire, C. 1980. An Inquiry into the Evolutionary Status and Apparent Identity of San Hunter-Gatherers. *Human Ecology* 8:9–32.

———, (ed.). 1984. *Past and Present in Hunter-Gatherer Societies*. San Francisco: Academic Press.

———. 1992. The Archaeological Identity of Hunters and Herders at the Cape over the Last 2000 Years: A Critique. *South African Archaeological Bulletin* 47:62–64.

Sealy, J., and S. Pfeiffer. 2000. Diet, Body Size, and Landscape Use among Holocene People in the Southern Cape, South Africa. *Current Anthropology* 41:642–654.

Sealy, J., and R. J. Yates. 1994. The Chronology of the Introduction of Pastoralism to the Cape, South Africa. *Antiquity* 68:58–67.

Seeman, M. 1994. Intercluster Lithic Patterning at Nobles Pond: A Case for Disembedded Procurement among Early Paleoindian Societies. *American Antiquity* 59:273–288.

Semaw, S., P. Renne, J. W. K. Harris, C. S. Feibel, R. L. Bernor, N. Fesseka, et al. 1997. 2.5-Million-Year-Old Stone Tools from Gona, Ethiopia. *Nature* 385:333–336.

Service, E. 1962. *Primitive Social Organization.* New York: Random House.

Shaw, P. A., and D. S. G. Thomas. 1996. The Quaternary Paleoenvironmental History of the Kalahari, Southern Africa. *Journal of Arid Environments* 32:9–22.

Shea, J., Z. Davis, and K. Brown. 2001. Experimental Tests of Middle Paleolithic Spear Points Using a Calibrated Crossbow. *Journal of Archaeological Science* 28:807–816.

Shelley, P. H. 1993. A Geoarchaeological Approach to the Analysis of Secondary Lithic Deposits. *Geoarchaeology* 8:59–72.

Shott, M. 1986. Technological Organization and Settlement Mobility: An Ethnographic Examination. *Journal of Anthropological Research* 42:15–52.

———. 1989. Bipolar Industries: Ethnographic Evidence and Archaeological Implications. *North American Archaeologist* 10:1–24.

———. 1992. On Recent Trends in the Anthropology of Foragers: Kalahari Revisionism and Its Archaeological Implications. *Man* 27:843–871.

Siegel, P. 1985. Edge Angle as a Functional Indicator: A Test. *Lithic Technology* 14:90–94.

Silberbauer, G. 1991. Morbid Reflexivity and Overgeneralization in Mosarwa Studies. *Current Anthropology* 32:96–99.

Sillen, A., G. Hall, and R. Armstrong. 1995. Strontium calcium ratios (Sr/Ca) and strontium isotopic ratios ($^{87}Sr/^{86}Sr$) of *Australopithecus robustus* and *Homo* sp. from Swartkrans. *Journal of Human Evolution* 28:277–285.

Sillen, A., and A. Morris. 1996. Diagenesis of Bone from Border Cave—Implications for the Age of the Border Cave Hominids. *Journal of Human Evolution* 31(6):499–506.

Singer, R., and J. J. Wymer. 1982. *The Middle Stone Age at Klasies River Mouth in South Africa.* Chicago: University of Chicago Press.

Smith, A., and R. Lee. 1997. Cho/ana: A *hxaro* Meeting Place in Northeastern Namibia. *South African Archaeological Bulletin* 32:118–127.

Smith, A. B. 1992. *Pastoralism in Africa: Origins and Development Ecology.* London: Hurst and Company.

———. 1998. Keeping People on the Periphery: The Ideology of Social Hierarchies between Hunters and Herders. *Journal of Anthropological Archaeology* 17:201–215.

Smith, A. B., K. Sadr, J. Gribble, and R. Yates. 1991. Excavations in the South-Western Cape, South Africa, and the Archaeological Identity of Prehistoric Hunter-Gatherers within the Last 2000 Years. *South African Archaeological Bulletin* 47:62–64.

Smith, B. 1998. *The Emergence of Agriculture*. New York: Scientific American Library.

———. 2001. Low-Level Food Production. *Journal of Archaeological Research* 9:1–43.

Smith, E. A. 1983. Anthropological Applications of Optimal Foraging Theory: A Critical Review. *Current Anthropology* 24:625–651.

———. 1988. Risk and Uncertainty in the "Original Affluent Society": Evolutionary Ecology of Resource Sharing and Land Tenure. In *Hunter-Gatherers I: History, Evolution, and Social Change*. T. Ingold, D. Riches, and J. Woodburn, eds. Pp. 222–252. Oxford: Berg.

———. 2001. Hunting and Gathering for Data on Hunters and Gatherers. *Evolutionary Anthropology* 10:187–189.

Smith, E. A., and B. Winterhalder. 1992. *Evolutionary Ecology and Human Behavior*. New York: Aldine de Gruyter.

Smith, E. A., and M. Wishnie. 2000. Conservation and Subsistence in Small-Scale Societies. *Annual Review of Anthropology* 29:493–524.

Smith, F. H. 1993. Models and Realities in Modern Human Origins: The African Fossil Evidence. In *The Origins of Modern Humans and the Impact of Chronometric Dating*. M. J. Aitken, C. B. Striner, and P. A. Mellars, eds. Pp. 234–248. Princeton, N.J.: Princeton University Press.

Soffer, O. 1989. The Middle to Upper Paleolithic Transition on the Russian Plain. In *The Human Revolution: Behavioral and Biological Perspectives on the Origins of Modern Humans*. P. Mellans and C. Stringer, eds. Pp. 714–742. Princeton, N.J.: Princeton University Press.

Soffer, O., J. M. Adovasio, J. S. Illingworth, H. A. Amirkhanov, N. D. Praslov, and M. Street. 2000. Paleolithic Perishables Made Permanent. *Antiquity* 74:812–821.

Solway, J., and R. Lee. 1990. Foragers, Genuine or Spurious? Situating the Kalahari San in History. *Current Anthropology* 31(2):109–122.

Sowunmi, M. A. 1991. Late Quaternary Environments in Equatorial Africa: Palynological Evidence. *Paleoecology of Africa* 22:213–239.

Speth, J. 1990. Seasonality, Resource Stress, and Food Sharing in So-Called 'Egalitarian' Foraging Societies. *Journal of Anthropological Archaeology* 8:148–188.

Speth, J., and K. Spielmann. 1983. Energy Source, Protein Metabolism, and Hunter-Gatherer Subsistence Strategies. *Journal of Anthropological Archaeology* 2:1–31.

Stahl, A. B. 1993. Intensification in the West African Late Stone Age: A View from Central Ghana. In *The Archaeology of Africa: Food, Metals and Towns*. T. Shaw, P. Sinclair, B. Andah, and A. Okpoko, eds. Pp. 261–273. London/New York: Routledge.

Stannus, H. 1915. Pre-Bantu Occupants of East Africa. *Man* 15:131–132.

Steward, J. 1938. Basin Plateau Aboriginal Sociopolitical Groups. *Bureau of American Ethnology Bulletin* 120. Washington, D.C.

Stiles, D. N. 1979. Early Acheulean and Developed Oldowan. *Current Anthropology* 20:126–129.

———. 1980. Archaeological and Ethnographic Studies of Pastoral Groups of Northern Kenya. *Nyame Akuma* 17:20–24.

———. 1981. Hunters of the Northern East African Coast: Origins and Historical Processes. *Africa* 51:848–862.

———. 1982. A History of Hunting Peoples on the Northern East African Coast. *Paideuma* 28:165–174.

———. 1992. The Hunter-Gatherer Revisionist Debate. *Anthropology Today* 8:13–17.

———. 1994. On Evolutionary Ecology and Cultural Realities. *Current Anthropology* 35:438–440.

Stiner, M. C. 1990. An Interspecific Perspective on the Emergence of the Modern Human Predatory Niche. In *Human Predators and Prey Mortality*. M. C. Stiner, ed. Pp. 149–185. Boulder, Colo.: Westview.

———. 1993. Small Animal Exploitation and Its Relation to Hunting, Scavenging, and Gathering in the Italian Mousterian. In *Hunting and Animal Exploitation in the Later Paleolithic and Mesolithic of Eurasia*. G. Larsen Peterkin, H. Bricker, and P. Mellars, eds. Pp. 107–126. Archaeological Papers of the American Anthropological Association, Volume 4.

Stiner, M. C., and S. Kuhn. 1992. Subsistence, Technology, and Adaptive Variation in Middle Paleolithic Italy. *American Anthropologist* 94:306–339.

Stiner, M. C., N. D. Munro, and T. A. Surovell. 2000. The Tortoise and the Hare: Small Game Use, the Broad Spectrum Revolution and Paleolithic Demography. *Current Anthropology* 412:39–73.

Straube, J. 1963. *Westkuschitische Völker Südäthiopiens*. Stuttgart: Kohlhammer Verlag.

Street, F. A., and A. T. Grove. 1976. Environmental and Climatic Implications of Late Quaternary Lake-Level Fluctuations in Africa. *Nature* 261:285–390.

Stringer, C. 1995. The Evolution and Distribution of Later Pleistocene Human Populations. In *Paleoclimate and Evolution*. E. S. Vrba, G. H. Denton, T. C. Partridge, and L. H. Burckle, eds. Pp. 524–531. New Haven, Conn.: Yale University Press.

Sugiyama, M. 2001. Food, Foragers, and Folklore: The Role of Narrative in Human Subsistence. *Evolution and Human Behavior* 22:221–240.

Sutton, J. E. G. 1977. The African Aqualithic. *Antiquity* 51:25–54.

———. 1994–1995. The Growth of Farming and the Bantu Settlement on and South of the Equator. *Azania* 29–30:1–14.

Templeton, A. R. 1997. Testing the Out of Africa Replacement Hypothesis with Mitochondrial DNA Data. In *Conceptual Issues in Modern Human Origins Research*. G. A. Clark and C. M. Willermet, eds. Pp. 329–360. New York: Aldine de Gruyter.

———. 1998. Human Races: A Genetic and Evolutionary Perspective. *American Anthropologist* 100:632–650.

Terrell, J. 1986. Causal Pathways and Causal Processes: Studying the Evolutionary Prehistory of Human Diversity in Language, Customs, and Biology. *Journal of Anthropological Archaeology* 5:187–198.

Testart, A. 1982. The Significance of Food Storage among Hunter-Gatherers: Residence Patterns, Population Densities, and Social Inequalities. *Current Anthropology* 23:523–530.

——. 1987. Game Sharing Systems and Kinship Systems among Hunter-Gatherers. *Man* 22:287–304.

——. 1988. Some Major Problems in the Social Anthropology of Hunter-Gatherers. *Current Anthropology* 29:1–31.

Thackeray, A. 1992. The Middle Stone Age South of the Limpopo River. *Journal of World Prehistory* 6:385–440.

Theime, H. 1997. Lower Paleolithic Hunting Spears from Germany. *Nature* 385:807–810.

Thorbahn, P. 1979. Precolonial Ivory Trade of East Africa: Reconstruction of a Human-Elephant Ecosystem. Ph.D. diss., University of Massachusetts—Amherst.

Thorp, C. R. 1996. A Preliminary Report on Evidence of Interaction between Hunter-Gatherers and Farmers along a Hypothesized Frontier in the Eastern Free State. *South African Archaeological Bulletin* 51:57–63.

——. 1997. Evidence for Interaction from Recent Hunter-Gatherer Sites in the Caledon Valley. *African Archaeological Review* 14:231–256.

——. 2000. Hunter-Gatherers and Farmers: An Enduring Frontier in the Caledon Valley, South Africa. Cambridge Monographs in African Archaeology 50. *British Archaeological Reports S860.*

Tomasello, M. 2001. The Human Adaptation for Culture. *Annual Review of Anthropology* 28:509–529.

Torrence, R. 1983. Time Budgeting and Hunter-Gatherer Technology. In *Hunter-Gatherer Economy in Prehistory.* G. Bailey, ed. Pp. 11–22. Cambridge: Cambridge University Press.

——. 1994. Strategies for Moving on in Lithic Studies. In *The Organization of North American Prehistoric Chipped Stone Tool Technologies.* P. J. Carr, ed. Pp. 123–136. Archaeological Series 7. Ann Arbor: International Monographs in Prehistory.

Trigger, B. 1990. The History of African Archaeology in World Perspective. In *A History of African Archaeology.* P. Robertshaw, ed. Pp. 309–319. London: James Currey.

Truswell, A. Stewart, and J. D. Hansen. 1976. Medical Research among the !Kung. In *Kalahari Hunter-Gatherers: Studies of !Kung San and Their Neighbors.* R. Lee and I. DeVore, eds. Pp. 166–194. Cambridge, Mass.: Harvard University Press.

Tryon, C., and S. McBrearty. 2002. Tephrostratigraphy and the Acheulean to Middle Stone Age Transition in the Kapthurin Formation, Kenya. *Journal of Human Evolution* 42:211–235.

Tunnel, G. 1996. Comment on Rose, L., and F. Marshall, Meat Eating, Hominid Sociality, and Home Bases Revisited. *Current Anthropology* 37:307–338.

Turnbull, C. M. 1965. *Wayward Servants: The Two Worlds of the African Pygmies.* London: Eyre and Spottiswoode.

———. 1983. *The Mbuti Pygmies: Change and Adaptation*. Orlando: Harcourt Brace Jovanovich College Publishers.

van Neer, W. 1989. Contribution to the Archaeozoology of Central Africa. *Annales (Sciences Géologiques) du Musée Royal de l'Afrique Centrale* (Tervuren, Belgium) 259.

Van Noten, F. 1977 Excavations at Matupi Cave. *Antiquity* 51:35–40.

Van Zinderen. 1976. The Evolution of Late Quaternary Paleoclimates of Southern Africa. *Palaeoecology of Africa* 9:160–202.

Vansina, J. 1990. *Paths in the Rainforest: Toward a History of Political Tradition in Equatorial Africa*. Madison: University of Wisconsin Press.

———. 1994–1995. A Slow Revolution: Farming in Subequatorial Africa. *Azania* 29–30:15–26.

Vayda, A., and B. McKay. 1975. New Directions in Ecology and Ecological Anthropology. *Annual Review of Anthropology* 4:293–306.

Vermeersch, P., E. Paulissen, and W. van Neer. 1989. The Late Paleolithic Makhadama Site (Egypt): Environment and Subsistence. In *Late Prehistory of the Nile Basin and the Sahara*. L. Krzyzaniak and M. Kobusiewicz, eds. Pp. 87–116. Poznan: Poznan Archaeology Museum.

Vierich, H. 1982. Adaptive Flexibility in a Multi-Ethnic Setting: The Basarwa of the Southern Kalahari. In *Politics and History in Band Societies*. E. Leacock and R. Lee, eds. Pp. 213–222. Cambridge: Cambridge University Press.

Villa, P., and F. D'Errico. 2001. Bone and Ivory Points in the Lower and Middle Paleolithic of Europe. *Journal of Human Evolution* 41:69–112.

Vincens, A. 1991. Végétation et climat dans le bassin sud-tanganyika entre 25,000 et 9,000 B.P.: Nouvelles données palynologiques. *Paleoecology of Africa* 22:253–263.

Vogel, J. 2001. Personal Communication.

Volman, T. P. 1981. The Middle Stone Age in the Southern Cape, South Africa. Ph.D. diss., University of Chicago.

Vrba, E. 1988. Late Pliocene Climatic Events and Hominid Evolution. In *Evolutionary History of the Robust Australopithecines*. F. E. Grine, ed. Pp. 405–426. New York: Aldine de Gruyter.

Wadley, L. 1993. The Pleistocene Later Stone Age South of the Limpopo River. *Journal of World Prehistory* 7:243–296.

———. 1996. Changes in the Social Relations of Precolonial Hunter-Gatherers after Agropastoralist Contact: An Example from the Magaliesburg, South Africa. *Journal of Anthropological Archaeology* 15:205–217.

———. 2001. Who Lived in Mauermanshoek Shelter, Korannaberg, South Africa. *African Archaeological Review* 18:153–179.

Wadley, L. and J. Binneman. 1995. Arrowheads or Pen Knives? A Microwear Analysis of Mid-Holocene Stone Segments from Jubilee Shelter, Transvaal. *South African Journal of Science* 91:153–155.

Wadley, L., and P. Harper. 1989. Rose Cottage Cave Revisited: Malan's Middle Stone Age Collection. *South African Archaeological Bulletin* 44:23–32.

Walker, A. and R. Leakey. 1993. *The Nariokotome* Homo erectus *Skeleton*. Cambridge: Harvard University Press.

Walker, N. 1995. *Late Pleistocene and Holocene Hunter-Gatherers of the Matopos: An Archaeological Study of Change and Continuity in Zimbabwe*. Uppsala: Societas Archaeologica Upsaliensis.

Waller, R. 1990. Tsetse Fly in Western Narok, Kenya. *Journal of African History* 31:81–101.

Wasylikowa, K., J. Mitka, F. Wendorf, and R. Schild. 1997. Exploitation of Wild Plants by the Early Neolithic Hunter-Gatherers in the Western Desert of Egypt: Nabta Playa as a Case-Study. *Antiquity* 71:932–941.

Weedman, K. J. 2000. An Ethnoarchaeological Study of Stone Scrapers among the Gamo People of Southern Ethiopia. Ph.D. diss., University of Florida.

Wendorf, F., and R. Schild. 1980. *Prehistory of the Eastern Sahara*. New York: Academic Press.

———. 1992. The Middle Paleolithic of North Africa: A Status Report. In *New Light on the Northeast African Past*. F. Klees and R. Kuper, eds. Pp. 39–80. Current Prehistoric Research. Cologne: Hinrich-Barth-Institut.

———. 1998. Nabta Playa and Its Role in Northeastern African Prehistory. *Journal of Anthropological Anthropology* 17(2):97–123.

Wendorf, F., R. Schild, and A. Close. 1986. *The Prehistory of Wadi Kubbaniya Volume 1: The Wadi Kubbaniyia Skeleton: A Late Paleolithic Burial from Southern Egypt*. Dallas, Tex.: Southern Methodist University Press.

Wetterstrom, W. 1993. Foraging and Farming in Egypt: The Transition from Hunting and Gathering to Horticulture in the Nile Valley. In *The Archaeology of Africa: Food, Metals, and Towns*. T. Shaw, P. Sinclair, B. Andah, and A. Okpoko, eds. Pp. 165–226. London/New York: Routledge.

White, F. 1983. *The Vegetation of Africa: A Descriptive Memoir to Accompany the UNESCO/AETFAT/UNSO Vegetation Map of Africa*. UNESCO Natural Resources Research Volume 20. Paris: UNESCO.

White, J. P., and D. H. Thomas. 1972. What Mean These Stones? Ethnotaxonomic Models and Archaeological Interpretations in the New Guinea Highlands. In *Models in Archaeology*. D. L. Clarke, ed. Pp. 275–308. London: Methuen.

White, R. 1985. Thoughts on Social Relationships and Language in Hominid Evolution. *Journal of Social and Personal Relationships* 2:95–115.

———. 1989. Production Complexity and Standardization in Early Aurignacian Bead and Pendant Manufacture: Evolutionary Implications. In *The Human Revolution: Behavioral and Biological Perspectives on the Origins of Modern Humans*. P. Mellars and C. Stringer, eds. Pp. 366–390. Edinburgh: Edinburgh University Press.

———. 1992. Beyond Art: Toward an Understanding of the Origins of Material Representation in Europe. *Annual Reviews in Anthropology* 21:537–564.

Whiten, A., J. Goodall, W. C. McGrew, T. Nishida, V. Reynolds, Y. Sugiyama, C. E. G. Tutin, R. W. Wrangham, C. Boesch. 1999. Cultures in Chimpanzees. *Nature* 399:682–685.

Wickens, G. E. 1982. The Baobab—Africa's Upside-Down Tree. *Kew Bulletin* 37:173–209.

Wiessner, P. 1982a. Risk, Reciprocity, and Social Influences on !Kung San Economics. In *Politics and History in Band Societies*. E. Leacock and R. Lee, eds. Pp. 61–84. Cambridge: Cambridge University Press.

———. 1982b. Beyond Willow Smoke and Dog's Tails: A Comment on Binford's Analysis of Hunter-Gatherer Settlement Systems. *American Antiquity* 57(1):171–178.

———. 1983. Style and Social Information in Kalahari San Projectile Points. *American Antiquity* 48:253–276.

———. 1984. Reconsidering the Behavioral Basis of Style: A Case Study among the Kalahari San. *Journal of Anthropological Archaeology* 3:190–234.

———. 1986. !Kung San Networks in a Generational Perspective. In *The Past and Future of !Kung Ethnography*. M. Biesele, R. Gordon, and R. Lee, eds. Pp. 103–136. Hamburg: Helmut Buske Verlag.

———. 1994. The Pathways of the Past: !Kung San Hxaro Exchange and History. In *Überleben Strategien in Afrika*. M. Bollig and F. Klees, eds. Pp. 101–123. Colloquium Africanum 1. Cologne, Germany: Heinrich-Barth-Institut.

———. 1996. Leveling the Hunter: Constraints on the Status Quest in Foraging Societies. In *Food and the Status Quest: An Interdisciplinary Perspective*. P. Wiessner and W. Schiefenhovel, eds. Pp. 171–191. Providence: Berghahn Books.

Wijngaarden, W. V., and V. W. P. van Engelen. 1985. *Soils and Vegetation of the Tsavo Area*. Nairobi: Geological Survey of Kenya.

Williams, N. M., and E. S. Hunn, eds. 1982. *Resource Managers: North American and Australian Hunter-Gatherers*. Boulder, Colo.: Westview Press.

Wilmsen, E. 1973. Interaction, Spacing Behavior, and the Organization of Hunting Bands. *Journal of Anthropological Research* 29:1–31.

———. 1989. *Land Filled with Flies: A Political Economy of the Kalahari*. Chicago: University of Chicago Press.

Wilmsen, E. N., and J. R. Denbow. 1990. Paradigmatic History of San-Speaking Peoples and Current Attempts at Revision. *Current Anthropology* 31:489–524.

Winterhalder, B. 1986. Diet Choice, Risk, and Food Sharing in a Stochastic Environment. *Journal of Anthropological Archaeology* 5:369–392.

———. 1996. Social Foraging and the Behavioral Ecology of Intra-Group Resource Transfers. *Evolutionary Anthropology* 5:46–57.

———. 2001a. The Behavioral Ecology of Hunter-Gatherers. In *Hunter-Gatherers: An Interdisciplinary Perspective*. C. Panter-Brick, R. H. Layton, and P. Rowley-Conwy, eds. Pp. 12–38. Cambridge: Cambridge University Press.

———. 2001b. Intra-Group Resource Transfers: Comparative Evidence, Models, and Implications for Human Evolution. In *Meat Eating and Human Evolution*. C. B. Stanford and H. T. Bunn, eds. Pp. 279–301. Oxford: Oxford University Press.

Winterhalder, B., and E. A. Smith, eds. 1981. *Hunter and Gatherer Foraging Strategies: Ethnographic and Archaeological Analyses.* Chicago: University of Chicago Press.

Wobst, H. 1977. Stylistic Behavior and Information Exchange. In *For the Director: Research Essays in Honor of James B. Griffin.* C. Cleland, ed. Pp. 317–342. Museum of Anthropology, University of Michigan Papers 61.

———. 1978. The Archaeo-ethnology of Hunter-Gatherers, or The Tyranny of the Ethnographic Record in Archaeology. *American Antiquity* 43:303–309.

Wolf, E. 1982. *Europe and the People without History.* Berkeley: University of California Press.

Wolpoff, M., A. G. Thorne, F. H. Smith, D. W. Frayer, and G. G. Pope. 1994. Multiregional Evolution: A World-wide Source for Modern Human Populations. In *Origins of Anatomically Modern Humans.* M. H. Nitecki and D. V. Nitecki, eds. Pp. 175–199. New York: Plenum.

Woodburn, J. 1972. Ecology, Nomadic Movement, and the Composition of the Local Group among Hunters and Gatherers. In *Man, Settlement, and Urbanism.* P. Ucko, R. Tringham, and G. Dimbleby, eds. Pp. 193–206. London: Duckworth.

———. 1979. Minimal Politics: The Political Organization of the Hadza of Tanzania. In *Politics in Leadership: A Comparative Perspective.* P. Cohen and W. Shack, eds. Pp. 244–246. Oxford: Clarendon.

———. 1982. Egalitarian Societies. *Man* 17:431–451.

———. 1988. African Hunter-Gatherer Social Organization: Is It Best Seen as a Product of Encapsulation? In *Hunters and Gatherers, Volume 1: History, Evolution, and Social Change.* T. Ingold, J. Riches, and J. Woodburn, eds. Pp. 31–64. London: Berg.

Wright, R. 1993. Technological Styles: Transforming a Natural Material into a Cultural Object. In *History from Things: Essays on Material Culture.* S. Lubar and W. D. Kingery, eds. Pp. 242–269. Washington D.C.: Smithsonian Institution Press.

Wurz, S. 1999. The Howieson's Poort Backed Artifacts from Klasies River: An Argument for Symbolic Behavior. *South African Archaeological Bulletin* 54:38–50.

———. 2000. The Middle Stone Age at Klasies River, South Africa. Ph.D. diss. University of Stellenbosch.

———. 2000. Personal Communication.

Wynn, T. 1989. The Evolution of Spatial Competence. *University of Illinois Studies in Anthropology* 17.

———. 1993a. Two Developments in the Mind of Early *Homo. Journal of Anthropological Archaeology* 12:299–322.

———. 1993b. Layers of Thinking in Tool Behavior. In *Tools and Cognition in Human Evolution.* K. Gibson and T. Ingold, eds. Pp. 389–406. Cambridge: Cambridge University Press.

Yee, D. 1994. More on Why Hunter-Gatherers Work. *Current Anthropology* 35:287–289.

Yellen, J. E. 1977. *Archaeological Approaches to the Present: Models for Reconstructing the Past.* New York: Academic Press.

———. 1998. Barbed Bone Points: Tradition and Continuity in Saharan and Sub-Saharan Africa. *African Archaeological Review* 15:173–198.

Yellen, J., and A. Brooks. 1989. The Late Stone Age Archaeology of the !Kangwa and /Xai/xai Valleys, Ngamiland, Botswana. *Botswana Notes and Records* 20:5–27.

Yellen, J. E., and H. Harpending. 1972. Hunter-Gatherer Populations and Archaeological Inference. *World Archaeology* 4:244–253.

Yen, D. E. 1989. The Domestication of Environment. In *Foraging and Farming: The Evolution of Plant Exploitation.* D. Harris and G. C. Hillman, eds. Pp. 55–72. London: Unwin Hyman.

Young, R., and G. Thompson. 1999. Missing Plant Foods? Where Is the Archaeobotanical Evidence for Sorghum and Finger Millet in East Africa? In *The Exploitation of Plant Resources in Ancient Africa.* Marijke van der Veen, ed. Pp. 63–72. New York: Kluwer Academic/Plenum.

Index

About the Author

Sibel Kusimba is an assistant professor of anthropology at Lawrence University and an adjunct curator of anthropology at the Field Museum in Chicago.